Whittington to World Financial Centre

The City of London and its Lord Mayor

Sir John Stuttard – Lord Mayor of the City of London, 2006-2007.

WHITTINGTON TO WORLD FINANCIAL CENTRE

The City of London and its Lord Mayor

JOHN STUTTARD

 PHILLIMORE

2008

Published by
PHILLIMORE & CO. LTD
Chichester, West Sussex, England
www.phillimore.co.uk
www.thehistorypress.co.uk

© John Stuttard, 2008
ISBN 978-1-86077-586-4

Printed and bound in Great Britain
by Cambridge University Press

Contents

To Lesley,
A Very Special Lady Mayoress

Acknowledgements

The author is very grateful to David Lascelles who encouraged him at each stage, providing advice on the financial sector both during the Mayoralty and when writing the book, and also in identifying the publisher. He is also very grateful to Geoffrey Daish for helping defray a major part of the costs of printing. He would like to thank the many friends who have read and commented upon the text of the book to ensure its accuracy and its good English, and for their support in the preparation of this book, in particular: Alderman Michael Bear, David Bradbury, Kay Brock, LVO, Paul Double, Chris Duffield, Alderman Roger Gifford, Tony Halmos, Alderman Sir David Howard Bt, Anne-Marie Jubber, Alderman Sir Paul Judge, David Lascelles, Alderman Lord Levene KBE, Alderman Ian Luder, David Milnes, Professor Michael Mainelli, Peter Nelson, Sir Peter Ricketts KCMG, Paul Sizeland, Professor David Wallace CBE, John Whiting OBE, Greg Williams, Peter Wyman CBE, and my wife, Lesley.

The author would also like to thank John Fisher, Sheldon Hind, Emma Hutchings and Lesley Mair – all of the City of London Corporation – for help in identifying the photos that have been used and the following persons and organisations for supplying photographs and other illustrative material. These illustrations have added greatly to communicating the content of Sir John Stuttard's year of Office as Lord Mayor of the City of London. Reference numbers after each name refer to the photograph or illustration provided and included in this book.

James Abelson: 80; Petri Anderson: 107; Barbara Bear: 152, 155; Geremy Butler Photography: 13; Cass Business School: 4; City of London Corporation (Public Relations Office): 2, 5, 53, 79, 83, 84, 89, 90, 91, 103; City of London Corporation (Guildhall Library): 3, 7, 18, 31, 52, 76; City of London Corporation (Lesley Mair): 142, 143; City of London (Rebecca Sandles): 148; The Cook & The Butler Event Company: 81; Sheila Cracknell: 105; David Drummond Collection: Cover main illustration, 11; Phil Fisk: 82; Paul Francis Photography and Pro-Manchester: 97; David Gee: 129; Peter Golding: 35; Reverend William Gulliford: 162; Peter Holland: 28, 29, 51, 54, 55, 58, 59, 65, 66, 67, 72, 124; The Honourable Artillery Company: 68; Andrew Illes: 120; Tim Jenkins: Cover bottom left, Frontispiece, 1, 56, 57; Sir Paul Judge: 23, 26, 92, 95, 127, 131, 132, 138, 139, 140, 144, 146, 149, 150, 154, 156, 157, 158, 160; King Edward's School Witley: 115; Grant Macdonald: 39, 40, 45; Nick Panagakis: 71; Wendy Parmley: 87; Photographic Techniques Ltd: Inside flap, 123 ; Photoshot: 96; PwC Kazakhstan: 141; Gerald Sharp Photography: (Cover top left, 6, 8, 9, 10, 14, 15, 16, 17, 19, 21, 24, 25, 27, 32, 33, 34, 41, 48, 73, 74, 75, 85, 88, 94, 101, 102, 106, 108, 109, 117, 120, 121, 130, 133, 134, 159, 163; John Snelling: 30; Coriander Stuttard: 104; Taysec: 137; H Tempest Limited and City University: 93; The United Society for the Propagation of the Gospel (USPG) Photographic Collection No 428: 113, 114; Clive Totman: 12, 20, 22, 37, 38, 43, 44, 47, 49, 50, 60, 61, 62, 63, 64, 70, 86, 98, 99, 116, 118, 128; VSO/Ben Langdon: 110, 119, 136; Phil Way and St Paul's Cathedral: 36.

Most of all, the author would like to thank the publisher, Phillimore and Co. and, in particular, Noel Osborne and Andrew Illes for their courtesy, good humour and the professional way in which they have managed this project.

About the Author

Sir John Stuttard was Lord Mayor of London in 2006-07. He is the 679th Lord Mayor in a line which stretches back to 1189.

Born in Burnley, Lancashire, Sir John was educated at Shrewsbury School and Churchill College Cambridge. After a year teaching English with Voluntary Service Overseas in Borneo, where he also read the news on Radio Brunei, he embarked on a career in accountancy, becoming a partner in 1975 in the London office of Coopers & Lybrand, now PricewaterhouseCoopers. Retiring as a partner in 2005, he continued as an adviser and is Vice Chairman of the UK firm's Advisory Panel.

His career was mostly spent assisting multinational City Corporations achieve their cross-border ambitions. He has helped companies acquire and sell businesses in other countries and has acted as reporting accountant to numerous stock exchange listings. He has also advised on corporate strategy, financial reporting and corporate governance. He spent two years in the UK Cabinet Office Think Tank in the early '80s, advising the Government on the management and privatisation of the UK's nationalised industries. He then led the privatisation of Royal Ordnance and worked on the privatisation of the electricity industry before advising many Scandinavian companies on stock exchange listings and acquisitions. For his services to Finnish industry in 1995 he was made a Knight First Class of the Order of the Lion of Finland, upgraded to Commander in 2004, and was awarded the Silver Medal of Helsinki. He served as Chairman of the Finnish British Chamber of Commerce, of which he is a Life President. He spent just over five years as Chairman and Chief Executive of Coopers & Lybrand (afterwards PwC) in China, developing the firm from a staff of 50 to over 1,500 when he left in 1999. His involvement in China continued as a director of the UK's China Britain Business Council and he is the author of a leading business guide to China, *The New Silk Road – Secrets of Business Success in China Today* (published by John Wiley & Sons).

Elected as an Alderman of the City of London in 2001, he was Sheriff of London in 2005. He is a Court Assistant of three Livery companies, the Worshipful Company of Glaziers & Painters of Glass, the Chartered Accountants and the Plumbers. He is also the Sponsoring Alderman of the Guild of Educators. He is a Knight of Justice of the Order of St John and a Companion of the League of Mercy. He was made a Knight Bachelor in 2008.

His longstanding interest in education and training resulted in his being appointed a director of the Cambridge University Appointments Board in the late 1970s. He has been elected a By-Fellow of the Møller Centre at Churchill College, Cambridge, an Honorary Fellow of the Foreign Policy Association in the US, an Honorary Fellow of the Securities and Investment Institute and an Honorary Member of the ACCA. His charitable activities now include Pro-Chancellor of the City University London, Trustee of Charities Aid Foundation, Governor of King Edward's School Witley, Trustee of Morden College and Adviser to St Paul's Foundation. During his year as Lord Mayor, he raised charitable funds to encourage cross-border learning through Voluntary Service Overseas and other educational schemes.

He is a keen collector of old cars that he rallies. In 1997 he drove his 1934 Rolls-Royce, painted pink as a result of sponsorship and coverage by the *Financial Times*, on the 10,000-mile journey from Peking to Paris. He is married to Lesley and has two sons, Tom and Jamie, and two grandchildren, Cassia and Henry.

1   *The Lord Mayor and Lady Mayoress at Mansion House prior to the Lord Mayor's Banquet.*

Introduction

Monday 13 October 2008 was an extraordinary day on which to be making the final amendments to, and signing off the final proof of this book. In several centuries of British financial history, there has rarely been a day as unprecedented as this for the UK banking industry.

The Prime Minister and the Chancellor of the Exchequer announced that the Government would be investing £37 billion to strengthen the share capital of three major UK banks, taking a majority equity interest in one, Royal Bank of Scotland (RBS). As part of a larger £500 billion financial support package, the UK Government has taken exceptional measures, including part-privatisation, to help restore confidence in the ailing banking sector – a sector which has suffered greatly as a result of the credit crunch, caused by injudicious lending, particularly in the US sub-prime market.

At an emergency summit in Paris the previous day, a Sunday, the eurozone leaders agreed on a region-wide bank rescue plan, mirroring Gordon Brown's lead. In total, European Governments committed to a rescue package of around £1.5 trillion, including capital injections, credit guarantees and additional liquidity. A further US$700 billion had already been approved by the US Congress.

After a depressing few months, in which the FTSE sank to below 4,000, its lowest level for many years, there was a rise of over 300 points on the day. Perhaps this is the turning point that we have all been hoping for. Only time will tell.

On the same day, the Met Office predicted a fine outlook, with a temperature of over 20 degrees, for the second day running. After a miserable, wet summer, is this the Indian Summer that we have all been hoping for?

Forecasting, at least of financial markets, is fraught with uncertainty. Who, two years ago, would have predicted the trauma in the global financial sector? Some economists and analysts claim to have done so, but they are the few. In 2006, financial markets were seemingly unstoppable. But, in the last 12 months, financial institutions have failed, employees have been laid off and pension funds have lost over one-third of their value. Yet, London remains the leading international financial centre.

The City of London has witnessed turbulent times in the past – destruction, plague, fire and financial disaster. But it has also witnessed great success as a world city and as the centre of the UK and global economy. Over the centuries, the Office of Lord Mayor has been an enduring factor, in difficult times as well as in times of prosperity. The Office exists to support and represent the people and businesses of the City in a unique and very special way.

After I completed my year as Lord Mayor, many friends asked Lesley and me which event stood out as the most memorable.

With 1,844 engagements, including 466 formal lunches and dinners, 764 speeches and 133 media interviews; with over 100 nights spent abroad in 23 countries; with hardly a free day at home during the year; being Lord Mayor is a full-time activity. It was difficult to single out one particular event. Every day was different. Every day was special.

I had kept a diary. After the year was over, during the five months of purdah, when the Late Lord Mayor, as he is unfortunately referred to, must stay away from civic affairs, I looked back on what we had done in the Mayoral year.

Of course, the events involving The Queen and other Heads of State stand out. But so does the welcome home in Guildhall Yard for the soldiers of the London Regiment from Afghanistan. Nothing, of course, will beat that first weekend – the Lord Mayor's Show, the fireworks on the Thames, the British Legion's Act of Remembrance at the Royal Albert Hall, the Remembrance Service at St Paul's and the Lord Mayor's Banquet.

However, the Lord Mayor's role, these days, is supporting, representing and promoting the UK financial services industry and so most of my meetings and events were associated with fulfilling this responsibility. I also promoted the UK as a centre for business education and professional skills development with the promotional theme 'City of London – City of Learning'.

But while most of the time was spent on ambassadorial and City financial work, there was still time, and something of a relief, to have the opportunity to welcome to Mansion House so many guests and friends, particularly from my Livery companies, the Lime Street Ward Club, Shrewsbury School and Churchill College, Cambridge, as well as PricewaterhouseCoopers. My Lord Mayor's charitable Appeal, in support of cross-border learning, was also fun and successful, thanks to VSO.

One moment I was dealing with the sub-prime crisis, Northern Rock or carbon emissions trading. The next I was visiting a hospice or handing out prizes at a school speech day. The content of the Mayoral diary is hugely variable. It is also hugely rewarding.

I realised that I was fortunate to have been given the baton to hold for a year and I hope, like my predecessors, that I left the office in good shape for my successor. But, so many people contribute to making the role a success – the City of London Corporation, the Foreign Office and UKTI, City businesses and trade associations, the Livery movement, charitable organisations and, of course, the staff at Mansion House. The Lady Mayoress is also a key figure, with her own programme of activities, as well as fulfilling a vital supporting role.

I would like to thank them all for their support and help. I am also grateful to so many people – fellow Aldermen, officials in the City Corporation, colleagues at PwC and other friends – for reading and commenting on earlier drafts of this book.

The book is aimed at describing the role of the Lord Mayor – ancient and modern. It is a unique office. It is as relevant today as it has ever been. I was proud to have been the 679th Lord Mayor, particularly at a time when London became the prime international financial centre in the world.

In the final chapter of this book, I reflect on the difficulties which surfaced in a major way in August 2007, after I had been in Office for nine months. I have described these, including the Northern Rock incident, in detail up to the date I left Office in November 2007. During these last three months, I stayed close to events as they unfurled, reacting as I could with the help of many around me – from business, the regulators and Government.

Hindsight is a great teacher and I have also given my views on some of the causes of the problems we have witnessed and the steps which, I believe, need to be taken to improve the governance and regulatory environment.

While the City of London has suffered, in the short term, not least because of its dependence on the financial sector, it still remains the world's prime international financial centre. As such, it needs strong leadership. The Office of Lord Mayor exists to support the people and businesses of the City and to help the UK authorities address the issues of the day and to ensure renewed and continuing success.

Sir John Stuttard
13 October 2008

2 *City of London from the River Thames.*

Part I

LONDON –
THE FINANCIAL
CAPITAL OF THE WORLD

The true portraicture of RICHARD WHITINGTON thrise Lord Maior
of London a vertuous and godly man full of good Works (and those famous) he builded
the Gate of London called Newegate, which before was a miserable doungeon. He builded
Whitington Colledge & made it an Almose house for poore people Also he builded a
greate parte of ý hospitall of S. Bartholomewes in westsmithfield in London. He also
builded the beautifull Library at ý Gray Friers in Londõ, called Christes Hospitall
Also he builded the Guilde Halle Chappell and increased a greate parte of the East
ende of the saied halle, beside many other good workes.

R. Elstrack Sculpsit.

The true portraicture of RICHARD WHITINGTON thrise Lord Ma
of London a vertuous and godly man full of good Works and those famous he builde
the Gate of London called Newegate which before was a miserable doungeon. He builde

The Role of the Lord Mayor

The Office of Lord Mayor dates back to around 1189, the first year of the reign of King Richard I, the Lionheart. In 1215, his younger brother and successor, King John, sealed the Magna Carta at Runnymede and, in the same year, John sealed another charter giving the Barons of the City of London (today's 25 elected Aldermen of the 25 wards in the Square Mile) the right to choose their own Mayor. The title 'Lord Mayor' came to be used in the 14th century and, by the 16th century, the prefix 'The Right Honourable' was added.

The Lord Mayor has, for the last 800 or so years, had the responsibility of representing, supporting and promoting the people and the businesses of the City of London. In the 13th century, the City had a large resident population and their businesses comprised every day trades such as bakers, butchers, carpenters, drapers, fishmongers, glass sellers, mercers and weavers, as well as those for specialist purposes such as armourers, glaziers, goldsmiths, painters and scriveners.

Over the centuries, the City of London developed as a major business and trading centre. There was always plenty of money to be made and, increasingly, available to be lent. So, not unnaturally, when the King or Queen wanted to embark on a crusade or fight a foreign war (usually against the French and, occasionally, against the Spanish or the Dutch) the merchants of the City obliged, or were obliged, to pay money to the Crown in return for privileges, such as a monopoly right to trade. Special rights were granted to the City so that its status grew far greater than any other city in the land. Favours and acts, such as the killing by the Mayor of the leader of the Peasants' Revolt, Wat Tyler, in 1381, further enhanced the City's powers.

To this day, the Lord Mayor attends at Whitehall, standing in line on the dais in Horseguards after the Prime Minister, Foreign Secretary and Home Secretary, when the Monarch greets a visiting Head of State to London. And the Lord Mayor gives splendid Banquets in the City in honour of visiting Heads of State and to commemorate special anniversaries or successes. During my year, I was honoured to greet The Queen and the Duke of Edinburgh when they came to celebrate the centenary of the Old Bailey and the 25th anniversary of the Barbican Centre. I was equally honoured to hold banquets for the President of Ghana and the King of Saudi Arabia, as well as to welcome Baroness Thatcher

3 *Medieval cartoon of Richard Whittington.*

3

and the Duke & Duchess of Gloucester for a dinner to commemorate the 25th anniversary of the Falklands War. At the Lord Mayor's Banquet, held each year in Guildhall for the previous Lord Mayor, the guests of honour consist of the Prime Minister, the Archbishop of Canterbury and the Lord Chancellor – and they each have a speaking part.

The Lord Mayor is head of the City of London Corporation, which is a corporation by prescription, with its own financial resources, used to fund a wide range of public benefit activities. These include the promotion of the UK-based financial services sector by the Lord Mayor. They also include some special responsibilities derived from its historical past, namely the upkeep of numerous open spaces in and around London, such as Epping Forest, and education, including the renowned Guildhall School of Music and Drama. The City Corporation makes a substantial contribution to the cultural life of the Capital through the Barbican Arts Centre. For the Square Mile, using statutory powers, the Common Council is the City Corporation's main operating arm providing local government services and is also constituted as a police authority.

With this wide range of historical responsibilities, with a private core and statutory local authority powers, the main role of the City Corporation is to help ensure the right physical, educational and regulatory environment within which the City's businesses can thrive and succeed. And this makes the City of London Corporation very different from other local authorities. In the City, with so few residents, the electoral franchise is dominated by business voters.

The Lord Mayor is also considered to be a figurehead for the Livery movement – the 108 Livery companies and also the guilds that represent the ancient as well as the modern trades and professions of London. In addition, he or she is the titular head of the London Regiment, the City of London scout group and many charities. The Lord Mayor attends many ceremonial events, particularly at Guildhall and St Paul's. He automatically becomes the Chancellor of City University and the Admiral of the Port of London, although this latter seems to come without any responsibilities and, at least so far as I could ascertain, neither uniform nor a hat.

But the Lord Mayor's main 'day job' continues, as it always has, to represent the people and the businesses of the City. And, over the centuries, these have changed, quite significantly.

THE CITY IN THE 21ST CENTURY

Today, there are fewer than 9,000 inhabitants in the Square Mile, as the City of London is known. The 340,000 people who work there commute on a daily basis from the other London Boroughs and from farther afield. And the businesses are no longer armourers, bowyers and fletchers. While Smithfield still thrives as a meat market, it is very much alone as a traditional trade in a city that is the heart, indeed the capital, of the world's financial industry.

Today, the businesses of the City comprise accountants, actuaries, bankers, fund managers, investment advisers, head hunters, insurers, management consultants, property managers and valuers, securities traders, ship brokers, solicitors and tax advisers.

And today, these businesses are no longer just domestic in nature. Not only are they international but many of them are foreign owned. Indeed recent surveys have shown that a large percentage, perhaps more than 50 per cent, of the activity in the financial sector comprises companies whose ultimate parent company has a head office outside the UK. Almost 50 per cent of the office buildings in the City are owned by foreign institutions, with around 25 per cent owned by German pension funds. It is ironic that what Mr Hitler failed to destroy during the Second World War is now in the hands of the trustees of funds for German pensioners. They must be grateful to the RAF and the Home Guard.

Reflecting this enormous change in the composition of the City's businesses, the content of the Lord Mayor's role has had to change, as well as the requirements for the job.

A further impetus to change resulted from the decision in the late '90s to focus the role of the Bank of England, and its Governor, on managing the monetary supply to control the rate of inflation, using the mechanism of changing interest rates. The wider responsibility of the Bank as the steward and leader of the City has all but disappeared, except in relation to the banking system. Based on the increasing importance of the Financial Sector to the economy, the Economic Secretary to the Treasury has taken a much greater interest in the City in recent years and, indeed, when he held that office, Ed Balls MP was dubbed 'City Minister' and his successor, Kitty Ussher MP followed suit. But, despite Government interest, there is a clear need for someone in the City of London – a City figure – to represent, support and promote the Financial Sector – and who better to do this than the Lord Mayor, whose job it has historically been. The apolitical nature of the Lord Mayor, independent of any political party, means that he is able to stand up to politicians, pointing out to them, either privately or in public, when the interests of the City are threatened. In the last year, Heathrow airport, visas for immigrants, capital gains tax changes, Northern Rock and suggested changes to non-domicile tax arrangements have all been subjects on which either I or my successor spoke – without fear of upsetting the party whip. This is one of London's strengths. The City has its spokesman – the Lord Mayor.

Increasingly, other financial centres in the UK (Edinburgh, Leeds and Manchester) have developed so that the Financial Sector is no longer a local affair. Companies headquartered in the regions such as Aviva, Bradford & Bingley, HBOS, Leeds Permanent and Royal Bank of Scotland have become national, if not international players. They appreciate as much assistance from the Lord Mayor and City of London Corporation as do HSBC, Lloyds, Prudential and Standard Chartered, which are based in London. The location of business in the UK is not an issue; the Lord Mayor serves the entire financial industry in the country, working with Whitehall, lobbying Brussels and promoting the Financial Sector in established as well as emerging markets. The term 'The City' now describes the UK's Financial Sector as a whole, not just the businesses of the City of London.

Furthermore, the Financial Sector is today dominated by companies many of whom have registered offices outside the UK. Citi, Credit Suisse, Deutsche Bank, JP Morgan, Merrill Lynch, Morgan Stanley, among others, have been key to the success of the industry, as have the foreign nationals working in it, estimated to be more than 200,000 in London alone.

THE CITY'S KEY SUCCESS FACTORS

In recent years, various studies have been published analysing London's strengths, weaknesses and threats. One such important report, *The Competitive Position of London as a Global Financial Centre*, was published in November 2005 by Z/Yen Limited, commissioned by the City of London Corporation and based on a survey of perceptions of companies in the financial sector.

The Z/Yen report listed the most important competitive factors for financial centres. In descending order of importance they were judged to be:

- Availability of skilled personnel
- Regulatory environment
- Access to international financial markets
- Availability of business infrastructure
- Access to business customers
- A fair and just business environment
- Government responsiveness
- Corporate tax regime

The study ranked financial centres based on perceptions in the industry and concluded that London and New York came out top, well above Paris and Frankfurt.

In preparing for my year as Lord Mayor I saw my main role as promoting the strengths of the City, as well as lobbying for changes to help remove any weaknesses or threats, complementing and following the strategies of the City of London Corporation.

This prime task, in 2007, was made a great deal easier as a result of the growing success of the financial sector in the UK, as confirmed by the Z/Yen and other reports.

In November 2006, the month that I took office, Oxford Economic Forecasting published a report, *London's Place in the UK Economy 2006-07*, commissioned by the City of London Corporation. This report concluded that:

- GDP growth in London was 3.9% compared to an average of 2.6% for the UK as a whole
- The Financial Services industry has played a large part in driving the acceleration in London's growth and, in 2006, accounted for 9% of the UK's GDP compared to 5% in 1980

- London has benefited from strong immigration from abroad, including large inflows of graduates and skilled professional and managerial workers
- Nearly one-third of London's workforce possess degrees or higher education qualifications
- London has become a 'world city' with more FT Global 500 companies having their headquarters in London than in any other city in the world
- London is a significant net contributor to the Exchequer
- Skills and education are a key issue for the future, including for London's universities

This last comment echoed the first finding of the Z/Yen report. This confirmed my belief that skills should be put at the top of the agenda. It confirmed my plan to launch, during my year, a campaign to promote London as a centre for business education and professional skills development – recognising the strengths of our professional institutes and universities. I have described this campaign 'City of London – City of Learning' in another chapter.

But back to the City's strengths and its enhanced global position.

Another report was published, also in November 2006, *International Financial Markets in the UK*, which confirmed London's position as the leading financial centre in terms of its share of international financial markets. This was prepared by International Financial Service, London (IFSL) which exists to promote the international activities of UK-based financial institutions and professional and business services, including maritime services. The facts were compelling:

- London has 32% of global foreign exchange trading
- London has 43% of global OTC derivatives turnover
- The London Stock Exchange has more foreign listed companies than any other exchange
- London accounts for 41% of all global foreign equity trades
- London has the most foreign banks – ahead of New York, Paris and Frankfurt
- The UK is the largest centre for cross-border banking with 20% of international bank lending and 22% of cross-border borrowing
- The UK insurance industry is the largest in Europe
- London is the leading worldwide centre for the supply of services to the maritime industry

It's much easier, when undertaking the role of Lord Mayor, to promote something where the reality supports the marketing messages you wish to give. This report gave me the ammunition I needed. But to make the story interesting and to provide additional substance and credibility in my impending discussions with overseas Ministers, Bank Governors and Regulators, I needed more qualitative as well as quantitative data.

In addition, I was at pains to stress that the City's success should not be taken for granted. In my speech in November 2006, at the Lord Mayor's Banquet, attended by Prime Minister Tony Blair MP, the Most Reverend Primate the Archbishop of Canterbury Dr Rowan Williams and the Lord Chancellor Lord Falconer, I made some remarks to this effect:

> But we need to be sensitive as to what can go wrong. In 1912, the Lancashire textile industry employed no fewer than 1.2 million people. Between the wars, as mills closed, 350,000 people lost their jobs – this is roughly the same number as commute each day into the Square Mile. My father, a chartered accountant in Burnley, witnessed many of his clients go to the wall. The decline in the cotton industry had a devastating effect on the whole community, which we still feel today. I learnt, from that experience, that we can never afford to be complacent. Success cannot be taken for granted.

With hindsight, these remarks have proved to be regrettably prophetic.

STRENGTHS AND THREATS

In recent years, the City's key strengths have been analysed by a number of organisations, the media and researchers, not least Z/Yen and IFSL. They have concluded that the City's strengths stem from a number of features – many historic. Taking these reports, and based on my own reading of history and economics and my own experience of working with global companies, I summarised the strengths as follows.

VALUES AND THE RULE OF LAW

The UK has a culture and a system of values that form the bedrock of, and are conducive to, the success of a financial services industry. These include an appreciation of integrity and fairness, as well as equity, tort, contract, confidentiality and professionalism, where 'one's word is one's bond', where you can sue for specific performance or damages, and where courts are independent and fair. Many of these principles date from Saxon times. Then, in 1215 King John signed the Magna Carta ceding certain rights to the Barons of England, including the Mayor of London. This restraint on the absolute powers of the monarch, and the balance of power that was thereby introduced, might justifiably be considered to be the beginnings of corporate governance. These essential cultural and legal attributes are often either overlooked or minimised in importance. We tend to take them for granted. Those major global cities where these values and mores exist, at least to any significant degree, include New York, Singapore and Hong Kong as well as London – all cities where standards of corporate governance are also judged to be strong and all three of which rank highly in global assessments of integrity. They are, not surprisingly, seen as the world's top four financial centres.

THE OPENING-UP OF THE MARKET AND
REMOVAL OF RESTRICTIVE PRACTICES ('BIG BANG')

London is the living embodiment of the success of Free Trade. 20 years ago we were very concerned that London might lose out to Paris or Frankfurt as the financial centre of Europe. Then when the decision was made to base the European Central Bank in Frankfurt, we thought that the game was up. But that has not happened. Today, the City of London is not just the financial capital of Europe but of the world. A key reason for this is that in 1986, inspired by Margaret Thatcher, the UK Government removed all restrictive practices and barriers to entry in the UK's Financial Sector. The result was immediate and outstanding. Encouraged also by London's time zone and the use of the English language, foreign financial institutions, from the US, Germany, Switzerland and elsewhere, increased the size and scope of their operations in London. A further important factor is the lack of protectionism when it comes to foreign ownership of businesses. When Dubai Ports acquired P&O, the US Congress and Administration went into overdrive to prevent an 'Arab' takeover of the administration of certain US ports. Not so the UK when NASDAQ made a hostile takeover bid for the London Stock Exchange. The City and Government view was that it didn't matter who owned the company and what nationality they had. The key issue was how they managed the business and, if it needed to be regulated, how it was regulated. So, the Treasury, under Ed Balls' leadership, decided that they would absolutely not introduce legislation to bar a potential foreign takeover, but that they would introduce legislation to prevent any subsequent regulation of an acquired LSE by the SEC.

THE POOL OF PROFESSIONAL TALENT

The Financial Sector in the UK, and London in particular, has attracted some of the best brains from university over a 50-year period. It would be incorrect and contentious to state that all the best graduates went into the City. However, compared with Germany where manufacturing and engineering have been sought-after occupations, and compared with France where administration is highly regarded as a career, in the UK the professions and the finance industry have

been seen as offering lifelong prospects and high reward. Foreign students and foreign graduates flock to London for training and work experience. This influx of young talent, from home and abroad, benefits the financial services industry and is a key success factor. In the Z/Yen survey, the availability of skilled personnel was ranked as the single most important factor in London's competitiveness.

4 *Lord Mayor with students at Cass Business School.*

THE ROBUST, YET BENIGN, REGULATORY ENVIRONMENT

In my 40 years as an accountant dealing with global companies, I had come across US accounting standards, US financial reporting and US filing requirements, and SEC rules. They are detailed, prescriptive and inflexible. They 'have to be followed'. If one ticks the box, then it is deemed to be OK, almost regardless of whether it seems to make sense. There is little, if any, chance to override or to deviate. To do so would subject one to the full might of the law and to the US courts. On the other hand, UK accounting and auditing was based much more on a 'true and fair view' of the financial results and position and of what makes sense in the circumstances of each case. Regrettably, in an effort to develop internationally accepted standards, this key difference between the US and UK approaches has been eroded. The lawyers and bureaucrats in the SEC have won the day. In my view, the International Accounting Standards Board has caved in and, thereby, has failed us. To their credit, they have introduced international accounting standards but, my goodness, at what cost.

In the field of UK corporate governance, however, the concept of a principles rather than a rules-based approach has been retained – and to good effect. This is reflected in the requirement that the Combined Code on Corporate Governance must be followed or, in the case of a deviation, the reason for such deviation explained. So deviation is allowed. In the UK, it has been generally accepted that rules are there sometimes to be broken and to be reinterpreted when it can be justified and when it makes sense to do so.

This 'commonsense attitude' to regulation has its roots in English history. Indeed, it was King Alfred – the king, who is better known for 'burning the cakes' than anything else – who conceptualised this English approach. During his reign (871-899), King Alfred recaptured London from the Vikings and restored Saxon fortunes. But he also commissioned the consolidation of English law into a single work *The Book of Dooms* and, in the preamble, he wrote, 'I have not dared to presume to set down in writing many laws of my own, for I cannot tell what will meet with the approval of our successors'. What vision, but also what simplicity.

From clear Saxon principles rather than rigid (Latin or Napoleonic) rules emerged English Common Law, with simple concepts such as tort, contract, specific performance, damages and equity. The legal framework was flexible and it is this flexibility that has been embraced by the financial regulatory environment and adopted in the UK, in recent years, by the Financial Services Authority and the Financial Reporting Council into principles. The UK has developed a system of business and financial regulation based on principles and an assessment of risk, rather than rigid compliance with rules. In an industry, such as financial services, where products, areas of activity and new ideas are being formulated and introduced on an ongoing basis, a rules-based approach is ineffective. It slows things down. Rules are always out of date. They take longer to be devised or to amend, not least because regulators are inevitably one step behind those they regulate. Instead, the UK system places reliance on the directors of companies assessing and managing their own risks when entering areas of new business or introducing new products. As a result, the costs of regulation are lower. Regulatory contact is a lot easier. Decisions are made faster. The environment for the introduction of new products is more benign.

Thus, Islamic Finance, Forward Freight Derivatives and Carbon Emissions Trading, to name but a few new business areas, have all been developed faster and more successfully in the UK than in other countries where a rules-based regulatory environment is in force. For these reasons, the major global players, in particular the US, German and Swiss finance houses have moved their international operations to London. Almost all the Sovereign Wealth Funds have offices in the City. London has become the place to be, if you are, or aspire to be, a major international financial business.

And, during my travels around the world, Ministers, Regulators and Central Bank Governors wanted to know the secrets of London's regulatory success. All were looking forward to participating in the International Centre of Financial Regulation that Gordon Brown, as Chancellor, announced would be established in the City of London.

I have dealt in the final chapter with the sub-prime crisis in the US and the Northern Rock incident in the UK, as these have highlighted shortcomings in both regulatory regimes. The impact of the former is far greater than the latter. Both problems have, however, emphasised the increased need for regulators, as well as regulated, to pay more attention to assessing risk in business. Yet more rules and more box ticking will not help. Instead it is essential that boards of directors understand the risks associated with new business activities and it is essential that the regulators have greater dialogue, at a senior level, with chief executives and company boards in respect of such matters.

It has been failure to do this that, in my view, resulted in the sub-prime crisis in the US and the Northern Rock incident in the UK, described on pages 269-88.

THE PHYSICAL ENVIRONMENT

The City of London Corporation's studies show that businesses want a secure environment in which to operate – with minimum risk to disruption from terrorist activities, fire, flooding and crime – and want an efficient environment in which to interact with their customers and grow their businesses.

Security is their first concern and the City of London is fortunate in having its own dedicated police force that is highly regarded, that relates well to its customers and that is the centre of excellence in the UK for combating and solving financial crime. Not long after the IRA bombing campaigns of the 1970s and '80s, vast improvements in camera technology made it possible to track movements in the Square Mile. A camera system and police checks were introduced into the City. Known as the 'Ring of Steel', this had the huge benefit of deterring terrorists as well as other criminal activity. Over the years, the 'Ring of Steel' has been complemented by hundreds of video cameras installed

5 *The skyline of the City of London today – tower cranes show that construction of new buildings continues.*

by occupiers of buildings to help protect their businesses. In addition, City businesses now work with the City Police Force, through a campaign known as 'Project Griffin', to try to identify potential terrorists and to minimise the risk of harm and disruption.

A second priority is the provision of modern office accommodation, where the City Corporation's Planning Department has done an excellent job over the years in encouraging the replacement of ageing office stock with new buildings – imaginatively designed and with the latest interior layouts. Retailing has been encouraged back into the Square Mile, which is now a most agreeable place in which to work, with many restaurants, bars and, of course, the Barbican Centre with its outstanding music and drama. This has been enhanced by the City's 'Street Improvement Scene', a programme of tree planting, pedestrianisation, fountains and benches, all of which improves the ambiance and attractiveness of London. Of greater relevance to the business and legal City was the decision in December 2006 to establish the Commercial Court in a new building in Fetter Lane. I was telephoned separately on 1 December 2006 by both the Lord Chancellor and the Lord Chief Justice to ask if I would allow Mansion House to be the venue for a Press Conference to announce the construction of a new building in Fetter Lane in which to house a new Commercial Court. I immediately agreed, not least since many of my predecessors had been campaigning for this for some time.

The present premises in Fetter Lane were well below standard. The proposition would help ensure that London remains the centre for commercial disputes and arbitration. I was pleased to help.

A third priority is effective transport, which, in recent years, has been a weakness. The population of London has increased markedly over the last 20 years, yet the transport system in many instances dates from the 19th century. Outdated rolling stock, complex old-fashioned wiring, and lack of air-conditioning all contribute to a less than satisfactory travelling experience. Since the formation of the GLA and the election of the 'other Mayor' (until recently, Ken Livingstone, now Boris Johnson), improvements have been made in ground-based public transport and there is now an effective network of buses. The Underground system, largely dating from the Victorian era, is gradually being updated, as are some of the over-ground train lines. There has been investment in Thameslink and the Docklands Light Railway has been built.

For very many years, successive Lord Mayors and the City of London Corporation have been pressing for a new railway line (Crossrail) linking Heathrow and the City (including Canary Wharf) and working closely with the Mayor of London to achieve this. It was with some satisfaction, therefore, that Prime Minister Gordon Brown announced, in October 2007, towards the end of my Mayoralty, that Crossrail would be built. The political impetus of a possible General Election (that was never called) resulted in the Treasury seeking financial commitments from the City, which were bravely and sensibly given, after a historic debate in the City's Court of Common Council ably led by the Chairman of Policy & Resources, Michael Snyder (now Sir Michael Snyder). The 25-year wait was over. But it will be 2015, at least, before it is built.

A further issue, which developed as a major matter during my Mayoralty, was that of air travel to and through the UK, particularly Heathrow. International businesses need efficient air travel to be effective. Heathrow was a post-war phenomenon which was added to, piecemeal, as London's air traffic increased. Now, out of date, scruffy, and with the added burden of additional security checks, Heathrow was failing and becoming a place which international travellers wanted to avoid. The 'one bag' rule introduced after terrorist incidents and alerts in the capital slowed down progress through the airport, whether one was leaving, entering or merely transiting. On my overseas travels, this became the single key issue that foreign executives would raise with me. In Kuwait, for example, the head of the Kuwait Investment Authority complained about the security arrangements at Heathrow which delayed his senior people accessing the UK. Later, in Denmark, a senior executive at Møller/Maersk, the largest container shipping company in the world complained about the one bag policy. I reported these complaints to Ed Balls and to his successor, Kitty Ussher.

On 20 June 2007, Gordon Brown was my chief guest at Mansion House, on his last appearance as Chancellor of the Exchequer, at the Banquet for Merchants & Bankers. I took the opportunity to praise him for what he had done in the previous 10 years and for developing an excellent relationship between the Treasury and the City of London. But I also took the opportunity to refer to Heathrow and its shortcomings.

As a result of these and other incidents drawn to their attention (for example Michael Snyder's late arrival for a meeting at No 11 caused by delays at Heathrow), the Treasury took a high profile response. In her inaugural speech as Economic Secretary, Kitty Ussher made specific reference to the failings of Heathrow. In discussion with the Department of Transport and, presumably, British Airports Authority, changes were gradually made. The British Ambassador to Denmark, David Frost, even arranged a visit of Danish businessmen, including a senior representative of Møller/Maersk, to inspect the new Terminal 5 at Heathrow and then to have lunch with me at Mansion House. As it happened, someone decided, that day, to dig up the road around Fleet Street and my visitors were 45 minutes late for their lunch engagement. The main achievement, though, is that through continuous lobbying, we managed to get everyone, led by the Treasury, to accept that there was a serious problem that needed to be resolved. Ken Livingstone also joined in, but not to the extent of arguing for a further runway. The Heathrow phenomenon convinced me, however, that the privatisation of London's airports had been seriously flawed. It made the planning and provision of public transport in the country's capital city, indeed the world's financial centre, a lot more difficult. London must have the best airport in the world if it is to continue to be the world's leading financial centre. There can be no compromise.

It was, of course, a further sadness to watch, some months after my Mayoralty was over, the shambles that developed as Heathrow's Terminal 5 was opened. This is exactly not what the City needs. Public transport is too important a subject to be left to the private sector alone. Much as I favour competition and private enterprise, Government has a role, from which it must not shirk, when it comes to the delivery of public services. Fortunately Terminal 5 is now operating well, but its opening has left an unfortunate legacy.

TAXATION – A PLUS AND A MINUS

A key advantage, often overlooked in the UK, is the tax regime. Some commentators have written, in the past, that the UK was in fact a tax haven. This stemmed partly from our 'Non Dom' rules, as they are referred to. Until the Budget of 2008, these rules permitted those foreigners who were not 'domiciled' in the UK (that is, did not intend to settle permanently) to be taxed in the UK only on their UK income and such of their non-UK income and gains as they remitted to the UK. This was of great benefit to many foreign nationals, not just wealthy Greek ship owners, but financial executives, Russian oligarchs and, even, students. For many years, there was a tacit agreement with the Treasury and the other political parties that this was an 'untouchable area' – to be left well alone.

The Greek ship-owning community left New York en masse when the fiscal environment changed there. Almost simultaneously, the UK Chancellor of the day wisely introduced tonnage tax which made the UK more attractive to foreign ship owners to establish their businesses in London. In fact they flocked to London and enhanced the success of the City's maritime sector – ship broking, marine insurance and ship finance.

In my discussions with the financial and maritime services industry, everyone pleaded with me – 'Please ensure that the Treasury doesn't attack Non Dom. It would do so much to harm UK plc. Remember what happened to New York'. Regrettably, at the Conservative conference in October 2007, the Shadow Chancellor George Osborne, suggested that one way of funding their proposed increase in the inheritance tax exemption was to introduce a new flat rate of tax of £25,000 for foreigners. The cat was out of the bag. The Treasury and probably also HM Customs & Revenue officials, who had been dying to attack non-doms for years, offered some draconian proposals. In the context of the election that never was, the Government went ahead, encouraged by the unions who wanted to tax fat cats. Foreigners began to feel unwanted. They began to plan their migration elsewhere – and with them the drivers of much wealth and business investment in the economy. I felt sick and was pleased to see Lord (Digby) Jones come out against the proposals. Then, later, universities and others representing the less well off non-doms joined in the condemnation. It seemed to me that the proposals had been poorly thought through, with inadequate

6   Left to right: Lord Mayor, Lady Mayoress, Gordon Brown, Mervyn King, Alderman and Sheriff David Lewis, Sheriff Richard Regan, Lord Mayor's Chaplain William Gulliford.

consultation, and were a most unfortunate response to George Osborne's politically inspired suggestions. Fortunately, after much lobbying, the Chancellor agreed to modify some (but by no means all) of the changes which would have adversely affected the tax position of non-doms. However, the damage had been done. The image of the UK being a welcoming environment for foreigners had received a bad knock.

During my term of office, the whole issue of UK taxation emerged as a potential major problem and I had cause to raise it in a number of speeches and in meetings, as a matter of serious concern. There were a number of aspects to this.

First, increased public spending has to be funded by Government borrowing or increased taxation. In good times, tax revenues increase as the economy expands. However, in recent years, the increase in public spending was such that it could be only be met by a higher fiscal burden. Thus, while some headline rates of tax have been reduced (namely the basic rate of income tax and the main corporation tax rate), the total tax take in the UK as a percentage of earnings had not, unlike in other countries, declined (due to changes in the tax base, for example the reforms to the capital allowances system).

Second, the Treasury had taken responsibility for fiscal policy from HM Revenue and Customs and did not have the same in-depth, grass roots experience. They were one step removed from the companies and individuals who were subject to any proposed new fiscal measures.

Then, the merger of the Inland Revenue and the Customs & Excise had created an unfortunate culture. The IR were, generally speaking, well educated and gentlemanly, trying to help ensure that tax charges were correct, while at the same time trying to prevent and penalise tax evasion and cut out loopholes. The Customs & Excise were used to a different clientele – for example, smugglers. Their response typically matched their clients' behaviour. I had not appreciated this until, while I was travelling in the Gulf on Mayoral business in February 2007, my wife received a letter from the newly merged HM Revenue & Customs to the effect that my personal tax payment was overdue and that, unless paid by a certain date, bailiffs would be retained to distrain my possessions (namely

7 *'The industrious 'prentice Lord Mayor of London' by William Hogarth.*

seize my household furniture). To receive such a notice while I was on 'public service' for my country was one thing. For my wife to have to deal with this in my absence was another. PricewaterhouseCoopers quickly came to the rescue and confirmed that my tax had been paid by the due date and the problem had arisen because one HMRC office had not communicated with another. Disturbingly, my wife was informed that the HMRC never issues apologies. This

17

incident confirmed what I had heard from practising accountants and it showed me how the culture and attitudes of our Revenue Authorities had changed – for the worse. This incident was confirmed by my former Tax partners at PwC as being typical.

Perhaps more important, HMRC officials had become fixated on meeting targets for tax collection, perhaps driven by a desire to increase fiscal revenues. There were instances of very senior HMRC officials contacting PLC chairmen and chief executives to discuss their company's approach to tax planning. There was a seemingly deliberate confusing of legitimate tax avoidance with illegal tax evasion – and demonising the former. There was greater uncertainty creeping into the system.

In time, these factors will conspire to make the UK uncompetitive as a country in which to do business. It is interesting that, in the period after I have stepped down as Lord Mayor, the issue of taxation is viewed as more important and not just a potential but a very real Achilles heel. Changes to capital gains tax, the taxation of non-doms and fiscal threats to the overseas profits of multinational companies have become issues of potential competitive disadvantage to the UK. I am sorry to see what has happened. Against that, there is undoubtedly hope – the Treasury deserves real credit for promoting Islamic Finance and for making changes to the tax system to facilitate Sharia'a compliant business. If only that enlightened, City-motivated stance suffused more of the way our tax system has been developed in recent years.

During my Mayoralty, I had intended to focus more on the worsening fiscal environment, but the Northern Rock incident and the sub-prime crisis intervened and I was deflected off course. Notwithstanding this, like others, I believe that a competitive fiscal environment is essential to maintaining the competitiveness and success of the City of London and I believe that currently things are not going in the right direction.

A WELCOMING CITY

A final factor in London's success seems to be that it is a welcoming place. Foreigners feel relatively at ease when they come to live in London. London has always accepted, and benefited from, an influx of foreign nationals – Huguenots, Jews, Poles, East African Asians, Bangladeshis and, now, Americans, French, Chinese, Indians, Middle Eastern Arabs and Russians.

London is also a very cosmopolitan place. There are restaurants with food from all countries of the world. Many languages are spoken. Indeed, London has always been that way. If you had lived in the City of London in Roman times, you would have heard foreign languages spoken, from Gaul, Germany, Greece, Italy and North Africa. In the 13th century, the chronicler, Matthew Paris, complained of too many foreigners. In the 1450s there was much suspicion of Italian bankers and merchants. In the late 16th there was concern over the large numbers of Huguenot immigrants. Then, in the 19th century, revolutionaries

from the Austro-Hungarian Empire and from Russia came to Britain to escape the regimes in those countries. And there were periodic bursts of Jewish traders and craftsmen fleeing persecution on the Continent and bringing with them business acumen, music and the visual arts. Latter-day immigrants have been Irish, Greek Cypriots, West Indians, Chinese, Bangladeshis, Poles and French. Not all have been appreciated. But the general picture is one of net immigration from other cities and towns in the UK and from other countries throughout the world. The City has a culture of welcoming foreigners to its midst and, generally, they have been welcomed. London is a city that foreigners actually like.

8 Ready to receive in the Salon of the Mansion House before the Judges' Banquet.

Today, outside Mansion House, you are as likely to hear Mandarin or Russian or French or American spoken as The Queen's English, since the financial sector has become truly international and London has become a truly international city. On my travels I used to declare that I was not the Mayor of a 'British' city but the Mayor of a truly 'international' city. This has been one of London's characteristics and strengths over the years.

However, in the nine months since I completed my year of office, the fiscal changes together with changes in visa arrangements have created the impression that foreigners are not as welcome as they used to be. This is sad. It is also potentially damaging. The UK has always done well when it has been open and has welcomed people from abroad.

THE SUCCESSES AND CHALLENGES OF 2006-07

The year started well in November 2006. London was reported to be the prime international financial centre of the world. This was confirmed in March 2007 when Z/Yen, headed by Professor Michael Mainelli, produced the first Global Financial Centres Index (the GFCI) with business and personal tax data from PricewaterhouseCoopers. The index charts how financial centres relate to each other and showed London and New York as the only two truly global financial centres, well ahead of the two Asian centres of Hong Kong and Singapore, in 3rd and 4th places respectively.

London's successes and reasons for them were clear and I included them in my speeches and I explained them in discussions with foreigners visiting Mansion House and on overseas Mayoral visits:
- Culture, values and rule of law
- Global market share and open access
- Benign yet robust regulatory environment
- Pool of talent and professional skill base
- Welcoming environment, including benign fiscal regime
- English language and time zone

Whoever I saw and wherever I went, everyone wanted to know the secrets of London success. I reiterated the mantra.

But I had to keep in touch with the businesses in the City and this was achieved through a series of meetings and structured events. These included:
- Periodic meetings and lunches with various interest groups, eg the Baltic Exchange, Swiss Re, HSBC, Lloyds TSB, Lloyd's of London, London Stock Exchange, Euronext LIFFE, the British Bankers Association, the Association of Foreign Banks, the International Underwriting Association etc
- A monthly meeting of City luminaries brought together in Mansion House and known as the City No 1 Breakfast Group. This comprised the leaders of the FSA, the Bank of England, the exchanges and the major Finance Houses
- My friends and colleagues at PricewaterhouseCoopers and clients, who helped enormously to ensure that I was properly briefed on issues of the moment

During my year, I promoted the City's strengths but I also pointed out the challenges – in my speeches, to the media and, not least, to the Treasury. They were:
- Transport, in particular Heathrow
- The fiscal environment
- Visas for foreign executives and for overseas students

In 2006-07, the City of London could do no wrong. We were seen, undisputedly, as the prime international financial centre of the world. Our method of regulation was seen as the best and to be emulated by all. The world's global finance houses had to have major operations in London. Many, like Morgan Stanley, centred their international operations in the City. If you were an aspiring executive in the global financial services industry, you had to have a spell in London. This was the Mecca.

Indeed, as Lord Mayor, I felt the sort of buzz that the Victorian entrepreneurs and civic leaders must have felt. A renewed confidence was evident. There was almost full employment. The economy, particularly the financial sector, was buoyant. General inflation was under control. Property prices in the capital were soaring. The Stock Market was back at a near all-time high. There was a real feel good factor.

Then came the Sub-Prime Crisis and Northern Rock. Then came the proposed changes to capital gains tax. Then came the attack on Non-Doms. Towards the end of my Mayoralty these became the key issues which I had to address. The first is described in detail on pages 269-88. The last is an ongoing saga. Then came the chaotic opening of Heathrow's Terminal 5. After I left Office, further poorly thought-out proposals were made to tax companies' overseas profits. All the good work that had been done was in danger of being eroded – and with it, London's supremacy as the world's leading financial centre and the driver of many jobs and much prosperity. Reputations take a long time to build, but can be lost over night. The end of 2007 and the beginning of 2008 were not good times for the City of London.

THE CHANGING ROLE OF THE LORD MAYOR

The office of Lord Mayor has continued for over 800 years. During all of this time, the individual elected to this role has sought to represent, support and promote the City of London. The City has changed and therefore the content of the role has changed. The office of Lord Mayor is a curious, very British phenomenon.

9 *The Lord Mayor with the Foreign Secretary, Margaret Beckett, and the Doyen of the Diplomatic Corps, His Excellency Khaled Al-Duwaisan, GCVO, at the Easter Banquet at Mansion House where the Lord Mayor entertains the diplomatic community.*

It is flexible enough to adapt to the far reaching developments that have taken place. Yet, it has an enduring quality that enables the incumbent to preside over a city that was a successful trading centre in Roman times and then, some 2,000 years later, is the world's prime international financial centre.

The Lord Mayor wears many hats and carries many banners. He represents business, the City of London Corporation, the Livery movement and charitable endeavour. He is a staunch advocate of Free Trade; the guardian of values and ethics; the promoter of good governance and best practice; the enthusiastic supporter of education and learning; and the champion of the disadvantaged and the poor. All these attributes have been found at different times in Lord Mayors of London.

There is a link between the innovative and successful city of today, which is universally acclaimed as the financial centre of the world, and the tradition, the ceremonies and the values of our ancestors. The Lord Mayor is part of this link. Most important, he is apolitical. He represents the businesses in the financial sector and the people of the City, without following any party whip. This gives him greater credibility and enhances his standing. This makes the Mayoralty a unique role.

To understand the enduring nature of the Office and the secrets of its success, let's go back a little in time. Let's begin with the City's most famous Mayor, Dick Whittington.

10 *The Lord Mayor's Show – the Lord Mayor in his coach, which dates from 1757.*

Part II

THE TRADITIONAL
ROLE OF THE LORD MAYOR

Dick Whittington

London 4 Miles

David Allen & Sons Ltd
London
Belfast · Manchester
& Harrow Copyright 1899

Dick Whittington – London's Most Famous Mayor – and his Cat

THE PANTOMIME STORY

Legend has it that Dick Whittington was a poor orphan from the country who came to London to seek his fortune. He had heard that the streets were paved with gold. After finding work in the kitchen of a rich merchant, he was ill treated by the cook and ran away. On his way home (to Gloucestershire) he stopped on Highgate Hill when he heard the bells peel out 'Turn again, Dick Whittington, thrice Mayor of London'. He returned to find that his cat had been sold for a very large sum to the King of the Barbary Coast, to put down a plague of rats. This made him rich. He married the merchant's daughter, Alice, and became very successful. After being Mayor three times, he did many noble things and, when he died, he left all his money to charity.

THE LIME STREET CONNECTION

In 1406 when Richard Whittington was Mayor for the third time, he was, like me, the Alderman for Lime Street. He lived in Leadenhall Street, which is in my Ward, next to the ancient and attractive Leadenhall Market and the world's leading insurance market, Lloyd's of London. As the Alderman for Lime Street and since my Mayoralty coincided with the 600th anniversary of his election, I naturally took a keen interest in Richard Whittington and wanted to learn more about him and what he did.

INVESTIGATING THE FACTS

My curiosity was further aroused when, as one of the two Sheriffs of London in 2005-06, I accompanied my predecessor as Lord Mayor, Sir David Brewer, CMG, together with many Mayors from the other London Boroughs, on the annual 'Whittington Walk' from Whittington Hospital, past the 'Whittington Stone' on Highgate Hill, down to Mansion House.

The fable of Dick Whittington was repeated by our guide, and the accompanying Town Cryer, namely that Dick was walking home to Gloucestershire up Highgate Hill when he stopped as the bells rang out 'Turn again, Dick Whittington, thrice Mayor of London'.

11 *Poster of Dick Whittington.*

12 London's Mayors on the annual Whittington Walk from Highgate to Mansion House.

But, I thought to myself, and as everyone knows, if you want to go home from London to Gloucestershire, you don't go up Highgate Hill. So what was the real story?

It is generally believed that Richard Whittington was born in Gloucestershire in the late 1350s. His father, Sir William de Whittington, owned an estate, at Pauntley, which Dick, as the younger son, did not inherit. Consequently he was sent to London to learn the trade of a mercer.

Contrary to the pantomime story he travelled by horse, not on foot, and after a successful apprenticeship under Sir Ivo Fitzwarren, whose daughter Alice he subsequently married, he became a successful trader, dealing in valuable imports such as silk and velvet. He became Master of the Mercers' Company on three occasions and he sold goods to the Court and to King Richard II. He also engaged in money-lending and he was owed large sums by the King, who had to finance armies to deal with unrest both at home and in Ireland. This constant need for finance had, no doubt, caused the King to seize some of the City of London's lands, through alleged misgovernment. When the then Mayor of London, Adam Bamme, died in office in 1397, the King needed a friend in the City and chose Richard Whittington, to whom he was also indebted, to fill the vacancy. But wily Whittington negotiated a deal to restore the City's rights and a grateful London public elected him Mayor in October 1398. He was elected a second time in 1406 and finally again in 1419. Thus, Richard Whittington was elected Mayor of London three times but actually served on four separate occasions.

So the first myth was exposed. He was Mayor *four* times.

The second question is the matter of Dick's intended destination when he left London, journeying up Highgate Hill. Where was he going to?

A quick canter through the Internet, after typing in the words 'Richard Whittington', reveals Whittington Castle near Oswestry in Shropshire where, allegedly, Dick lived as a boy and, some say, was his home. There is another strange connection in that the Fitz Waryn (Fitzwarren) family, into which Richard married, owned Whittington Castle at various times in the 13th and 14th centuries. It has also been suggested that Richard's father's family hailed from nearby, in the Midlands, before they acquired property in Gloucestershire.

Is it possible, therefore, that when Dick Whittington was on the point of leaving London because he was unhappy, he was not on his way back 'home' to Gloucestershire but to Shropshire where he knew he would receive a friendlier welcome? After all, he had apparently left Pauntley because his elder brother had inherited their father's estate – and big brother would not be best pleased to see him return. Whittington Castle was, on the other hand, perhaps a more likely place of refuge for an unloved and unhappy apprentice from London. Who knows?

RELATING THE WHITTINGTON STORY – ONE OF CHARITY AND VOLUNTEERING

The Whittington debate makes a good story, but I had an additional reason for publicising Dick Whittington. During my Mayoralty I wished to promote, inter alia, volunteering and charity (the subject of a separate chapter in this book).

Richard Whittington is a role model for modern-day City executives. After all, over the centuries, the City has had many wealthy charitable donors – for example Sir John Cass and Sir Thomas Gresham. In addition, each Lord Mayor has in his year of office a dedicated Lord Mayor's Appeal for a charitable cause. And the City Bridge Trust managed by the City of London Corporation makes substantial donations to community activities.

Whittington was the Bill Gates of his day, extremely generous and he certainly demonstrated 'public service'. During his life, he did a great deal for the City and was a major donor – money which would be used for construction – the rebuilding of Guildhall, a ward for unmarried mothers at St Thomas' Hospital, the rebuilding of his parish church (St Michael Paternoster Royal) and public toilets (a 64-seater no less) in St Martin Vintry that were cleaned automatically by the River Thames at high tide. He had a caring nature which led him to pass a law prohibiting the washing of animal skins, by apprentices, in the River Thames, because so many boys had died of hypothermia in cold, wet weather, or in the strong river currents. He undertook great public service, being Mayor four times and also a Member of Parliament, serving on many Royal Commissions and sitting as a Magistrate and as a Judge.

13 *Stained glass portrait of Richard Whittington in Old Library, Guildhall.*

Richard Whittington died childless, in 1423, his wife Alice having predeceased him in 1411. Like many wealthy businessmen, who die without issue, he left his fortune (£7,000) to charity in the City that had made him successful. This legacy financed the first library in Guildhall, repairs to St Bartholomew's Hospital, almshouses (now the Whittington College, where poor homeless people could live), a priests' college, repairs to Newgate Gaol (indicating his interest in the rights of prisoners) and a public water supply.

But there was a further reason for publicising Dick Whittington. My predecessor, Sir David Brewer and his wife, Tessa, had a dog, Figaro, who lived with them for their year in Mansion House. On the other hand, Lesley and I had cats – two lovely British Blues, Spot and Cato, half sisters with orange eyes and blue-grey fluffy coats. While, realistically, they would prefer to stay at our home in Totteridge, we decided to take with us their 'stuffed' substitutes, Sean and Nick (named after the efficient and fun-loving footmen who had looked after us when I was Sheriff at the Old Bailey). We placed Sean and Nick in our Private Quarters at Mansion House and they looked quite lifelike. After the Year of the Dog, this was to be the Year of the Cat.

And, of course, in the pantomime story, Dick Whittington had a cat, called Tommy – a cat that had been sold to the King of the Barbary Coast and which had made his early fortune. There is actually no evidence that Richard Whittington ever had a cat in real life. Mention was first made of his cat in the play, based on the pantomime, *The History of Richard Whittington, of his lowe byrth, his great fortune*, which first appeared in 1605. It has been suggested that the origin of the cat was the type of boat, called a 'catt', which Whittington used to transport cloth from Holland to England. Again, who knows? But it doesn't matter. So far as the public is concerned, Dick Whittington had a cat and 2007 was going to be the Year of the Cat, for all sorts of (Regulatory) reasons which will become apparent later in the book.

On 8 November 2006, two days before I took Office, a Press release was issued from the City Corporation headed 'City of London's new cat-loving Lord Mayor backs Shropshire's claim on Dick Whittington'. The text ran as follows:

> Leading City of London accountant John Stuttard, 61, steps into office on Friday 10 November as the ambassador for the UK's world-beating financial services industry – but also into a controversy over where predecessor Dick Whittington was born.
>
> Lord Mayor Elect Stuttard (who just happens to have been educated at Shrewsbury School) took time out from preparing to promote London and

14 *A group from the Lord Mayor's alma mater, Shrewsbury School, joins the show.*

the UK's Square Mile business centre to fuel controversy over the true-life Dick Whittington – claimed by both Gloucestershire and Shropshire.

Speaking before this Saturday's Lord Mayor's Show and fireworks, he said: 'Dick Whittington was a great example, like me, of an economic migrant; someone who moved to where the work was and maximised the value of his talent. The legend says he "turned again" at Highgate Hill in North London – but you would only go that way if you were travelling to Shropshire – not Gloucestershire.'

Burnley-born John Stuttard and wife Lesley have two British Blue cats, Spot and Cato (both six), but neither will see much of him during his year in the City of London's Mansion House as his main job will be promoting the financial services industry abroad for three months – and receiving ministers and business delegations.

At school from age 13 to 18 in Shrewsbury, the Lord Mayor Elect remembers well Morris's store and the tale of the unfortunate Mr Done, the toll-keeper on Kingsland Bridge. After schoolboys pushed the keeper in the river, the angry headmaster cancelled half-day term-time holidays and told a chastened assembly: 'This was an outrage. You have done to Done that which you ought not to have done.'

Father-of-two John Stuttard, who until recently was a senior partner with global accountants PricewaterhouseCoopers, puts his Whittington-like success down to his own upbringing – both in Lancashire and Shropshire.

Lord Mayor Elect Stuttard, who will meet Prime Ministers and leading business figures regularly during his term of office, will help UK jobs by promoting London as a financial centre during more than three months of delegation visits to two dozen countries including China, India, Russia, and Brazil – the four nations likely to become world leaders this century.

ENDS

BBC Radio Gloucester telephoned immediately, demanding to speak to the new Lord Mayor and seek an apology. I was interviewed on the very morning of my taking Office. The interview went roughly like this:

Interviewer: The new Lord Mayor of London, Alderman John Stuttard, who is with us this morning, has claimed that our local hero Dick Whittington came from Shropshire and not Gloucester as everyone popularly believes. This has come as a bit of shock to many here in Gloucester and we have been finding out what people think. First, at the 'Dick Whittington' pub in Gloucester, Sir, what do you think of this claim?

Local in pub (in heavy west country accent): I think it's a damned cheek. Who do he think he be, this Lawrd Mayor, trying to steal our Dick Whittington? Everyone knows he's ours.

Interviewer: And now we have the Archivist from the Gloucester Library and Archives Department. Sir what light can you shed on this?

Archivist: Well, there's definite proof that Richard Whittington came from Pauntley in Gloucestershire, where his father had an estate. The estate was left to the elder son and so Richard had to leave home, looking for work, and he went to London, where he became a great success.

Interviewer: First, Mr Stuttard, congratulations on becoming Lord Mayor, but now I think you have upset some folks here in Gloucester with your comments about Dick Whittington. You have heard what has been said. I think you need to explain yourself.

JS: Thank you and good morning. Yes, there are claims that Dick Whittington lived in Shropshire as well as Gloucestershire. In truth, he probably came from both. You know, Dick Whittington is a real role model. He belongs to all of us. He came to London to study and learn. He worked hard and became very wealthy and, when he died, he left all his money to charity. Don't you think that's something we should all emulate?

Interviewer: But I get the impression that because you were educated at Shrewsbury you favour Shropshire and you don't like Gloucestershire, my Lord Mayor.

JS: Oh yes, I do. When I was a little boy I used to come and stay with my aunt who lived in Lennox House just near the Spa. I remember climbing all the way to the top of Gloucester Cathedral. It's a very nice place. I have a very soft spot for Gloucester.

Interviewer: Well, perhaps you're not such a bad chap after all. Thank you for being with us and good luck.

CATS ARE EFFICIENT REGULATORS

And so the story was repeated during my Mayoralty and the cat theme was developed. In my speeches, I added two more (non original) cat jokes, to amuse and also to get across the benefits of cats in a regulatory setting, so promoting the form of financial regulation in London. Thus:

15 *The Lord Mayor's Children's Christmas Party – ready to receive – together with Georgie the Cat.*

- But, we are fortunate to be with you today. I am certainly luckier than the cat who was referred to recently in the Westmoreland Gazette, under the column 'Lost & Found' – 'Lost in Cartmel – One-eyed Ginger Tom – Recently Castrated – Answers to the name of Lucky'; and:

- And while on the subject of cats, we were all very sorry to learn of the recent passing of Humphrey, the Downing Street cat. A serial killer, he served under three Prime Ministers, ridding Whitehall of vermin. In a 120-page file on Humphrey released recently by the Cabinet Office, one official wrote that he caught hundreds of mice and the odd rat, whereas after he retired from public service his successors, Rentokil, haven't caught a thing. The file added: 'He is a workaholic who spends nearly all his time in the office, does not socialise a great deal or go to many parties and has not been involved in any sex or drugs scandal – at least so far as we are aware'. When asked about Humphrey's gender and whether he had sired any offspring, the same official responded that Humphrey had indeed been positively vetted

- I pointed out often that, like our form of financial regulation in the City of London, cats don't blindly follow rules. They use their intuition and they have a very effective touch when it comes to dealing with vermin.

2007 – 'Year of the Cat'

For the cover of our 2007 Christmas card we had chosen, with the help of David Bradbury and John Fisher of the City of London Corporation's Libraries & Archives Department, a photo of a 19th-century pantomime poster, owned

16 *Colin and James bring in the Lady Mayoress' cats, Sean and Nick, at the Lord Mayor's Children's Christmas Party.*

by collector David Drummond of Cecil Court off Charing Cross Road, depicting Dick Whittington on his way to London with a black cat.

Then, at the Lord Mayor's Children's Fancy Dress Christmas Party at Mansion House in January 2007, attended by around 400 young children, there was a definite cat theme. First, our two stuffed cats were carried in, on foot stools, by Colin Tucker and James Macdonald, Mansion House Steward and Footman respectively, as part of the formal procession led by the City Marshal, Common Cryer and the Pikemen & Musketeers. Then, Georgie, the daughter of June and Gerry Pulman, the City Corporation's Chief Commoner, came dressed in a cat suit and charmed all the other little girls who had dressed in theirs. In one very special moment, the 'kittens' were seen huddled together around Georgie on the side of the stage, listening very intently to her – presumably learning about the niceties of hunting mice and what cakes they might expect for afternoon tea in Mansion House Ballroom.

17   *The Chief Commoner, Gerry Pulman, Pearly Queen and young pearls at the Lord Mayor's Children's Christmas Party.*

2007 was to be the Year of the Cat, but it was also a year in which we promoted the City's risk-based regulation and the benefits of volunteering and charitable giving, as well as having a lot of fun.

And, of course, we spread the word about the benefits of coming to London for a business education and to learn professional skills. Richard Whittington, like me, was an economic migrant. He came to London to be apprenticed, to study, to work hard – and he found the streets paved with gold. And many, like Richard Whittington, went on to become public servants and philanthropists. It's great to receive, but it's even better to give.

18 *Painting by Logsdail of the Lord Mayor's Procession in front of the Royal Exchange.*

The Ceremonies and the Grand Events of the City

THE POPULAR PUBLIC IMAGE OF THE LORD MAYOR

If you 'Google' the 'Lord Mayor of London', invariably you are presented on your computer screen with an image of someone dressed in a scarlet gown, wearing a gold chain around his shoulders, waving a black-feathered tricorne hat and travelling in a gold coach, attended by Pikemen in 17th-century costume.

THE LORD MAYOR'S SHOW

This is, without doubt, a photograph of the Lord Mayor on the day of his Show. In his 18th-century carriage, which weighs almost three tons, each year the new Lord Mayor is conveyed from Guildhall to the Royal Courts of Justice, to be 'shown' to the public en route and then to make his declaration of office before the Lord Chief Justice, the Master of the Rolls and judges of the Supreme Court, together with representatives of the City, his family and friends.

Only the Monarch is entitled to more horses – eight to be precise. The rest of us have to make do with two or, if we've just received a large bonus, four. But, the Lord Mayor may have six and they look magnificent as they plod in stately fashion along Cheapside, New Change, down Ludgate Hill and then up Fleet Street, with thousands of cheering and waving spectators and many millions more watching at home on television. This is the Lord Mayor's Show which takes place annually on the second Saturday in November.

The Show comprises hundreds of different entrants or 'floats', as they are known, since the procession was originally waterborne from the City to the Inns of Court. A Canaletto painting, dated 1747, of *The River Thames on Lord Mayor's Day*, depicts barges, rowing boats and yachts colourfully and enthusiastically accompanying the Lord Mayor to Westminster. Today, the floats are commissioned and prepared by various organisations and businesses in the City of London. They are many and they are varied – soldiers and cadets, some on horseback, some with big guns, some playing music, and all with smart uniforms; charities and community service volunteers; St John's Ambulance and Red Cross officers and cadets ready to come to anyone's assistance; schools with marching bands

19 *The Pikemen and Musketeers are the Lord Mayor's bodyguard.*

20 *Early morning rehearsal for the Lord Mayor's Show.*

and displays; colourful and wild horsemen from Kazakhstan; Chinese lion dancers and acrobats; the latest Rolls-Royce cars, as well as some vintage ones; a fleet of Morris Minors; Liverymen of the City, showing their wide ranging occupations and trades; and, of course, the Pikemen & Musketeers, the Lord Mayor's personal bodyguard from the Honourable Artillery Company; and the Light Cavalry, the Lady Mayoress' personal bodyguard. The Armed Forces, the charitable institutions,

the schools, the Livery companies and the City's businesses all play an important part. It is a happy day, a day for cheering and waving, and a day of smiling faces.

The Lord Mayor's Show is the longest, unrehearsed parade in the world – three miles long, but over a distance of just 2½ miles, so that the first float finishes before the last float has started. For many years now, this amazing parade has been a family business. Dominic Reid, OBE took over from his father as the Pageantmaster who ensures, together with a team of volunteer Marshals, that everything works with split second precision timing. It is an amazing accomplishment. It is a wonderful thing to watch and is much enjoyed by everyone – young and old.

In preparation for my Show, in November 2006, I found out that this would be the 250th time that the coach, made in 1757, would be used. Currently insured for £1.5 million the Lord Mayor's Coach was designed by Sir Robert Taylor, an architect, and built by Joseph Berry, a coachbuilder from Holborn, at a total cost of around £860. Its exterior is gilded rococo woodwork with allegorical painted panels attributed to Italian painter Giovanni Battista Cipriani, depicting the genius of the City of London in the form of Truth, Temperance, Justice and Fortitude. The walls and ceiling of the interior are covered in a red silk fabric. After the Coronation coach it ranks second in terms of importance in the kingdom. Now on its 250th outing, it was important that this anniversary, this accomplishment, should be recognised in some way. So we arranged a competition of paintings of the coach by schoolchildren. 'Arts for All' is a charity run by Caroline Barlow and Richard Tait aimed at encouraging youngsters from the East End to explore and enjoy their artistic talents by drawing, painting and making things. For many years it has been supported by the Worshipful Company of Blacksmiths. In July, Caroline and Richard brought the kids with their exhibits to the Old Bailey, where we were living while I was one of the two Sheriffs of London. The judges included Dominic Reid, Sheldon Hind from the City Corporation's Public Relations Office and the Show programme designers, PSP Communications. The paintings were all so imaginative. In the end, we chose a painting by a young 15-year-old Somali boy, Ilias Muhudin, whose parents were refugees. He won the first prize of £250 and, as well as seeing his painting reproduced on the front cover of the Lord Mayor's programme, he was invited for lunch at Mansion House on the day of the Show. When he was interviewed by the BBC outside broadcast team, he responded magnificently.

Bearing in mind the importance of international companies, foreign nationals and overseas students to the success of the City of London, I discussed with Dominic how we might make the Show more international in character. I had fortunately met the amiable and able Ambassador from Kazakhstan, Erlan Idrissov, partly in preparation for my official visit to his country and also because Kazakh companies were increasingly coming to London for

21 *The Lord Mayor inspects the Guard, from HMS Illustrious, together with the Sheriffs and the Pageantmaster, Dominic Reid.*

22 *Ilias Muhudin and his painting of the Lord Mayor's coach.*

23 *Gog and Magog in the 2006 Lord Mayor's Show.*

business as well as share issues and listings on the London Stock Exchange. The President of Kazakhstan was also due to come to London in November to raise the profile of his country. I suggested a Kazakh entry in the Show, little realising that they would bring a group of fierce looking horsemen from the Steppes. But two conditions were first communicated by His Excellency: (1) could we guarantee television coverage? (2) could we find the horses? It was clear that (1) would be no problem. A group of wild looking Kazakh warriors riding through the streets of London would create quite a stir. Any television channel worth its salt would dearly like to cover this. But the second condition might be less easy to satisfy. Dominic had an idea. He had a friend who could put him in touch with the owner of some polo ponies, which would be strong and wiry enough

24 *Kazakh horsemen steal the show.*

to cope with wild Kazakh horsemen. So the scene was set for something out of Tamburlaine, but hopefully without the blood. In the event, we had an extra piece of good fortune when the film about an imaginary Kazakh, Borat, was released a few weeks before the Show. Initially the Kazakh authorities found the association of such poor behaviour with their nation to be unacceptable. But when the film became popular and the character of Borat became well known, they saw the marketing benefits of the film in putting little known Kazakhstan well and truly on the map. Some media reported that, during the Show, the Kazakh warriors had been seen leaving the City and charging off to the West End after hearing of a rumour that Sacha Baron Cohen had been spotted there.

We also approached the Hong Kong Economic & Trade Office in London. The Director-General, Sarah Wu, agreed that, given its importance as a financial centre, Hong Kong should have an entry – a bun tower, to be erected at the corner of Cornhill and the Royal Exchange, with acrobats climbing the tower picking 'buns'. It was certainly different and very visual.

25 *The Finnish float in the Lord Mayor's Show featured the first ever 'official' State visit to the UK of the real Father Christmas.*

The international theme continued with the Hamburg Guild participating for the second time in three years commemorating the centuries old relationship between the Hanseatic League and the City of London. The China-Britain Business Council, of which I had been a director for six years, organised a traditional Chinese lion dance. Then, the Finnish British Chamber of Commerce, of which I had been chairman, decided that their float should be a Father Christmas sitting on a sledge, pulled by a stuffed reindeer. Coming up to the Christmas season, this was good marketing for the Finnish tourist industry offering snowbound holiday excursions in Lapland – and it was also the first ever 'official State visit' of Santa Claus to the UK.

I was personally pleased to see my old school, Shrewsbury, enter the Show, helping increase the links between Shropshire and London – and giving the school the chance to publicise its rowing prowess, confirmed during my Mayoral year when the First Eight won the Princess Elizabeth Cup at Henley Regatta. Other organisations with which I was involved also entered floats – PricewaterhouseCoopers, where I had worked for almost 40 years; the Ward Club for Lime Street,

26 The Lord Mayor's 1934 Rolls-Royce acts as the 'float' for the Guild of Educators in the 2006 Lord Mayor's Show.

where I am the elected Alderman, represented in an old London bus, sponsored by Richard Walduck of Imperial Hotels; King Edward's School Witley, of which I am a governor; the Guild of Educators, an embryo Livery company for which I am the Sponsoring Alderman and to whom I had lent my two old Rolls-Royces for the Show; the Worshipful Company of Plumbers, where I am an Honorary Court Assistant; the Worshipful Company of Chartered Accountants in England & Wales, where I am a Court Assistant; City University, of which I as the Lord Mayor became Chancellor for the year; and the Worshipful Company of Glaziers and Painters of Glass, my Mother Livery company, where I am also a Court Assistant, in lead position in the Show ahead of all the other Livery companies.

27 The Glaziers Float, led by Past Master Phillida Shaw.

39

The Glaziers float was spectacular, with Liverymen and their children dressed variously as lords and ladies, lions and angels, dancers and banner carriers – weaving around a horse drawn bus and behind it an image of the new Lord Mayor in a stained glass panel. The Glaziers' Mayoralty Committee, chaired by Phillida Shaw, a Past Master of the Company, had worked amazingly hard with the float designer, Jane Lyster, and involved youngsters from the South East London Army Cadet Force and pupils from the Cathedral School in Southwark carrying transparent umbrellas. Altogether the Glaziers' float had 102 people either on it or around it.

The Show starts at Guildhall, after the Lord Mayor has attended a Presentation ceremony, choreographed by the City's Remembrancer, Paul Double, where the organisations with whom the Lord Mayor is associated present him with a gift. I received some wonderful presents – a frame of 17th-century Swiss stained and painted glass from the Glaziers Livery company; two inscribed photograph albums from the Chartered Accountants Livery company; a distinguished visitors' book with beautifully inscribed coats of arms for use at Mansion House from the Plumbers' Livery company; six personalised moleskin note books (to record daily events and impressions) from the United Wards Club; a Georgian silver shell butter dish and toast rack, plus some throat pastilles (to counter the large number of speeches) from the Lime Street Ward Club; a silver salver from the Guild of Educators; a engraved decanter and glasses from the Guildable Manor of Southwark; a double photo frame from the City Livery Club; and a leather document case, with my initials embossed on it, from PricewaterhouseCoopers. The gifts were presented by representatives of each organisation, with a short speech and a flourish. It was a very happy occasion. Then, breakfast was served in the newly refurbished Old Library in Guildhall, with the warning not to drink too much coffee, as it takes a long time to travel in a carriage from Guildhall to the Law Courts.

28 *Left. Presentation Ceremony before the Lord Mayor's Show – a gift from the Glaziers.*

29 *Right. Presentation Ceremony before the Lord Mayor's Show – a gift from the Plumbers.*

30 *Lord Mayor's Show – waiting to board the coach in Guildhall Yard.*

After breakfast, the Aldermen, all dressed in their scarlet gowns, cheer the Lord Mayor as he steps into his coach to be taken to Mansion House, with his chaplain, to watch the procession. Accompanying the Aldermen, and the Lord Mayor, at all such ceremonials are the Ward Beadles, in traditional uniform and carrying their Ward mace, the symbol of the Monarch and of authority. My beadle, Edward Kipping, was the longest serving and oldest beadle. I had often joked in previous years that he was the one that should have been in the carriage while I walked, yet he was obliged to walk alongside the coach and, on this occasion, he would not consider any other option. When I was Sheriff, I had chosen as my chaplain, the Reverend William Gulliford, the incumbent of St Dunstan-in-the-West, for a number of reasons. It is usual that the person chosen as Sheriff's chaplain subsequently becomes Lord Mayor's chaplain, assuming the Sheriff progresses to be Lord Mayor. Our sixth-floor flat in the City looks out, at eye level, on to the lantern tower of St Dunstan's in Fleet Street. From our window, we can also see directly down into William's study to observe that he is working hard, preparing his sermons on time. Proximity of his church to our London flat was one reason for choosing William, but there were others. Like me, he was educated at Cambridge. He had also served as Assistant to the Bishop of London and so knew the protocols of the Church of England well. He was young, in his mid-30s, and I thought it would be beneficial to

31 *Nineteenth-century view of Fleet Street showing St Dunstan-in-the-West.*

32 The City Marshal ensures that everyone is ready before leading the procession into dinner with the Lord Mayor's Chaplain and the Common Cryer.

appoint, as chaplain to the Lord Mayor, a bright, young, talented man perhaps destined for higher office. It would give him a unique opportunity and another perspective of City life.

By tradition, the Lord Mayor arrives at Mansion House before the floats so that he, the Lady Mayoress, the outgoing Lord Mayor and his family, and all their friends can watch the entire procession. On Princes Street, just before reaching the Royal Exchange, I had my first television interview with Clare Balding of the BBC. 'What did it feel like with all these people cheering me?' I responded that it was wonderful but that they hadn't come to cheer me, but the Lord Mayor. As the 679th Lord Mayor, one realises that one is performing a role for a year, upholding a wonderful tradition and that one is not a celebrity, at least not in one's own right.

33 The Lord Mayor and Late Lord Mayor watch the Show from the balcony at Mansion House.

Many of our friends joined us on the grandstand erected in front of Mansion House to watch the Show. The Late Lord Mayor, Sir David Brewer, stood next to me with the two Sheriffs, Alderman David Lewis and Richard Regan, immediately behind. And around us were our families – Lesley, now the Lady Mayoress; and our two sons, Tom and Jamie, and their wives, Louise and a very pregnant Cori. Cori's baby was actually due that very day but, being her first, the baby was late. As we watched the procession, Clare Balding

34 *Lord Mayor's Show – Master Chartered Accountant, Peter Wyman, Master Glass Seller, Dr Jo Thomas, and Master Actuary, (the late) Robert Thomas, greet Alderman Sir Michael Savory. Master Cutler, Peter Roberts, looks on.*

came to interview me again and asked if our grandchild had been born. 'No', I replied, 'She's in the tummy of the lady sitting behind us.' Without realising it and without knowing the sex of the unborn baby, I had said 'She' and this turned out to be the case. Our first grandchild, Cassia, was born a week later. This was excellent timing, as it enabled her Mother not only to watch the Show but to attend the Lord Mayor's Banquet as well. And, indeed, at the Banquet, referring to Cori, the Prime Minister Tony Blair said he hoped that his speech wouldn't have unintended consequences.

Then it was time for us to join the Show and Lesley and I boarded our separate coaches, in glorious sunshine, escorted by the Pikemen & Musketeers and the Light Cavalry. I was accompanied by my chaplain, William, and by the Swordbearer, Neill O'Connor, and the Common Cryer, Richard Martin, bearing the mace. Being the formal representation of the Monarch, the mace always precedes the Lord Mayor but in any procession the Lord Mayor is positioned immediately behind the sword. So, in the coach, the Lord Mayor sits in the back (on the right-hand side) opposite the Swordbearer who is on the front seat, facing backwards, alongside the Common Cryer.

In the Lord Mayor's Show, the public expect to get a good view of

35 *The Lady Mayoress, in the Lord Mayor's Show, with daughter-in-law Louise and Tessa and Olivia Brewer.*

the Lord Mayor. To achieve this, I had to stand up for most of the journey and lean out of the coach, each window in turn, waving my hat. In principle this doesn't present a problem. You just have to be a little energetic, darting from side to side and holding on tight. However, from time to time the procession stops and, on each occasion, the coach lurches forward quite violently, so you have to grab hold of whatever you can. A further difficulty is caused by ornate gilded carving immediately above the coach windows, such that if you're not careful each lurch results in a sharp bang to the head – and ornate gilded carvings can hurt. I noticed that evening that I had two slight wounds on the top of my head. Perhaps 18th-century Lord Mayors didn't stand up to wave to the crowds. My other concern was that, while waving, I might drop my tricorne hat. Tricorne hats are quite heavy and don't have an obvious place where you can get a good grip. I had learnt this during the previous week when I went for a hat waving session with Barry Ward, Keeper of the Robes, at Guildhall. I had visions of my precious hat, a gift from the Worshipful Company of Feltmakers, falling to the ground and being crunched by one of the shire horses. Fortunately, despite tennis elbow, I managed to keep hold of it throughout.

The coaches stopped in front of the West Door, the main door, of St Paul's Cathedral where Lesley and I were greeted by the Acting Dean, Canon Edward Newell, and the Chapter, with the choir singing in the background. There we knelt, so that Ed could bless us and give us each a bible. It was a very special moment. The last time we were blessed together was on our Wedding Day. By happy coincidence, Peter Chapman, a former fellow partner at PricewaterhouseCoopers,

36 *The Lord Mayor and Lady Mayoress are blessed by the Acting Dean, Canon Edward Newell, on the West steps of St Paul's Cathedral, while Peter Chapman, Lay Canon, and the Pikeman and Musketeers look on.*

was present in his role as Lay Canon at St Paul's. And so was my old mentor from Coopers & Lybrand, Sir Brian Jenkins, GBE, and his wife Ann, standing to the north of the main steps, witnessing this magical moment and cheering us on. I owe much to Brian, since he introduced me to the civic City and to this special condition known as 'Aldermania'.

Then onto the Law Courts for the formal oath to the Monarch, followed by smoked salmon sandwiches and a glass of champagne. The formal swearing (by me) was accompanied by some lovely speeches from the Recorder of London, His Honour Judge Peter Beaumont QC, the Lord Chief Justice Baron (Nicholas) Phillips of Worth Matravers and the Master of the Rolls the Rt Hon Sir Anthony Clarke, all choreographed by

The Queen's Remembrancer, Master Robert Turner, with assistance from Jill Jacobs, a fellow Glazier. It is a lovely ceremony where, for some reason, each speaker has to recite some Milton and does so in a most enthusiastic manner, often with contrived relevance to the individuals they are praising. It is all performed in a very stylish manner, made slightly macabre when the five judges sitting at the bench doff their tricorne hats in unison three times, saluting the Lord Mayor. The coaches are then reboarded and the procession makes its return journey to Mansion House and lunch.

Later that afternoon, after a short rest and a quick change into black tie, the whole family and our house guests were taken down to HQS Wellington, the floating home of the Honourable Company of Master Mariners, on the Thames Embankment, to watch the fireworks which I, as Lord Mayor, had to start by firing a Verey pistol. Our son Jamie's mother-in-law, Jeni Aird, came with us in the Mayoral Rolls-Royce (registration number LMO) and became very excited, waving to the crowds as the car sped along. For our guests this was the end to a wonderful day. But for Lesley and me, it didn't stop there.

A further most important engagement began at 19.00 at the Royal Albert Hall, the annual Festival of Remembrance, organised by the Royal British Legion and attended by nearly every member of the Royal Family. It is a most moving event, with military displays by current members of the Armed Forces, choral performances and prayers. It ends with a parade of banners and the release of poppy petals from the roof. Lesley and I were escorted to the 'Lord Mayor's Box' where our other guests were the Prime Minister and Cherie Blair, the Rt Rev and Rt Hon Bishop of London Richard Chartres and his daughter Sophie, the Rt Hon The Lord Mayor of Westminster Alexander Nicoll and Grania Nicoll, and the Chief of the Defence Staff, Air Chief Marshal Sir Jock Stirrup, GCB, AFC, with his wife, Mary. A particularly spine-chilling moment was the procession of young war widows and their young children, who lost their husbands and their fathers in the recent campaigns in Iraq and Afghanistan.

THE SILENT CEREMONY

The Lord Mayor's Show is one of the best events of the Mayoral Year, coming the day after the Silent Ceremony when the new Lord Mayor is first sworn in and takes over from his predecessor – who is then somewhat cadaverously referred to as the 'Late Lord Mayor'.

Dating back many centuries, the Silent Ceremony is the most magical and mystical of all the City's ceremonies. It follows practice adopted in Coronations the world over, where power is transferred from one person to another – this time in Great Hall, Guildhall, the seat of government and power house of the City of London Corporation. Watched by around 200 people, including the other Aldermen, the High Officers of the City, Livery Masters and other guests, the ceremony takes around 45 minutes. It is undertaken in total silence apart from the incoming Lord Mayor who swears two oaths and then signs two declarations – to undertake the Office of Lord Mayor and to safeguard the City Corporation's assets (the silver and furniture at Mansion House). After the oaths, the outgoing Lord Mayor beckons the incoming Lord Mayor to sit in his seat in the centre of Great Hall and, as he does so, removes his tricorne hat at precisely the same moment as the incoming Lord Mayor puts his on. Each bearer of a symbol of office then approaches the centre of Great Hall in silence, making three remembrances (bows from the waist), stopping after each one and then taking three steps before the next remembrance. The symbol of office in question (the mace, the sword, the seal and the purse) is handed first to the outgoing Lord Mayor who touches it. It is then passed to the incoming Lord Mayor who also touches it and puts the object on the table in front of him. The objects are then removed, individually, with similar remembrances by the officers, except these are made, somewhat unusually, as each bearer is walking backwards. After all who, these days, bows while walking backwards? After this procedure has been completed, each of the Aldermen and the High Officers congratulate the new Lord Mayor and the outgoing Lord Mayor, also in silence. It is timed to perfection. It is a piece of pure theatre that sends shivers down the spine as one recalls that this ceremony is centuries old.

The Silent Ceremony concludes with the outgoing Lord Mayor escorting the incoming Lord Mayor (this time processing on the right, as the senior of the two)

37   The new Lord Mayor takes over, after the Silent Ceremony November 2006, with Lady Mayoress, two sons, Tom and Jamie, and one daughter-in-law, Louise – the other, Cori, heavily pregnant and not present.

out of Great Hall into Guildhall Yard where the trumpeters of the Household Cavalry herald the Admission of the new Lord Mayor. The bells of the City's churches ring out. It is the beginning of a new era. The final act of transfer of power takes place in the Mayoral limousine, a Rolls-Royce PhantomVI, which conveys the incoming and outgoing Lord Mayors, the Swordbearer and the Common Cryer back to Mansion House. In the back of the car (where there's enough room for all four), the Swordbearer takes off his fur hat and retrieves the key, kept in the hat, to the seal of Christ's Hospital. He hands it to the outgoing Lord Mayor who gives to the incoming Lord Mayor who returns it to the Swordbearer who puts it back in his hat with the immortal words 'My Lord Mayor, I will keep it under my hat'. And so, the transfer of power from one Lord Mayor to the next has taken place – a ceremony that has been the same for many hundreds of years. It is, for all involved, a magical, almost religious experience.

But the first ceremony in the process of becoming Lord Mayor takes place many years before this.

38 The new Lord Mayor takes over after the Silent Ceremony, November 2007.

BECOMING AN ALDERMAN

To be considered for election as Lord Mayor, the candidate must first be elected as an Alderman, a requirement that dates from 1215 when King John sealed the first of two charters – the second, being the Magna Carta, is the more famous one. This provided that the Barons of the City of London had the right to elect their own Mayor from amongst their number. Today, for *Barons*, read *Aldermen*.

To become an Alderman, the individual must be a British subject and have been approved as suitable, by the Lord Chancellor's Advisory Committee, to be a Magistrate. And, of course, he or she must be elected by those entitled to vote in a Ward of the City of London. There are actually 25 wards – at one time there were 26, including one in Southwark, the ward of Bridge Without. Anyone can vote if they are a resident in the ward or registered as one of the agreed business voters in the ward – each firm has roughly two votes for every 10 employees. It is competitive and, very often, a hard-fought democratic election.

For the successful candidate, the first ceremony is the welcome into the Court of Aldermen, where the newcomer wears morning coat – yes, the City tries to keep to standards of dress, as well as values and ethics. The other Aldermen are all dressed, as they have for centuries, in their scarlet gowns (very similar to, but not quite the same as, the one worn by the Lord Mayor on Lord Mayor's Show Day). The new Alderman makes a short speech saying how pleased he or she is to be elected and, if he or she is sensible, never says anything contentious, at least not on this occasion.

The second ceremony is the welcome of the new Alderman to the Court of Common Council, the City's ancient Parliament, at one of its monthly meetings in Guildhall. The Court of Common Council consists of 25 Aldermen and 100 Common Councilmen. Although the Aldermen sit on a dais at one end of Great Hall, they have equal rights with the Common Councilmen when it comes to voting and sitting on committees. The only difference is that to become Lord Mayor, one has to be an Alderman. Research has shown that while Common Council and the country's Parliament evolved at the same period, and on similar lines, Parliament assumed more distinct outlines than Common Council. It is a legend that Parliament was modelled on the City Corporation. The fact that it has endured for so long demonstrates the effectiveness of a system of government that has lasted many centuries. Again, dressed in morning coat, the new Alderman makes a short speech saying how pleased he or she is to be elected and, again, if he or she is sensible, never says anything contentious. Occasionally, he or she breaks this norm and usually lives to regret it. After all, modesty and humility are precious and traditional traits in the City. Newcomers have much to learn. To express one's own (often ill-informed) views at one's first appearance does not bode well for future progression. But innovation and imagination are also rewarded. This is place where both constancy and change each has its place.

Interestingly, unlike in national or other local authority elections in the UK, all candidates standing for election as either Aldermen or Common Councilmen are independent of a political party. This apolitical nature of the City of London Corporation has stood it in good stead over the years. There is no party whip to obey. There is less need to focus on the broader political landscape although, of course, matters affecting the City such as planning and transport, as well as a fair allocation of business rate, are enormously important. But, each of the 125 members is independent and puts the City, its residents and its businesses first. The City's Parliament (the Court of Common Council) is therefore more consensual. When the Lord Mayor speaks in public, he is not biased or prejudiced as a result of party membership. He is speaking for the businesses of the City and has their interests exclusively at heart. This is part of the City of London's success.

The Role and Responsibilities of an Alderman

Aldermen of the City of London are constitutionally quite distinct from the Aldermen which used to be part of the local government political scene. In the latter case, they were selected by the local councillors of the local authorities. On the other hand, the City's Aldermen are directly elected from the City's wards. Since the very earliest times they have represented the City's commercial heritage. Today they continue that role through training for the Mayoralty which will see successful candidates representing the City brand around the world.

But the role of an Alderman is not confined to commercial concerns. They are assigned to City Corporation Committees, charities and City schools, as members, trustees, representatives and governors.

I was fortunate in being allocated first to the Open Spaces Committee, which looks after the City's 'green lungs' of Epping Forest, Burnham Beeches, Coulsdon Common and Highgate Wood. The Saturday morning visits to these sites gave me an excellent opportunity to understand the detailed issues being considered as well as to get to know other members of the Court of Common Council. It comes as a surprise to many people when they learn that the City of London has responsibility for these environmentally friendly, recreational areas, which also include Hampstead Heath, bequeathed to the City when the GLC was abolished. For me, during my Mayoralty, it was an added pleasure to visit Epping Forest to commemorate the 125th anniversary of the transfer of Wanstead Park to the City Corporation and to visit Golders Hill Park (part of Hampstead Heath) on the occasion of the centenary of the formation of Hampstead Garden Suburb. Later I visited Burnham Beeches and opened the Information Centre, Cafeteria and Toilets – by this stage I had become quite accomplished at opening public conveniences, mirroring the social amenity and tradition established by my predecessor, Richard Whittington, in the 15th century. I should explain. Not only was Dick Whittington a great donor to charity, he also introduced a number of social benefits, including, as mentioned above, the first public lavatory in the City – a 64-seater, no less – that was flushed every time the tide came in. This was too much of a temptation for me. Being the Alderman for Lime Street, I revelled in the prospect of opening public conveniences – at the visitor centre at the Monument in the City, at the British Embassy in Astana (Kazakhstan), and at the visitor and information centre at Burnham Beeches. This was true public service.

As a junior Alderman, I joined the Establishment Committee, the Planning & Transportation Committee and one of the Markets Committees. And, as an

Alderman, I attended the monthly meetings of the Court of Aldermen and of the Court of Common Council, the City's Parliament at Guildhall.

I was also fortunate to be allocated to the Royal Bridewell Hospital and its progeny, King Edward's School Witley, whose original site was gifted to the Lord Mayor and Aldermen in 1553 by the young Edward VI. After the dissolution of the monasteries by Henry VIII, starting in 1536, education for youngsters, particularly from poorer families, was badly hit. For many years, children suffered from not having a school to attend. So, up and down the country, local mayors and aldermen considered the alternatives. By the time Henry's son, Edward, came to the throne, plans were being developed for the establishment of new schools. Charters were signed by the Monarch and, today, there are Edward VI schools in many cities and towns throughout England. In 1552, Nicholas Ridley, the Bishop of London, preached a sermon which moved the King to ask for the co-operation of leading City merchants in dealing with the social problems of the day. The Bishop wrote separately to Sir William Cecil, the King's secretary, drawing attention to the existence of a 'wide, large empty house, belonging to the King, called Bridewell, which would wonderfully serve to lodge Christ in, if he might find good friends at court to procure in his cause'. Bridewell Palace, south of Fleet Street, had been built on the orders of Henry VIII as his home with his first wife, Catherine of Aragon. After their final quarrel and divorce, it was used by the French and Spanish Ambassadors for a while before becoming empty. So moved by Ridley's sermon, the King made a personal gift of Bridewell Palace to the City of London to provide for the 'correctness of a variety of misdemeanants of both sexes' and to apprentice children. Poor Ridley was later burnt at the stake, together with Bishop Latimer, at Oxford during Queen Mary's reign in 1555. But the School was founded and Mary confirmed the gift in 1556. With the desire to improve the educational environment and facilities, the School moved to Witley, in leafy Surrey, in 1867. It has since educated boys and girls, many from disadvantaged backgrounds, receiving bursaries from the Foundation and from other educational charities. It is, today, a wonderful school with an excellent academic record and a very happy atmosphere in which children can be educated and develop their unique talents. It relies on charity to fund bursaries for children from poorer families and approximately forty per cent of pupils receive funding to help with their education. It is an independent, foundation school, which adds greatly to our society and I have been very pleased to be associated with it and to have led its 450th anniversary appeal. During my Mayoral year, I was delighted that the School could be involved in so many of the events and ceremonies, not least the Lord Mayor's Show and the church service at St Dunstan's after the Silent Ceremony. I was also delighted to visit the School, in State, on the occasion of the 2007 Speech Day and award the prizes.

It will be evident that the roles of an Alderman are quite varied and are sometimes accompanied by colourful ceremonies that date back centuries. They also involve modern corporate governance practices that appertain to any 21st-century board.

WARD MOTES

The word 'Mote' is a derivation of 'Moot', Saxon for a meeting or assembly of people. Ward Motes are periodic meetings of the 25 wards in the City which allow members of each ward to elect their Aldermen, Common Councilmen, the Ward Beadle and the Honorary Ward Clerk and to consider any matters arising in the ward. The Alderman presides over the ward motes, which are usually annual. He or she wears a violet gown which is the symbol of civic authority. The violet colour probably dates from Roman times. He is, of course, preceded by the Ward Beadle, carrying a mace that typically dates from the 17th century. Crying 'Oyez, Oyez, Oyez', the Beadle bids those present to stand while the Alderman takes the chair for the meeting. Where an Aldermanic vacancy arises or where an existing Alderman seeks re-election, then the Lord Mayor attends, as Returning Officer, in full fig, and chairs the Ward Mote, accompanied by the City Marshal, the Sword and Mace. It is a ceremony that has been practised for centuries. It is a very basic and simple form of democracy that goes back to Saxon times. It is also very colourful.

ELECTIONS OF SHERIFFS AND THE LORD MAYOR

From Saxon times the Sheriffs had great powers, in particular to tax people and the name given to the City's seat of Government, Guildhall, has its origins in the payment of money or the making of a contribution – 'gild' or 'geld'. After 1189, powers of governance within the City were assumed by the Mayor, assisted by duly elected Aldermen. Although Parliamentary legislation now governs some aspects of the City's electoral franchise through private Acts, which the City Corporation has promoted, much remains subject to internal instruments known as Acts of Common Council. The election of Lord Mayor and Sheriffs are examples of the latter. They also involve very colourful, as well as traditional, ceremonies.

All 35,000 Liverymen of the City of London are entitled to vote in the Election of Sheriffs, held every summer on, or close to, Midsummer Day. This election takes place at Guildhall when anyone who is a Liveryman of one or more of the 108 Livery companies may attend and vote by raising his or her hand. Known as a Common Hall, it is a colourful occasion, when the masters, prime wardens and upper bailiff and the other wardens wear their gowns of office. Two Sheriffs are chosen to represent the City of London and are elected, unlike the High Sheriffs in other cities and

39 *John Stuttard's Shrieval Badge and Chain.*

40 *Lesley's Shrieval Brooch.*

counties of England whose names are recommended by the local community and then chosen (pricked) by the Monarch (with a bodkin). The London Sheriffs must be approved by the Monarch, although this takes place after they have been admitted at another ancient ceremony, the Quit Rents Ceremony, described later. If there are more than two candidates for the Offices of Sheriff, then a poll is demanded and Liverymen are summoned to vote in person on a subsequent date. Normally, at least one Sheriff is an Alderman of the City of London, who might some day progress to being Lord Mayor. Many centuries ago, the Court of Common Council determined that to be Lord Mayor the individual must have served the office of Sheriff. After election, the Sheriffs each make an acceptance speech.

The two Sheriffs are 'admitted' on the day before Michaelmas Day (or St Michael's Day, 29 September), as this latter is the date of the annual election of the Lord Mayor. It should be noticed that elections of both Sheriffs and the Lord Mayor take place on quarter days, saints' days, as in medieval times these were holidays. It was less disruptive to trade and business to require Liverymen to vote on holidays than on workdays. The Admission of Sheriffs is also held in Guildhall and is followed by an opportunity for celebration over a long lunch, known as the Sheriffs' Breakfast. Duly fed and watered, the Sheriffs then take up residence at the Central Criminal Court, Old Bailey, where they perform their traditional roles of looking after the judges. In former times, the Sheriffs had real power.

41 John Stuttard, as Sheriff, with Deputy Christine Cohen of Lime Street Ward at the Sheriffs' Breakfast, September 2005.

They would oversee executions and intervene where they believed this necessary. Today, they entertain civic and business guests at lunch each day with the judges; they support the Lord Mayor in carrying out his duties, often representing him and speaking on his behalf; they also understudy the Lord Mayor and, in the case of the Sheriff who is an Alderman, this is essential if one aspires to progress to this higher office. The two Sheriffs also supervise the Election of the Lord Mayor, which takes place the day after their own Admission.

The Election of Lord Mayor is the final stage in a process which takes many years – of preparation, review and examination. He, or she, must be capable of representing the businesses of the City, the City Corporation and the Livery. With around 750 speeches, he must be eloquent. Each year, the Lord Mayor has approximately 1,800 different engagements, meeting Heads of State and hundreds of Ministers, Ambassadors, business executives and community leaders. So, he (or she) must therefore be capable of holding his own, covering a wide range of subjects, often of a complex business and financial nature. The Lord Mayor represents the City's businesses, namely the UK's Financial Sector and he is their key spokesman. The ultimate choice of Lord Mayor lies with the Court of Alderman from two of their number selected by Common Hall.

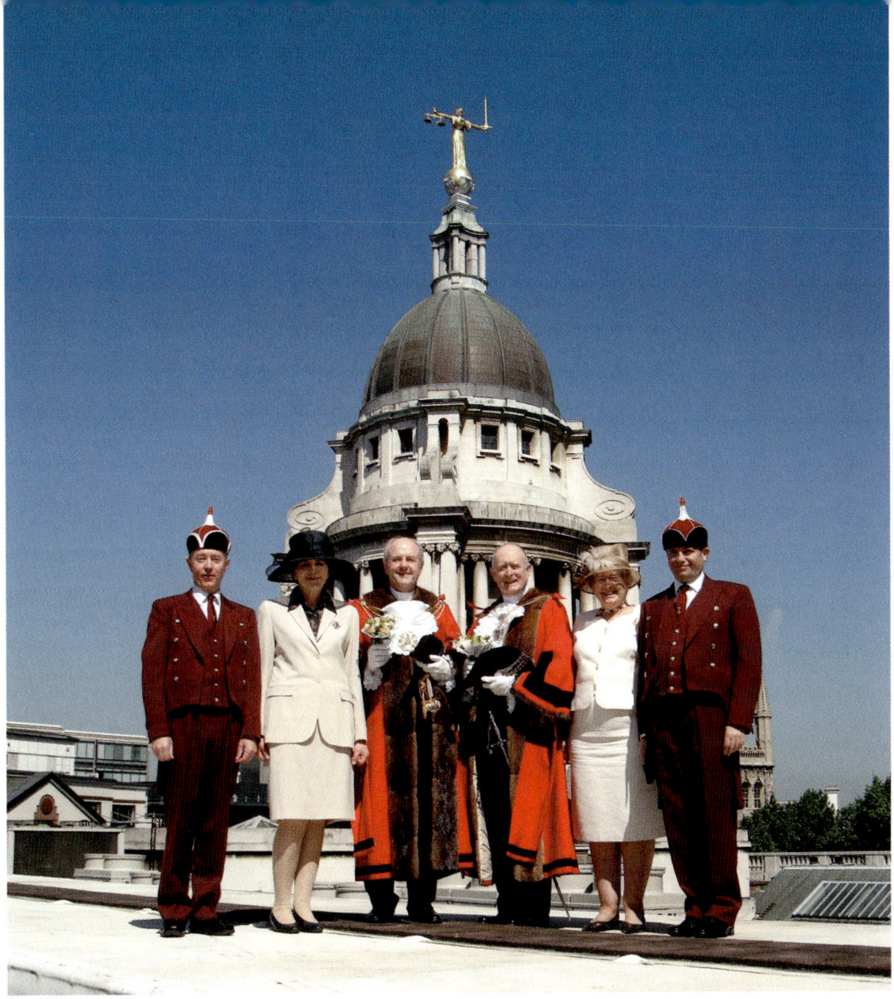

42 *Sheriffs and footmen at the Old Bailey – with splendid hats acquired during a Mayoral visit to Mongolia.*

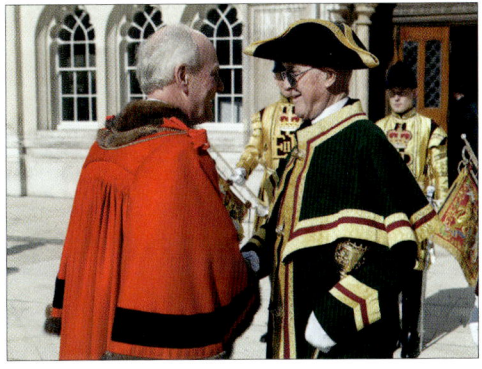

To ensure that this process conforms to modern corporate governance standards and is as transparent as possible, an appraisal panel has been established, including external independent members, to take references and interview prospective candidates. The results of these appraisals are communicated to all the other Aldermen, meeting confidentially as the Privileges Committee, who decide whom to support for the office of Lord Mayor. Great care is exercised to ensure that the chosen person is acceptable to the Livery, whom the Lord Mayor will represent, as well as possessing the qualities and experience to do the job.

43 *Election of the Lord Mayor on Michaelmas Day 2006. The Lord Mayor Elect is congratulated by his beadle, Edward Kipping.*

On the day of Election of Lord Mayor, a Common Hall is convened of Liverymen. Again, it is a very colourful affair with the masters, prime wardens and upper bailiff, together with their wardens, wearing their gowns of office. Anyone who is an Alderman who has served the office of Sheriff and has not previously served as Lord Mayor is in contention to be considered for election as Lord Mayor and each person's name is read out. By tradition, based on the outcome of the appraisal and the decision of the Privileges Committee, the chosen preferred

44 *Election of the Lord Mayor on Michaelmas Day 2006. The Lord Mayor David (now Sir David) Brewer, congratulates the Lord Mayor Elect John Stuttard.*

candidate's name is read out first, to which Liverymen respond 'All'. The favoured or chosen name for the following year is then read out, to which Liverymen respond 'Next Year', although this is not a binding decision for the future. In response to other names, Liverymen respond 'Later'. The names of the first two candidates are then communicated to the Aldermen, assembled in a separate room, who vote in secret on their choice of Lord Mayor for the year. It should be noted, however, that they have previously agreed, and communicated to the Livery, that they will support their chosen candidate, providing his or her name is one of the two returned to them by Common Hall. Thus the Aldermen make the final decision, based on the law of the land, but take note of the wishes of the Livery.

COAT OF ARMS

Early on in one's career as an Alderman, aspiring Sheriffs are encouraged to approach the College of Arms to obtain a grant of arms, if they don't already possess one. I had started this process some years earlier, when I was introduced by an old friend and former partner, Peter Walsh, to Peter Gwynn-Jones, then Lancaster Herald and later to become Garter Principal King of Arms.

I had wanted to include, in the design of my arms, reference to my work and experience that also fitted with our family. My father was a chartered accountant, as am I, and so is my elder son. Having qualified as an accountant with Cooper Brothers & Co, whose arms included a lion holding an abacus, and having spent five years in China, the concept of a Chinese abacus was an obvious starting point for my arms. So I asked Peter Gwynn-Jones if the design on the shield could allude to an abacus. Because I came from a family of four and because we are a family of four, Peter drew four red balls (four spheres crossed gules) pierced vertically (palewise) by black rods (enfiled by three pallets sable) on a gold (or) background. It looked dramatic and was a very clear simple design. On the battlefield, it would certainly have been possible, at 400 yards, to recognise that it was Stuttard and his troops entering the fray.

The crest was less easy to achieve. I wanted to have some reference to Finland in my arms. I had, at that time, been made a Knight of the Order of the Lion of Finland. I had also completed the 75kms cross-country skiing marathon, the Reppu Finlandia. So, I asked Peter if I could have a lion – cross-country skiing. There was a pause and I had an image of a Bateman cartoon where someone had said something that was socially incredibly inept and unacceptable. The response was swift 'Mr Stuttard, may I remind you that this is the College of Arms, not Disneyworld'. Trying to recover the position, I blurted out, 'But I've seen lions and other animals doing all sorts of things in heraldry'. 'Oh no you haven't' came the reply. 'In heraldry, animals are inanimate, they don't *do* things'. But Peter was imaginative as well as humorous. 'I have a suggestion. If your lion is in a salient position, with his feet together, standing on the crest wreath, holding his ski sticks, it will look as though he is skiing, but of course you must realise that he is not. Is that OK?' 'Absolutely', I replied. So that was it.

The only remaining decision was the motto. I had wanted something that reflected my approach to life and to challenges that I was faced with, along the lines of 'Nothing's Impossible'. In business, in any walk of life, if someone said to me that it wasn't possible, that was like a red rag to a bull. I knew it jolly well was possible. It was partly the will and partly the way. In life, if you want it to happen, it is always possible. My elder son, Tom, who was reading Classics at Cambridge, told me that a double negative is difficult in Latin. So he suggested turning the motto round to the much simpler and more positive '*Semper Potest*', namely 'Always Possible', and that stuck.

The Duke of Norfolk, Earl Marshal and Hereditary Marshal of England, duly made the grant of arms and the full emblazonment was beautifully executed on a parchment with the seals of Garter and Clarenceux, on 12 February 1996.

After the election of Sheriffs and of each Lord Mayor, a banner is made for each new incumbent with the design of his coat of arms. This is then carried in the Lord Mayor's Show by a cadet, organised, for many years, by Flight Lt Kevin Mehmet. The banners look wonderful, being held aloft next to the respective

45 *Sir John Stuttard's coat of arms.*

coach. After the Lord Mayor ceases his term of Office, the banner is hung in the Aldermen's Court Room at Guildhall.

The design of the coat of arms is also used on everything possible – invitations, menu cards, gifts and all the official records and decorations. And the arms may be passed down from father to sons, in perpetuity.

THE CHURCH SERVICES

One of the great pleasures of Aldermanic office is the number of religious services that one attends. Over the years, the City has benefited from the involvement of individuals of many faiths. Indeed the multifaceted nature of the community is one of London's strengths. Involvement in the traditional church and other religious services is seen by all Aldermen as part of fulfilling the role regardless of one's faith.

At the start of the City's civic year, in April, the Lord Mayor and Sheriffs process into the church of St Lawrence Jewry, which is situated at the south side of Guildhall Yard, for a service attended by members of the Court of Common Council. The Alderman & Sheriff's Chaplain attends and, in my Shrieval year, my Chaplain, the Reverend William Gulliford, preached a most moving sermon. At another service at St Lawrence Jewry, the Lord Mayor chooses the visiting preacher to give the Spital Sermon and, in my year as Lord Mayor, I asked The Right Reverend Tom Butler, Bishop of Southwark, in view of my association via the Glaziers' Livery company who worship at Southwark Cathedral.

Two of the City's schools, Christ's Hospital and King Edward's School Witley, visit the City each year for a church service and lunch at Guildhall. The pupils at Christ's Hospital always look magnificent in their individual blue robes as they march, in measured steps, through the City accompanied by the school's brass band. KES Witley, as it is known, return each year to St Bride's Church adjacent to the site of the Royal Bridewell Palace.

I have always thought of St Paul's as the City's church. Standing in a dominant position and having survived the Blitz, the cathedral has great significance for Londoners. The Lord Mayor has his own seat in St Paul's, on the north side of the Quire and east of the Choir Stalls, where there are brackets to hold the sword and mace. The first formal service of the new Mayoral Year takes place on the second Sunday of November, the day after the Lord Mayor's Show. At this service, the Lord Mayor reads the lesson, after a formal procession into the Cathedral. Welcomed by Canon Ed Newell, the Acting Dean, I was formally introduced, again, to the Chapter, who by this stage were great friends. On this occasion, the Mayoral Rolls-Royce was escorted by three City of London Police outriders to ensure our timely arrival at the West Entrance to St Paul's. By the end of the Mayoralty we were getting quite used to police escorts and found them a very convenient way of getting about town. After the service, Their Royal Highnesses Prince and Princess Michael of Kent joined us at Mansion House prior to a wreath-laying ceremony at the Royal Exchange, the first occasion on which they had attended this event. Prince Michael and I processed to the steps next to the

46 *Laying a wreath with HRH Prince Michael of Kent at the Royal Exchange on 12 November 2006.*

war memorial and laid our wreaths in turn. It was greatly appreciated that the Royal Family had been represented in the City for this Act of Remembrance, coinciding with the parallel and better known event at the Cenotaph at Whitehall. There followed a curry lunch in the Egyptian Hall at Mansion House for all who took part in the Act of Remembrance, including the old comrades, who sang some WWII songs. It was on meeting some of those who had served in the Merchant Navy that I learnt of the awful treatment meted out to those who lost their ship – immediately the call went out to abandon ship, the crew's wages were stopped, since seamen were employed by their ship and not their company. War is a savage and cruel affair, but for merchant seamen it seemed particularly so.

During the Mayoral Year, there are many wonderful services at St Paul's. Two stand out. The service for the Sons of the Clergy, an organisation established during Cromwell's time, when many clergymen lost their livings and a charity was formed by their sons to help their unemployed fathers. The service is an opportunity for bishops from across the UK to gather in their fine vestments and process with the Lord Mayor, Sheriffs and Aldermen. Another colourful service takes place the day after one of the splendid banquets at Mansion House, for the masters, prime wardens and upper bailiff. Known as the United Guilds Service, it is an occasion for the leaders of the Livery to don their gowns again and join together in an act of worship at St Paul's. Three choirs take part and, again, the Lord Mayor reads the lesson. My reading was taken from St John's Gospel and the sermon during my year was preached by His Grace the Archbishop of Canterbury, Dr Rowan Williams, who spoke about the contribution of the Livery companies to society and to charity.

But perhaps the most special of the church services during my Mayoral Year was given by my chaplain, William Gulliford, at his church, St Dunstan-in-the-West. After the Silent Ceremony at Guildhall, William planned a service of thanksgiving, attended by many of our friends. Ed Newell kindly preached the sermon and the choir of King Edward's School Witley sang Handel's Zadok The Priest, so well. It was a magical way to start my Mayoralty.

And at the end of the year, as Remembrance Sunday approached, two further Services were very special. First, the Act of Remembrance in the garden to the east of St Paul's, organised by the Royal British Legion, is one of the few occasions in the year when all 108 Livery companies are represented in a cross-planting ceremony, with wonderful hymns and the moving Kohima Prayer. Then, the annual ceremony at Lloyd's of London when the whole of the staff in the Richard Rogers designed building stand in silence, looking down on the Atrium, as the Lutine Bell is rung and the Last Post is sounded, before wreaths are laid on the rostrum in the middle of the underwriting floor.

47   John Stuttard, as Sheriff, with fellow Sheriff Kevin Kearney at Remembrance Service at St Paul's Churchyard.

THE MAJOR BANQUETS

Each year, the Lord Mayor hosts banquets for the different constituent major groups in the country:
- The Masters, Prime Wardens & Upper Bailiff, where Master Mercer and Master Grocer (Numbers 1 and 2, respectively, in the Livery company hierarchy) speak
- The Judges, where the Lord Chancellor and the Lord Chief Justice speak

- The Easter Banquet, attended by the Ambassadors of foreign countries, where the Foreign Secretary speaks
- The Merchants & Bankers, where the Chancellor of the Exchequer and the Governor of the Bank of England speak
- The Trade & Industry Dinner, where the Secretary of State for Trade & Industry (now Business, Enterprise & Regulatory Reform) speaks
- The City Banquet, where the Chairman of the Financial Services Authority speaks
- The London Government, where the Mayor of London speaks
- Dragon Awards, where awards are presented to organisations in the London area who have contributed to community and charitable causes. For many years, the former broadcaster, Martyn Lewis, has compered this event with great enthusiasm
- The Bishops, held in alternate years, where the leaders of the religious communities in the UK are invited and where the Archbishop of Canterbury speaks.

48 Line up in the Drawing Room of the Mansion House before the Judges' Banquet, with the Lord Chief Justice.

49 Dragon Awards.

50 *The Lady Mayoress greets the Archbishop of Canterbury, Dr Rowan Williams.*

And of course, the Lord Mayor speaks at all of them. These speeches are very important opportunities to get across messages and to show support, as appropriate, to various interest groups and sections of society. In preparation for these speeches, about four weeks in advance, I convened a meeting involving Kay Brock, the Lord Mayor's Private Secretary, Tony Halmos, Head of Public Relations, and Bill Beaver, the Lord Mayor's Speechwriter. We would discuss potential subjects in the light of current circumstances, after which Tony would produce a first draft, followed by comments from many others, consolidated by Bill Beaver. But I would always write the final version – in my own words. I refer in a later chapter to the content of some of the key speeches.

Also, by tradition, the Lord Mayor provides all the wine at the key banquets. With around 12 cases of red and eight cases of white consumed at each one (and double that at least for the Lord Mayor's Banquet), a certain amount of pre-planning is required. It is difficult, if not impossible, to acquire such large amounts of claret ready for drinking on the 'spot market'. So, over the years, the Aldermen have acquired wine a decade in advance as part of a syndicate to ensure that there are sufficient quantities laid down in Mansion House that can be called up as required. Derek Smedley, a vintner by profession, advises the syndicate and organises regular tastings to determine what to buy and when the stock is ready for drinking. White wine is purchased on the 'spot market', as this is more readily available. Interestingly, over the years, red wine is becoming more popular and white relatively less so – at one point 10 years ago, the quantities consumed were roughly 10 cases of each. Another change in drinking taste is that red burgundy is now less fashionable and the amount of port drunk has decreased at banquets.

It was said, many years ago, that you had to be a millionaire to be Lord Mayor. Certainly, in days gone by, the Lord Mayor was expected to pay for the costs of running the Mansion House – staff, furniture, cutlery, crockery etc as well as the wine and the grand banquets. Nowadays, the cost is modest – and anyone who has had a reasonably successful career will not find the out-of-pocket cost too exorbitant. But, of course, the real cost is the time commitment – first, of being first an Alderman for many years, then, Sheriff for a year and, finally, Lord Mayor. Over an elapsed period of between seven and ten years, this can amount to a minimum of at least four man years of one's life. And, in the Mayoral year the time required is much more than that required in a full time job. It is, to use modern parlance, a 24/7 role.

THE LORD MAYOR'S BANQUET AND THE LIGHTING-UP DINNER

Of all the banquets and dinners, perhaps the grandest and most memorable is the Lord Mayor's Banquet which has taken place annually at Guildhall since 1501. By tradition, the banquet is hosted jointly by the Lord Mayor and the two Sheriffs and is held on the Monday after the Lord Mayor's Show, in honour of the Late Lord Mayor. Preparation for this banquet begins many months beforehand, with choice of caterer, a tasting of sample menus, preparation of guest lists, choice of menu card and cover, decisions as to flower arrangements – and of course, the Lord Mayor's speech. The City Remembrancer, Paul Double, is ultimately responsible for the banquet, ably assisted by his team of Fiona Hoban, Michaela Whitbread and Neil Morris. However, a Lord Mayor & Sheriffs' Committee is appointed to oversee arrangements for the banquet and also the Lord Mayor's Show. The banquet is preceded, some 10 days earlier, by the Lighting-up Dinner, which is a sort of dress rehearsal for the banquet itself. The origin of this dinner is unclear, but it was usual in the 18th century for the Court of Aldermen to give instructions for fitting-up Guildhall and it seems likely that arrangements would

51 *Menu card and place setting for Lord Mayor's Banquet on 13 November.*

52 *The menu card for the Lighting-up Dinner.*

have been checked to ensure that all was in order. Lighting was a prominent feature of these occasions and it is known that some 3000 wax tapers were required for the Lord Mayor's Banquet of 1761, at which King George III was the principal guest. At the banquet in 1827, a board containing oil lamps in the design of an anchor crashed down on the Lord Mayor and the Lady Mayoress. Both escaped serious injury, but this incident gave added importance to the role of the Lord Mayor & Sheriffs' Committee.

Normally, around 700 guests are invited to the Lord Mayor's Banquet, with a much smaller number at the Lighting-up Dinner, traditionally held in the Guildhall Crypts. However, in 2006, renovation began of the Guildhall North Block, which dates from the 1950s. This work required the complete refurbishment of the kitchens and, as a result, with temporary kitchen facilities, the number that could be served at a banquet was limited to five hundred. To make up for this, it was agreed that a larger number of invitations would be issued for the Lighting-up Dinner and, also, that Aldermen and Common Councilmen should alternate between the two events for 2006 and 2007 since the limitation in numbers would apply to both years. These arrangements turned out to be a huge success, as both dinner and banquet were held in Great Hall and the dinner was indeed more like a dress rehearsal for the banquet. To make the dinner equally special, we devised a ceremonial lighting of the candles at the beginning of the dinner, after a procession of the Lord Mayor and Sheriffs' Committee bearing lanterns.

The food and wine were the same at the two events and we gave each course a theme and a name associated with a country or region with which we had connections, namely:

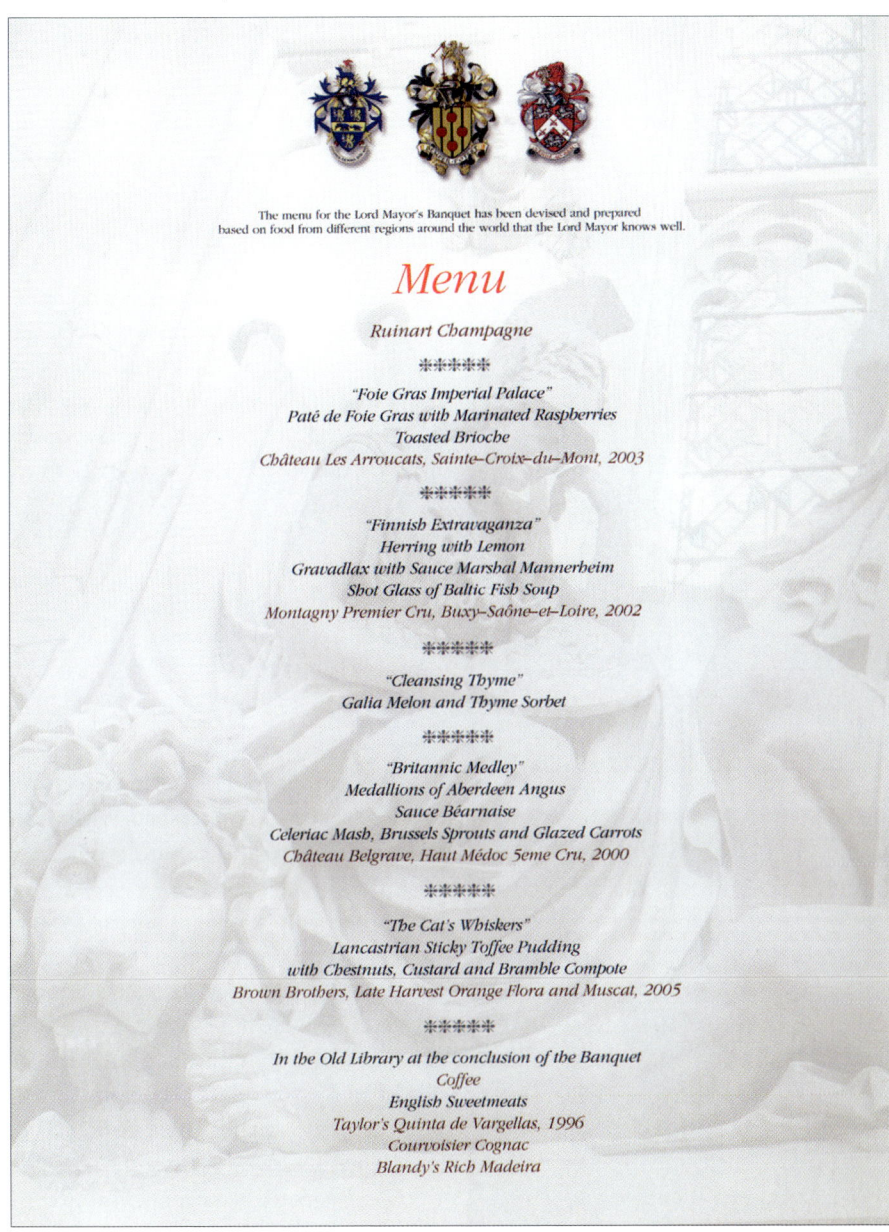

The menu for the Lord Mayor's Banquet has been devised and prepared based on food from different regions around the world that the Lord Mayor knows well.

Menu

Ruinart Champagne

✸✸✸✸✸

"Foie Gras Imperial Palace"
Paté de Foie Gras with Marinated Raspberries
Toasted Brioche
Château Les Arroucats, Sainte-Croix-du-Mont, 2003

✸✸✸✸✸

"Finnish Extravaganza"
Herring with Lemon
Gravadlax with Sauce Marshal Mannerheim
Shot Glass of Baltic Fish Soup
Montagny Premier Cru, Buxy-Saône-et-Loire, 2002

✸✸✸✸✸

"Cleansing Thyme"
Galia Melon and Thyme Sorbet

✸✸✸✸✸

"Britannic Medley"
Medallions of Aberdeen Angus
Sauce Béarnaise
Celeriac Mash, Brussels Sprouts and Glazed Carrots
Château Belgrave, Haut Médoc 5eme Cru, 2000

✸✸✸✸✸

"The Cat's Whiskers"
Lancastrian Sticky Toffee Pudding
with Chestnuts, Custard and Bramble Compote
Brown Brothers, Late Harvest Orange Flora and Muscat, 2005

✸✸✸✸✸

In the Old Library at the conclusion of the Banquet
Coffee
English Sweetmeats
Taylor's Quinta de Vargellas, 1996
Courvoisier Cognac
Blandy's Rich Madeira

53 *The menu card for the Lord Mayor's Banquet.*

The banquet and the dinner afford an opportunity to invite friends, as well as business, civic and other distinguished guests, and to involve some of them in the arrangements. The Lord Mayor and Sheriffs' Committee was chaired, by tradition, by my hugely supportive Deputy in my ward, Christine Cohen, OBE, and involved, among others, Dennis Cotgrove and the late Mary Lou Carrington, also Common Councilmen representing Lime Street. Friends, whom I nominated to be on the Committee, included Michael Beale (former, also hugely supportive, Deputy at Lime Street), Peter Beesley (Master Glazier), Peter Berry, CMG, David Colvin, CMG and Peter Wyman, CBE. My two Sheriffs, Alderman David Lewis and Richard Regan CC, chose eight members between them. I was also asked to nominate someone to perform the role of Deputy Gauger at the Lighting-up Dinner. In former times, the Deputy Gauger was a wine tester, dating from the days when the City was entitled to impose wine duties. Although the position is

54 Deputy Christine Cohen, the late Mary Lou Carrington and Michael Beale (members of the Lord Mayor and Sheriffs' Committee) wait the start of the Lord Mayor's Banquet.

now a sinecure, interestingly it is retained by contemporary Weights and Measures legislation. I needed someone who knew his wines and enjoyed tasting them. So I was pleased to nominate my father-in-law, Geoffrey Daish, who was delighted to so act and composed a verse which he read out at the Lighting-up Dinner, as follows:

> For I am the Deputy Gauger
> There is no one who could be sager
> Judge all the wines
> Their vintage and vines
> I'm bound to be lit up, I wager

The Lighting-up Dinner was a very friendly affair and no mishaps occurred. It was also an excellent dress rehearsal for the Banquet itself.

Perhaps, as a result, when it came to the Lord Mayor's Banquet, despite the formality, Lesley and I felt more relaxed. We were already three days into the Mayoralty with the Silent Ceremony, the Lord Mayor's Show, and the British Legion event at the Royal Albert Hall and Remembrance Sunday behind us. We were getting into the swing. Photographs of us in our finery, together with the family, the Sheriffs and Mansion House team, were taken at Mansion House before we left for Guildhall, again accompanied by a police escort.

55 The Lady Mayoress' father, Geoffrey Daish, as Deputy Gauger at the Lighting-up Dinner on 2 November 2006.

56   *The entire Mayoral Party at Mansion House prior to the Lord Mayor's Banquet.*

For these occasions, the Lord Mayor wears a black and gold gown, the Mayoral gown, with the black tricorne hat presented by the Feltmakers. The Lady Mayoress wears her tiara, which we had acquired when we knew that I would be Sheriff. Victorian and stately, it suits Lesley and, unlike many tiaras, is not glitzy, while

57   *The Lord Mayor and Lady Mayoress and family at Mansion House prior to the Lord Mayor's Banquet.*

containing an appropriate number of diamonds. She has fairly thick hair and therefore carries a tiara well.

On arrival at the portico to Guildhall, we were met by Deputy Christine Cohen, the Chairman of the Lord Mayor & Sheriffs' Committee, with a barrage of photographers such as one sees on television meeting stars at the Oscars. Lesley and I then walked to the Old Library of the Guildhall and waited there for the Prime Minister and Cherie Blair to arrive. This was the last occasion in which the guest of honour and the other chief guests were to process into the Old Library, between ranks of other guests who watched and clapped as each dignitary was announced. It was a little like a catwalk, where one can have a good look at someone well known as he or she processes up the aisle to be greeted by the Lord Mayor. And so it was with Tony and Cherie Blair. Lesley and I greeted them before the usual photographs and then a formal procession was called and we whisked them away for drinks in the Art Gallery and the signing of the Distinguished Visitors' Book. It was Tony Blair's last Lord Mayor's Banquet after announcing his intention of stepping down as PM in the summer. He clearly enjoyed it and I had a very relaxed evening discussing many subjects with him including the countries that I would be visiting as Lord Mayor. After my speech of welcome, the Prime Minister replied and was filmed for the 10 o'clock news. The other speakers were The Archbishop of Canterbury, praising the Late Lord Mayor, Sir David Brewer, who replied, and then Lord Falconer, also in his last appearance as Lord Chancellor, who was extremely funny.

58 *The Lord Mayor receives the Prime Minister and Mrs Blair at the Lord Mayor's Banquet on 13 November 2006.*

In my banquet speech, on which I started work in the summer, I noted London's pre-eminence as a financial centre but warned against complacency, giving the Lancashire cotton industry as an example of how the world can change. I argued against too much regulation and I stressed the importance of education. I then introduced my programme for the year, promoting London as a centre of excellence for business education and professional skills development 'City of London – City of Learning'. I also described the charitable nature of the City and introduced my charitable appeal for the year, managed by Voluntary Service Overseas.

The speeches were well received. It was a very successful and happy evening. Tony and Cherie Blair left immediately the banquet finished, as he had to prepare for a phone call with President Bush. As a result, Lesley and I were able to mingle and relax with friends in the Art Gallery over a cup of coffee and a glass of something.

THE STATE VISITS

There are usually two State visits each year – in the Spring and the Autumn. This timing avoids the busy summer season while at the same time avoiding the worst of the winter weather. After recommendations by the Foreign Office, State visits are agreed with the Palace and then notified to the Lord Mayor's Office via the City Remembrancer. In recent years, State visits have typically been of two nights' duration, with a welcome usually at Horseguards on the first day, a banquet that evening at Buckingham Palace or Windsor Castle, followed by a banquet on the second evening at Guildhall, at which The Queen is represented by a member of the Royal family.

I was fortunate to participate in four such visits – two as Sheriff (China and Brazil) and two as Lord Mayor (Ghana and Saudi Arabia). They stand out as highlights of my two years in office.

The quality of the preparation, as one can imagine, matches the quality of the events. A booklet is prepared by the Palace describing every detail of the visit, from the moment the Head of State arrives at Heathrow and is escorted to Horseguards for the formal welcome by The Queen. This is a special ceremony and the dress code is 'State'. For the Lord Mayor, this means Old Bailey (18th-century-style black cloth coat) with breeches, the Lord Mayor's gown, chain, badge and tricorne hat. It also demands special treatment, with a police escort from Mansion House to ensure prompt arrival in Whitehall.

Arriving at Horseguards, the Lord Mayor and the accompanying Sheriffs, wait in their Rolls-Royce cars until the appointed time and then line up on the dais in the following order: Prime Minister, Foreign Secretary, Home Secretary, Lord Mayor of the City of London, the two Sheriffs, Chief of the Defence Staff, First Sea Lord, Chief of the General Staff, Chief of the Air Staff, Lord Mayor of Westminster and the Metropolitan Police Commissioner. Dressed in our finery, we could resemble a scene from a Gilbert & Sullivan opera. On the parade ground, the Household Cavalry are lined up, looking magnificent, waiting for the arrival of the Monarch. It is quite a spectacle. The Ceremony begins with the Lord Lieutenant of London (Lord Imbert until 2008, now Sir David Brewer) welcoming members of the Royal Family, and then The Queen and Duke of Edinburgh, onto the dais, preceded by the National Anthem as the cars draw up. It is very precisely timed. Her Majesty has received many State visitors during her long reign and, on each of the four occasions I attended this ceremony, she looked very relaxed. Perhaps one of her most admirable gifts is her ability to remember who everyone is and where you last met. In my case, she referred to the event to commemorate the Centenary at the Old Bailey, when she unveiled a plaque to mark the occasion.

At the appointed hour, the visiting Head of State arrives with his entourage. After his national anthem, and greeting by The Queen, he inspects the guard, together with the Duke of Edinburgh, and is then escorted by The Queen for the introductions. The whole event is quite short but shows England at its very best.

59 Deputy Stuart Fraser chairs the Reception Committee for the Saudi Arabian Banquet, assisted by the Chief Commoner, Deputy Pauline Halliday, and the Remembrancer, Paul Double.

That evening, the Lord Mayor, in evening dress (white tie with decorations), and the Lady Mayoress, wearing her tiara, are invited to a sumptuous banquet at Buckingham Palace or Windsor Castle. For me, the frequent changes in dress did not present a problem. I got quite adept, with the help of the footmen at Mansion House, at washing, shaving and changing in 10 minutes flat. For Lesley, it was a little more complicated. A tiara has to be carefully fixed in a lady's hair, requiring the expert assistance of a hairdresser on each occasion. But the effect is terrific. There is nothing quite so sparkling as the sight of ladies at a State banquet, in their fine gowns and jewellery. And of course the men can look pretty dashing as well.

A police escort again ensures prompt arrival at the Palace, to be greeted by staff whose faces become increasingly familiar and who are always so welcoming and helpful. After the introductions to the Monarch and the Head of State, a procession is formed for the distinguished guests and, on the occasion of the Saudi banquet, Lesley found herself taking part in the Royal procession with the Prime Minister's wife, Sarah Brown, and the Home Secretary, Jacqui Smith, as there were no Saudi ladies present. She was escorted by HRH Prince Richard Duke of Gloucester and sat between HRH and David Cameron. By tradition, the speeches are given before the meal is served and are short and friendly. The banquet ends with a unit of the Band of the Highlanders marching around the banqueting hall playing the bagpipes. After dinner, there is always the opportunity of a discussion with a member of the visiting delegation or someone from the Foreign Office or the Palace, before a reasonably early night.

On the second night of a State visit, the Lord Mayor and the City Corporation host a banquet for the visiting Head of State at Guildhall. This is an extraordinary event, with all the glamour, pomp and ceremony that one can imagine, attended by around 500 guests. By tradition, a Reception Committee is appointed of members of the Court of Common Council, who oversee the detailed arrangements which are the responsibility of the Remembrancer – in recent years, Paul Double, assisted by Fiona Hoban and their able staff. To ensure it all goes to plan, a trial meal tasting is held and, on the morning of the banquet, a rehearsal takes place so that everyone knows the precise arrangements relating to greeting, processing and the speeches.

The Ghana State Banquet

My first State banquet as Lord Mayor was in March 2007, for the President of Ghana, His Excellency John Kufuor, whom I had met during my visit to Ghana in January 2007. Being the 50th anniversary of the country's independence and since Ghana was the first British colony to receive its independence, a State visit in 2007 by the Ghanaian President to the UK was highly appropriate and significant. During my stay in Accra, I had enjoyed my meeting with President Kufuor and our discussion at his palace. He kindly invited my Mayoral party to a reception the same evening to welcome home Kofi Annan, the retiring Secretary-General of the United Nations, whom it was also a pleasure and an honour to meet. Educated at Lincoln's Inn and Exeter College Oxford, the President is a very able, cultured man, who has gained the respect of leaders in many countries and was elected Chairman of the African Union for the 2007-08 session. When I saw him in Accra I asked him if he would wear national dress for the banquets in the UK during his State visit. He replied that he thought it might be too cold, since Ghanaian national dress comprises a length of colourful 'kente' cloth which is draped over one shoulder, leaving the other one bare. He feared for the weather in the UK in March and joked that he might have to hire white tie and tails. In the event, he attended both banquets in his national costume, something which was much appreciated. He looked magnificent.

For State banquets at Guildhall, the Lord Mayor wears 'Full State' dress, namely an ermine and maroon gown, on top of Old Bailey and breeches, with the chain and badge of course. The ermine gown has two tassels which hang in front, prompting the often naughty Ken Livingstone to say that anyone could tell the Mayor of London from the Lord Mayor of the City of London, as the latter had dangly bits. Escorted again by police outriders, I arrived with Lesley at Guildhall to be greeted by the Chairman of the City Corporation's Reception Committee, Deputy William Fraser, and his wife Penny. The plan is that the Lord Mayor and Lady Mayoress then wait under the porch to the main entrance to

60 *HRH The Duchess of Gloucester with the Lady Mayoress. Bill Fraser looks on.*

61 *The Recorder of London, His Honour Judge Peter Beaumont QC, reads the Address of Welcome to the President of Ghana.*

Guildhall for the distinguished guests to arrive. When the car carrying the members of the Royal Family draws up, the band plays the British National Anthem. We greet them and then we all await the arrival of the State guest. As his car approaches, the band plays the national anthem of the visitor's country.

The Ghanaian State Banquet was the first occasion that the regimental band on duty that evening had performed at such an important event. They knew that they had to start playing each anthem as the Rolls-Royce entered Guildhall Yard. But they didn't get it quite right. My car, LMO, entered the yard first, in accordance with the agreed procedures. But, as I began to alight from the car, I was startled to hear the first line of our National Anthem echoing around the yard. I scrambled to attention, after which the Remembrancer approached with the line 'My Lord Mayor, I think they've upgraded you'. But this wasn't all, when the Gloucesters arrived, the band played the Ghanaian national anthem. We had previously experienced an amusing incident with their Royal Highnesses on the occasion of a visit to the City by the King and Queen of Norway, so I explained all to the Duchess. She wondered what would happen when President Kufuor arrived. Fortunately someone had spoken to the band and the Ghanaian national anthem was played again. So far as the President was concerned everything was working smoothly.

At previous banquets, a formal reception had been held in the Old Library, where visitors were applauded as they walked up the aisle to be greeted by the Lord Mayor, Lady Mayoress and Sheriffs. Known as the 'cat walk', this was followed by the Recorder of London reading an Address of Welcome, which was then placed in a most attractive silver casket as a gift to the visitor. However, on this occasion, the Old Library was out of action, due to the Guildhall North Block refurbishment programme. Additionally, the concept of a cat walk was being seen, increasingly, as outdated. So, for the Ghana Banquet, after the introductions, a procession was formed to escort the President to the Guildhall Art Gallery for the Reception and to sign the Distinguished Visitors' Book. Prior to the start of

62 *HRH The Duchess of Gloucester with the Lord Mayor at the State Banquet at Guildhall for His Excellency John Kufuor, President of Ghana.*

the Banquet, another procession then escorted the President into Great Hall, to a fanfare from the Household Cavalry, after which the Recorder, His Honour Peter Beaumont QC, read the Address of Welcome in the Hall.

There is nothing quite like State trumpeters in Guildhall to demonstrate just how good the British are at pomp and ceremony. Prior to the grace and prior to each speech, there is a fanfare, which always gives the impression that something important is about to occur – which, of course, it is. Guildhall was decorated with flowers in the colours of the Ghanaian flag. With gleaming silver, sparkling glasses and hundreds of bright candles, Great Hall looked magnificent.

Having been to Ghana, and having met the President before, made the evening so easy and relaxed for both me and my distinguished guest. I learnt that his brother had been at Cambridge at the same time as me and that, like me, the President was a mason. Masonry is very popular in Ghana, as they like the structure of the craft and also its emphasis on friendship, community and charity. In my speech, I congratulated the President on his country's achievements since independence in 1957 and, referring to my visit there, I spoke of the pleasure of meeting him and the Asantahene (the King of Ashanti) in Kumasi, also the President's home town.

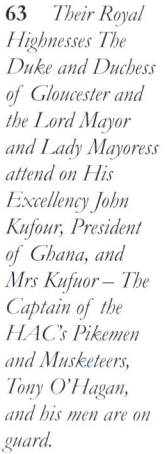

63 Their Royal Highnesses The Duke and Duchess of Gloucester and the Lord Mayor and Lady Mayoress attend on His Excellency John Kufour, President of Ghana, and Mrs Kufuor – The Captain of the HAC's Pikemen and Musketeers, Tony O'Hagan, and his men are on guard.

I also made reference to the good work being undertaken by Voluntary Service Overseas with the Ghanaian Government. The banquet was a huge success.

64 *Trumpeters from the Household Cavalry precede a speech at the Ghanaian State Banquet at Guildhall.*

THE SAUDI STATE BANQUET

My second State Banquet, as Lord Mayor, was in October 2007, for King Abdullah of Saudi Arabia, who has the title 'Custodian of the Two Holy Mosques'. The arrangements for the visit were very similar to those described above for Ghana, with some minor changes. First, the welcome at Horseguards seemed, not surprisingly, to be surrounded by a greater degree of security – policemen, men with bulges in their pockets, roof top observers and armed vehicles accompanying the Royal visitors' entourage, which in total numbered over 300 people. Then, at the banquets at both Buckingham Palace and Guildhall, while wine was served, it was less in evidence and, as a mark of respect to our guests, I had two alcohol free evenings.

I had visited Saudi Arabia in February 2006, as Sheriff, accompanying the previous Lord Mayor, Sir David Brewer. This helped enormously when it came to preparing my speech. I had also met Sir Sherard Cowper-Coles, our Ambassador

65 *The Lord Mayor greets HRH The Duke of York at Guildhall while the Sheriffs look on.*

66 *His Majesty The King of Saudi Arabia, attended by HRH The Duke of York, the Lord Mayor and the Lady Mayoress in the Art Gallery of Guildhall.*

to Saudi Arabia at the time of our visit and stayed at his residence in Riyadh. In addition to liking Sherard, I understood that he was an accomplished Arabist. I managed to track him down, in Afghanistan where he is now Ambassador, to seek his views on a suitable Arab quote. He did not fail me and I was able to include in my speech the following text:

> Friendship is based on mutual esteem and trust – and as you say in your country, 'a true friend tells you the truth rather than believes all you say.' Thus we have enjoyed a long relationship. And, our two kingdoms have so many common objectives.

67 *The Town Clerk and Chief Executive, Chris Duffield, is presented to His Majesty the King of Saudi Arabia, while Alderman Sir Michael Oliver looks on. Alderman Sir David Howard is in the background.*

I praised the King for his efforts to bring about peace in the Middle East and for his vision of reform in his kingdom and spoke about education, making a further reference as follows: 'It was the well known hadith of The Prophet Muhammad, peace be upon him, which enjoined the faithful to 'seek knowledge, even as far as China'.' He was equally gracious in his speech and, during the evening, we discussed the issues his country faces, as well as two of his passions: breeding horses and training falcons. Exchanging gifts is always a pleasant ritual and His Majesty's generosity extended to personal gifts for Lesley and me as well as a present for the City Corporation – a stunning model, in gold, of the fort in Riyadh which his father had captured in 1902, so starting the third ruling dynasty of the Saud family.

THE HONOURABLE ARTILLERY COMPANY – PRESENTATION OF COLOURS

One of the Lord Mayor's roles is President of the City of London Reserve Forces and Cadets Association. As a result, in my capacity as President and as Lord Mayor, I was involved in a number of events and meetings during my year where the Armed Forces featured.

One very special event took place on Friday 18 May when the Honourable Artillery Company was presented with new colours by Her Majesty The Queen.

The HAC holds a very special position in the life of the City. Incorporated by Royal Charter in 1537, the HAC is the oldest regiment in the British Army and the second most senior unit in the Territorial Army. Since 1641, the Company has owned its present estate of six acres on a site just north of the City's Barbican complex and its present home, the attractive Palladian style Armoury House, was built in 1735. Since the Restoration, the Company has provided guards of honour in the City for visits by members of the Royal Family and overseas Heads of State. The Company is also one of a few regiments that enjoys the privilege of marching through the City of London with drums beating, colours flying and bayonets fixed.

The custom dates from the 17th century or earlier and was designed to encourage recruitment. In those days, the Court of Aldermen appointed the chief officers and paid the professional soldiers who trained members of the Company. To this day, the Lord Mayor and Aldermen are honorary members of the HAC's Court of Assistants. The Pikemen & Musketeers and the Light Cavalry form the escort and bodyguards for the Lord Mayor and Lady Mayoress respectively and are often on duty at Mansion House and in the City at ceremonial and Livery events. It was a great pleasure that, in my year, the Captain of the Pikemen & Musketeers was Captain Tony O'Hagan, a former colleague at Coopers Brothers & Co. in the late 1960s. We got to see Tony and his colourful Company at many events during the year, and also enjoyed meeting Captain Reg Howe, Officer Commanding the Light Cavalry, and his cavalrymen. We all became great friends.

The HAC is known to have possessed Colours since the 17th century. More recently, Colours have been presented by Her Majesty The Queen in 1955 and 1980. These bear Battle Honours won in the two World Wars by both the Infantry Battalions and the Artillery Batteries, a unique honour. It was therefore an added bonus that new Colours were presented by The Queen during my Mayoral Year, which gave Lesley and me the opportunity of witnessing this spectacular event, as well as playing a very minor part. On a sunny May Day, dressed in morning coat, badge and top hat, I was driven to Armoury House and met by a friendly figure, the HAC Captain Commandant, General Sir Timothy Granville-Chapman, GBE, KCB, who is the Aide-de-Camp General to The Queen and Vice-Chief of the Defence Staff. Escorted by the HAC Court Secretary, Peter Patrick, and guided by Colonel Geoffrey Godbold, OBE, TD, DL who had recently joined Mansion House team, Lesley and I were taken to the stand, where around 1,800 guests were already seated. The ceremony began with all 64 members of the Company of

68 *Her Majesty The Queen presents new colours to the HAC.*

Pikemen & Musketeers, led by Tony O'Hagan, marching onto the Parade Ground and my brief moment of glory occurred when I took the salute. Geoffrey was there to advise me 'Hat off my Lord Mayor. Hat on my Lord Mayor.' These were invaluable instructions for someone who had been in the School CCF, but had progressed no further in the Armed Forces. The Chief Commandant then arrived for a General Salute by all 254 members of the Company, before the old Colours were marched off the Parade Ground, after being shown to the assembled gathering. At 12 o'clock sharp, Her Majesty The Queen arrived in the Royal Bentley, as the national anthem was played. After an inspection of the Company, she watched from the dais as the new Colours were brought in, unfurled and laid on an altar of drums prior to the blessing by the two padres. It was a very moving moment, as the Colours are given, in Regimental life, an almost religious significance. After a short speech, The Queen, who is the Captain-General of the HAC, formally handed the new Colours to the Regiment and then a few guests were introduced to her and Prince Philip. I had the pleasure of meeting the Duke of Edinburgh on a number of occasions and always enjoyed the quip or joke that he would typically make. On this occasion, he held up his hand, as though to shield his eyes, saying that he was dazzled by the sun shining on my diamond badge. He asked if they were real and I replied that there was a rumour that they were a love gift from Ivan The Terrible to Queen Elizabeth I. He laughed. The Ceremony finished, we all repaired to Armoury House for a pleasant lunch and the culmination of a very special event.

THE QUEEN VISITS THE CITY

In former times, when the Monarch visited the City of London, the Lord Mayor met him or her at the City boundary in full State dress carrying the pearl sword which had been presented to the City by Queen Elizabeth I on the occasion of her visit to open the Royal Exchange in 1571. Nowadays this elaborate ceremony is reserved for special events such as a Jubilee and it was my predecessor, Sir Michael Oliver, in 2002, who had the pleasure of handing the sword to the present Monarch on her visit to the City to commemorate the Golden Jubilee.

69 *Her Majesty The Queen unveils a plaque to commemorate the Centenary of the Central Criminal Court in Old Bailey.*

In my year, while the pearl sword was not used, I did have the honour of greeting Her Majesty on two occasions when she visited the City.

On the first of these, 27 February 2007, Queen Elizabeth came to the Central Criminal Court, The Old Bailey, to commemorate the centenary of the visit by her great grandfather, King Edward VII, to open the building in 1907. He had unveiled a plaque and an identical plaque, with appropriate wording, was manufactured for

70 Her Majesty The Queen attends a concert at the Barbican to mark its 25th anniversary. Sir John Tusa on left.

the centenary event for The Queen to unveil. In 1907, the building contained a lift. Not many lifts had been installed at that time and there was a rumour that Edward VII had an aversion to lifts and used the stairs. The Queen had no such fear and the lift carried a monarch probably for the first time in its history. I presented to Her Majesty the distinguished visitors present, namely the Lord Chancellor Lord Falconer, the Recorder His Honour Peter Beaumont QC, other judges and the Chief Commoner Gerry Pulman.

The second occasion was just one week later when The Queen came to celebrate the 25th anniversary of the opening of the Barbican Centre by attending a concert. She was very relaxed and I was pleased to be able to present to her Sir John Tusa, Managing Director of the Barbican centre, Graham Sheffield, the Artistic Director, and Sir Colin Davis, the evening's conductor. Prior to the arrival of the Royal Party, the Guildhall School of Music and Drama had played a brass version of *Spem in Alium* by Thomas Tallis. This gave me an idea for spectacular music at two Mansion House banquets (see p. 83).

25TH ANNIVERSARY OF THE FALKLANDS CAMPAIGN

In the middle of June 2007, the country recalled the events of 1982 when the Falkland Islands were attacked by the Argentinian Army and then recovered by British Forces under difficult circumstances. The South Atlantic Medal Association had been active in planning the 25th anniversary.

For me, this event began with a rehearsal at Guildhall on Friday morning the 15th to prepare for the dinner that evening at which the chief guests would be their Royal Highnesses the Gloucesters and Baroness Thatcher, plus all the top brass from the Armed Forces, headed by the Chief of the Defence Staff, Air Chief Marshal Sir Jock Stirrup, GCB, AFC with his wife, Mary. But before the dinner, there was a memorial service to attend, in front of Trinity House, at which HRH Prince Michael laid a wreath. Dressed, ready for dinner in Old Bailey and breeches, decorations, chain and badge, Mayoral gold and black gown and tricorne hat, I participated briefly before leaving for Guildhall to greet our guests.

During dinner, I sat next to Margaret Thatcher and the Duchess of Gloucester. HRH graciously suggested that I should focus my attention on the former Prime Minister and it was a fascinating evening. Still razor sharp, but with, I was informed, the after effects of a stroke, Margaret Thatcher responded to issues as she might well have done 25 years earlier. Tony Blair was about to step down as PM and

I cheekily asked her what she thought were the key attributes of a successful leader. Her first answer was predictable: 'One must be determined.' Her second was memorable: 'The secret of success is nurturing and releasing talent.' She also added that Churchill is a great role model when it comes to preparing and making speeches. In discussion with her, I pointed out that she had sat in the same seat many times as Prime Minister at Lord Mayor's Banquets and that from this position you could see statues of some famous people – Wellington, Nelson and Churchill. She looked me straight in the eye and with a quizzical look said: 'I wonder who's missing.' Another memorable evening.

The commemoration continued over the weekend with the ceremony of Trooping The Colour on Saturday in Horseguards, followed by lunch at the London home of General Officer Commanding London District Major-General Sebastian Roberts, KCVO, OBE and his wife Elizabeth. Then on Sunday, we were back at Horseguards, again in morning coat and Mayoral badge, for another spectacular parade which we watched from the VIP stand, together with The Reverend and Right Honourable Ian Paisley, Sir John Nott and David Cameron. As soon as this was over, we were whisked over to Victory Monument on the island in front of Buckingham Palace to watch, with His Royal Highness The Prince of Wales and the Prime Minister, the fly past of aircraft used in the Falklands Campaign.

WELCOMING HOME OUR LADS (AND LASSES) FROM THE LONDON REGIMENT

Another very special event took place on Sunday 14 October 2007, when 140 soldiers of the Somme Company of the London Regiment returned from Afghanistan and were given a welcome in the City. Dressed in Old Bailey with trousers, scarlet gown, chain, badge and tricorne hat, accompanied by the two Sheriffs, I was driven to Guildhall Yard where around 750 people had gathered

71 *Welcome home, at Guildhall, to the Somme Regiment from Afghanistan.*

to watch the men march in. I was met by a former Lord Mayor, Alderman Sir Michael Savory, who is the Regiment's Honorary Colonel, General Officer Commanding London District Major-General Bill Cubitt, CBE, the Commanding Officer Colonel Greg Truman, the Chief Commoner Deputy Pauline Halliday and the Vicar of St Lawrence Jewry, the Reverend David Burgess, who said prayers. Greg Truman and I spoke, after which I took the salute. On this occasion, Colonel Richard Martin, the City's Swordbearer was there to help me out. 'Hat off my Lord Mayor. Hat on my Lord Mayor.' Then, Bill Cubitt and I handed out campaign medals to every member of Somme Company present and had a chat to find out what they'd done and where they'd been. I met some brave people that day.

After the formalities we repaired to Great Hall for drinks and eats, where the soldiers met their families and there were some emotional moments. I was asked if one soldier could be permitted to propose to his girlfriend over the loudspeaker system. I responded that I would be delighted – provided he knew that she would accept. He went ahead and Lance Corporal Field's proposal was duly accepted, to a round of applause. For me this was one of the most memorable events of the Mayoralty. There had been criticism by the Head of the Army, General Sir Richard Dannatt, KCB, CBE, MC that public homecomings were becoming a rarity. It was therefore a pleasure for me and an honour that we in the City should have organised this parade to welcome home soldiers from the London Regiment who had so bravely served in Afghanistan.

THE STATE OPENING OF PARLIAMENT

Each year, the Lord Mayor of the City of London and the Lord Mayor of Westminster are invited to attend the State Opening of Parliament, watching from the narrow balcony that allows a wonderful view of the proceedings. As with all State or semi-State occasions, a motorcycle escort was on hand to ensure that we got to the House of Lords on time.

During my year, the timing of events was such that I attended two State Openings – the first, in November 2006, when Lord Falconer was the Lord Chancellor and the second, a year later, when Jack Straw had assumed the office. Jack reverted to custom followed in years prior to Lord Irvine, where the Lord Chancellor does not turn his back on the Monarch but retires, walking backwards down the steps, trying to avoid tripping over his train. It is amusing to watch, but shows respect for Her Majesty. The Queen wears the Imperial State crown and the parliamentary robe with a long train carried by two page boys. Two ladies in waiting are in attendance and she is accompanied by the Duke of Edinburgh. The lords are also in their finery, with wives sporting tiaras. As a visitor, Lesley was relieved not to have to wear hers.

It is a long Ceremony, if only because there is quite a lot of waiting at the beginning, to ensure that everyone who should be present is there – judges sitting on the woolsack and the Prime Minister and MPs having been summoned by

Black Rod from the Commons to stand at the bar of the House of Lords. It is one moment in the year when you could be forgiven for mistaking which House is senior. It is a spectacular occasion and one of the great British events in the calendar, as well as being extremely important from a constitutional viewpoint.

The formal Opening is followed by receptions. We were invited to one hosted by the Speaker of the House of Commons, which provides an excellent opportunity to network with MPs, Ambassadors and Ministers.

THE QUEEN'S DIPLOMATIC RECEPTION

Every year Her Majesty holds a reception at Buckingham Palace for ambassadors from other countries accredited to the Court of St James. Attended by senior figures in the judiciary, our own Foreign Office and Government, it is a colourful affair, with national costume worn by our foreign guests. The dress code for me was white tie and tails with decorations and Mayoral badge, but Lesley had to go to the hairdresser to have her tiara fixed.

With the large number of guests who attend this popular event, The Queen only has time to meet the foreign visitors. The evening ends with dancing after a buffet. It is a good opportunity to chat and to catch up.

BUCKINGHAM PALACE GARDEN PARTY

A great treat is the annual Garden Party invitation extended to the Lord Mayor and Lady Mayoress. Many thousands of people attend these events at Buckingham Palace each year and, on the first occasion I attended as an Alderman, I sought advice from a Senior Alderman and former Lord Mayor, Sir Paul Newall. Morning coat, black top hat, black waistcoat of course and an umbrella very tightly furled as carried by Patrick Macnee in the 1960s television series 'The Avengers', he said, definitely showing his age as well as his dress sense. As Lord Mayor, one is whisked off to the VIP tent where guests are introduced to Her Majesty and HRH The Duke of Edinburgh. On this occasion, Her Majesty asked about the plaque she had unveiled at the ceremony to commemorate the centenary of the Old Bailey and I agreed to find out if it had been put in place. It had and I sent a photograph to the Palace to show it in position and received a gracious letter of thanks for following this up.

THE ORDER OF ST JOHN

The Order of St John has contributed greatly to care in the City of London for many centuries, with an unfortunate hiatus of 300 years in the middle. In about 1140, the knights of the Order, which started in Jerusalem, built their British headquarters at Clerkenwell, just north of the City's boundaries. They prospered as a military religious order, caring for the sick as well as seeking to defend Christianity, until Henry VIII confiscated their land and dissolved the Order in the 16th century. In 1877, the St John Ambulance Association was formed, to provide First Aid and training in First Aid. And in 1888, Queen Victoria made the British Order a Royal Order of Chivalry. Today, the Order flourishes and comprises St John Ambulance, which is a leading first aid, transport and care charity, and the St John Eye Hospital in Jerusalem.

At every major event in the capital, St John Ambulance volunteers are conspicuous in their black uniforms with a white Maltese cross. The training of youngsters is a priority, starting at the age of five, where a child can become a Badger, and then at the age of 10 a full cadet. It is a challenging and rewarding training which enables the volunteers to be able to care for anyone injured or sick at public events, such as the Lord Mayor's Show.

Each year, on the nearest Saturday to St John's Day, the General Assembly of the British Order gather for their Annual Assembly at Mansion House, followed by lunch and then the annual service at St Paul's Cathedral. You might imagine that you had stumbled on a film set for a scene from a Harry Potter film. Men and women in long black capes, decorated with enormous Maltese crosses, escorted by men similarly dressed carrying banners. It is very picturesque and traditional, but the content of the Assembly is like any modern AGM with presentations on latest training techniques, on collaboration with local emergency services, on volunteering. St John adds enormously to the welfare of our community.

As Lord Mayor, I was invited to become a Knight of Justice of the Order and was very proud, during my year, to wear the Maltese cross as a neck decoration and as a badge on my left breast. The extra significance for me was that the Maltese cross was also the emblem of my prep school, The Leas at Hoylake in Cheshire.

A further pleasure was that my old mentor from Coopers & Lybrand, Sir Brian Jenkins, GBE, who was Lord Mayor in 1991-92, is now the Prior of England & the Islands and my aunt, Margaret Boothman, MBE, is a Dame of the Order.

Although my honour was announced and the decoration given to me by Sir Brian Jenkins and The Rt Hon Sir John Wheeler before my Mayoral year started, it was not until November 2007 that I was formally invested, by HRH Duke of Gloucester, at a magical ceremony at the Priory Church of St John, Clerkenwell. I was pleased that this was observed by Brian and Margaret, as well as by her younger son, Clive, all of whom had a part to play in the ceremony.

THE LEAGUE OF MERCY

The League of Mercy was founded in 1899 by Queen Victoria to establish a large body of voluntary workers who would assist with the maintenance of voluntary hospitals and 'otherwise relieve sickness and suffering'. In 1948 when the National Health Act abolished these hospitals, the League was wound up. It was then re-founded, by Sir Robert Balchin, as a charity in 1999 and encourages and recognises volunteers to assist and care for the sick, elderly and disabled. Each year, the League of Mercy Foundation makes around 50 awards to volunteers in charities. In 2007, I was honoured by the Foundation for work in the voluntary sector and received the Companion's badge.

Spem in Alium

Spem in Alium was composed by Thomas Tallis in about 1570 for eight choirs of five voices each. Believed to be influenced by an Italian composer, it is a work of outstanding genius, where the choirs sing a vocal line that is later repeated or varied slightly. This is described as homophonic, where the parts move together in harmony, creating chords. It is a work of exquisite beauty which presents a new idea, moves to a climax, subsides, presents another new idea and then climaxes again. Because of its complexity it is rarely performed. The effect on the listener is of being mesmerised and overwhelmed. I had heard it before but, on hearing it again at the Barbican Centre played by brass from the Guildhall School of Music and Drama, I was convinced that it would be memorable if it were played in the Egyptian Hall at Mansion House.

72 *The Chief Commoner, Deputy Pauline Halliday. with Alderman Dr Andrew Parmley, prior to the Saudi Arabian State Banquet.*

Initial enquiries by Mansion House staff showed that it would be difficult to arrange. It required 40 members of an orchestra or choristers. But, faced with a challenge, and knowing what a great impact it would have on any event at Mansion House, I approached Alderman Dr Andrew Parmley. Andrew is a good friend, as well as being a Fellow Alderman, and an accomplished musician, organist and music teacher. His contacts in the music profession are very wide. Quick as a flash, he was back with some ideas. And so, two of the most memorable performances of music I shall ever experience took place in Mansion House during my year.

The first was a choral rendition by 40 members of the English Chamber Choir who sang *Spem in Alium* at the Judges' Banquet on 17 July 2007. I thought that, of all people, the Judges would be the guests at Mansion House who would most appreciate a performance of this work. They loved it. It made the evening.

73 *The menu cover for the Judges' Banquet at Mansion House.*

The second was a brass rendition by 40 brass players from the Redbridge Brass Band and Zone 1 Brass, conducted by Frank Renton, a conductor, broadcaster and writer. Frank was the senior bandsman in the Army for many years, teaching and training musicians in the Army bands. During the afternoon of Saturday 22 September, I heard the two bands practise. It was magical. At the end of the rehearsal, Frank said to the musicians, 'Not bad. With a bit of

74 *Sandra Cross, the Lord Mayor's secretary at PwC, with Riitta Hiltunen from Finland.*

75 *Private Party at Mansion House — Sir Brian and Lady Jenkins, Sir Brandon and Lady Gough, David and Ann Hobson.*

luck it will be all right on the night'. And so it was. They played at a private banquet for our friends and all who had helped during my Mayoral year. The brass version was louder than the choral version. The sound filled the Egyptian Hall. It reverberated around the room, bouncing off the ceiling, coming to a climax, fading away and then filling the room again. It was quite magical, breath taking, sensational, memorable and made the evening a great success. A few of our guests came to see me after the dinner to say that it had moved them to tears. I owe a debt of gratitude to Andrew Parmley and Frank Renton for delivering something so special. It was a highlight of our year.

Mansion House –
Stately Home for a Year

THE CLOTHING CHECKLIST –
THE LORD MAYOR MUST BE CORRECTLY DRESSED

Preparation for living in Mansion House for a year is rather like preparing to go to a new school. A checklist of clothes is sent to the next Lord Mayor (the Senior Alderman below the Chair, as he is amusingly called) so that he can prepare for his busy year in office. Then, some weeks before he takes Office, various changes need to be made to the clothes and gowns. A tricorne hat has to be made, requiring measurement and fitting. The red Aldermanic gown has to be altered to add a train to it and a hood. Ribbons which can be tied in a bow have to be attached to the shoulders of the various coats in order for the Mayoral chain to be affixed. All this is engineered and managed by the Steward, Colin Tucker, with help from the three footmen, Neil Fletcher, John Hibbitt and James Macdonald.

The 'private side' of the House has been run by Colin for some years and he is extraordinarily knowledgeable about the dress requirements and about the operations of the domestic quarters in Mansion House where the Lord Mayor and the Lady Mayoress live.

With some 1,800 engagements during the Mayoral year, there are frequent changes of dress – from lounge suit to morning coat, to Old Bailey (black cloth tail coat, in 18th-century style) with trousers or breeches, with any one of four gowns (Aldermanic violet, Aldermanic scarlet, Lord Mayor's gold and black, and Lord Mayor's State ermine) to white tie or State (velvet coat with breeches). To ensure that the Lord Mayor is properly turned out in the right dress, and looking smart, requires a team in support. The Steward and the Footmen (Neil, John and James – one on duty at any time) do a wonderful job ensuring that there are no hiccups, that the shoes are properly cleaned, that the right decorations are in place as required, and that the Lord Mayor is always on time.

THE ORIGINS AND PURPOSE OF MANSION HOUSE

Mansion House was built in 1752 to provide the Lord Mayor and his family with a home for the year. Until then, each Lord Mayor had often lived in the hall of his Livery company, if his Livery had one and if there was room. It was

76 *18th-century engraving of Mansion House.*

not ideal. Large civic buildings were springing up across the country and abroad for mayors, governors and provosts. So the City of London had to have its own Mansion House for its own Lord Mayor.

Designed as the official residence of the Lord Mayor of the City of London 'for the time being', this was a place where business could be conducted, where justice could be dispensed (Mansion House had a justice room and was the City's Magistrates' Court for many years) and where guests could be entertained.

THE PRIVATE QUARTERS

77 *Guests at Mansion House.*

Living at Mansion House is like living in a stately home. The drawing room (known as the Lady Mayoress' Boudoir) is one of the finest rooms that one could possibly

imagine, with elaborate plasterwork on the walls and cornices. This is complemented by an enormous bedroom with four-poster bed, two bathrooms and a dressing room for the Lord Mayor that contains the plumpest plaster cherubs that you have ever seen. A small kitchen means that the occupants have the ability to prepare their own breakfasts and this also acts as a servery for receptions. But then there is a splendid small Private Dining Room which can hold up to 18 people and is very suitable for breakfasts, lunches and dinners. During the year, I entertained three Presidents (from Kazakhstan,

Mexico and the Czech Republic) there, as well as the Sultan of Selangor and many other Ministers, Ambassadors and distinguished guests.

For Lord Mayors with families, there are a further two bedrooms at their disposal, and our boys and their wives, as well as friends, used these very occasionally during the year.

The private quarters are, on the one hand, very cosy but, on the other, very grand and create just the right feeling and impression when one is entertaining distinguished guests. One can create a very homely atmosphere, yet maintain a sense of style and importance. They are quite perfect as a place for a Lord Mayor, and Lady Mayoress, to live and entertain for the year.

Essential to the efficient working and management of the private quarters are Karen and Lisa, both sisters, who have worked in Mansion House for years.

78 *Colin Tucker and Neil Fletcher in the Private Dining Room at Mansion House.*

THE STATE BEDROOMS

In days when security was not quite such an issue, heads of State and other distinguished visitors used to be accommodated at Mansion House when visiting the City. Today, a Presidential entourage extends to many attendants and security officers. So the two, very grand, State bedrooms are now, regrettably, rarely used by senior visitors. During our year we tried to use them as much as possible, for example as auction prizes at fundraising events, where bed and breakfast (the latter with the Lord Mayor and Lady Mayoress) might be an attraction.

THE OLD BALLROOM

Immediately adjacent to the State bedrooms is the Old Ballroom, with its magnificent plaster carvings of musical instruments and high gallery. Once used for grand balls, this is now a convenient room for large meetings and presentations, as well as lunches and dinners.

During my year we used the Ballroom on a number of occasions for lunches and dinners where the number of guests was less than one hundred. A memorable event was the lunch for the Mayor of Beijing, Wang Qishan, after he was admitted to the Freedom of the City of London in a ceremony in the Drawing Room of Mansion House. The ceremony was conducted, of course, in English and translated into Mandarin for the benefit of the Mayor, who burst out laughing when it came to the promise 'to obey the Lord Mayor of London and inform him of any misdoings or conspiracies'.

THE EGYPTIAN HALL, THE SALON, THE LONG PARLOUR AND THE DRAWING ROOMS

Most visitors to Mansion House see the ground floor (the Walbrook Entrance) and the grand rooms on the first floor. All are very special, with magnificent plasterwork, which is a notable feature of Mansion House, Empire-style furniture (The Nile Suite dating from 1803) and 17th-century Dutch paintings. It all works to create the atmosphere of a stately home that is also a museum. It is a pleasant place to visit for a reception or a dinner – on the one hand, friendly, at the same time, impressive.

79 *Plate butlers, Abderrazzak Sakim and Andrew Ford, at Mansion House.*

The Egyptian Hall can seat 350 people for dinner and is used for the great banquets as well as for lunches, conferences and briefings. It is multi-purpose and very splendid with its Corinthian columns, barrel vaulted plaster ceiling and statues around the walls.

The other rooms are used for receptions and the occasional dinner party. We very much enjoyed using the Salon for a dinner for about 50 guests when the Prime Minister of Qatar, His Excellency Hamad Bin Jassim Al Thani, visited London. On that occasion, we asked the Plate Butler, Andrew Ford, to bring out as much silver as he could from the Plate Room in the Basement. Some of this was designed by Paul De Lamerie and Paul Storr. It looked magnificent. I was able to joke that, while Qatar had reserves of oil and gas, we had reserves of silver.

We tried to combine the grand surroundings of the house with a personal, friendly welcome, like a home.

THE VENETIAN PARLOUR

Mansion House is also the office of the Lord Mayor and the daily programme is planned and executed by staff working there.

One of the most amazing offices that I have ever enjoyed is the Venetian Parlour, with its ornate plaster ceiling and grand furniture. Called Venetian, because of its arch-topped window, it is a wonderful place in which to work – most inspiring. Yet it is also a very impressive place to receive visitors and hold meetings of up to eight people, either around a table or, more comfortably, on the sofas and easy chairs.

MANSION HOUSE STAFF

Immediately next door, with an interconnecting door, is the office of the Private Secretary and Chief of Staff, Kay Brock, LVO. With very useful prior experience in the Civil Service, management consultancy, the European Commission and at Buckingham Palace, Kay was in overall charge of Mansion House and the support to the Lord Mayor. It is a difficult job, with so many engagements and with so many events in the house and so many outside links to build and maintain.

To assist her in performing these duties, she has a head of operations, Andrew McKie, who looks after the administration and the domestic side of the house, and Neil Chrimes, newly recruited from the Foreign Office, to head up programme planning and execution.

During my year, one of the Mayoral stalwarts, Anni Gale, MBE, was Diary Secretary to the Lord Mayor. She had served 25 Lord Mayors and knew the form, as well as possessing a sense of humour – essential in that job. She retired shortly after the end of my Mayoral year.

The programme managers, Lt Colonel Richard Martin (also the ceremonial Swordbearer) and Colonel Billy King-Harman, CBE (also the City Marshal), together with Neil Chrimes, planned the daily events, including the overseas visits. Assisted by Penny Shelley, MBE, another long-serving member of staff, and secondees from the Foreign Office, in my year Jonathan Nethersole, the team worked extremely hard to ensure that the busy programme worked well. They were joined by Colonel Geoffrey Godbold, OBE who was recruited on a part time basis to act in ceremonial events as Common Cryer and Serjeant-at-Arms.

The major banquets and dinners were organised by Olenka Hassell and her efficient team. With the need to seat guests in just the right place and with invitees inevitably dropping out at the last minute, their patience was endless.

80 *Kay Brock, the Lord Mayor's Private Secretary and Chief of Mansion House staff.*

81 *Shrove Tuesday in Guildhall Yard – The Worshipful Company of Poulters Pancake Race supported by Mark Groves and The Cook and The Butler Event Company. On the left is Gerry Pulman and Bill Beaver; while on the right Anni Gale catches her pancake.*

82 *The Mansion House team.*

During the year, I calculated that I ate 466 formal lunches and dinners. Not all of these were at Mansion House, but many were. So the catering team of Searcy's led by Peter Martin with chef, Mani, were essential to our wellbeing and the enjoyment of our guests. The choice of menu was typically the preserve of the organisation booking the Egyptian Hall for an event, for example a Livery company dinner or an association lunch. However, when it came to the key banquets and private events, Lesley would go off into a huddle with Colin and Mani. A delightful meal would result. We were pleased with the quality of food that we experienced and served to our guests during the year.

Of course, Mansion House can't function without very many people behind the scenes providing security, cleaning the rooms and polishing the silver. John Davis, Walbrook Hall Keeper, acted as guide to many organised tours of Mansion House, as well as standing in as Common Cryer, carrying the mace, the semblance of the Monarch, which precedes the Lord Mayor at all ceremonies. In all, it was a really great team, of dedicated people, who worked tirelessly for the Mayoralty, trying to ensure that everything went to plan and that the Lord Mayor arrived on time and performed his role effectively.

THE BUSINESS CONTENT AND THE SPEECHES

83 *City of London Corporation coat of arms.*

But a crucial element is the briefing and speechwriting for the Lord Mayor who has to give over 760 speeches and 130 media interviews. Frankly, this is the meat – and an increasingly important part of the job. Given its importance I have devoted a separate chapter to the messages, the speeches and the media interviews.

Part III

THE CITY OF LONDON CORPORATION AND THE CITY CIVIC

History of the City's Government

There is no record of the origin of the City of London as an administrative body, but there are indications of the establishment of corporate government in Roman times. The civic administration in the City and the freedoms of its inhabitants were recognised in a charter granted by William the Conqueror in 1067. In that charter he promised to recognise the rights, privileges and laws that the City had enjoyed since the reign of Edward the Confessor. These rights were then enhanced over the centuries, as concessions were gained from the Crown in return for loans and taxes to finance crusades and wars. London's importance as a trading centre and as a port helped the City to secure these privileges long before other cities in the land and, to this day, the City of London has much greater power and status, which is evidenced in many ways.

In Saxon London and after the Norman Conquest, authority was principally vested in the Aldermen (or elder men) who met in the City's ancient Court of Husting, whose administrative work was gradually absorbed by the Court of Aldermen. London, as with other cities, was subject to the authority of the Crown and this was exercised by the Sheriff, an ancient Office that dates from the seventh century. But by the 12th century, there was a move towards civic independence and the Office of Mayor was created, with Henry FitzAilwyn becoming the first incumbent in around 1189. In 1199, King John granted the citizens of London, uniquely in England, the right to elect their own Sheriff and in 1215 he granted the Barons of the City of London (today's Aldermen) the right to elect their own Mayor. In the 14th century the Mayor became known as the Lord Mayor.

The first tentative evidence of participation by representatives of the Commons of the City is supported by an Oath of the Commune in 1193, when *probi homines* were to be associated with the Mayor and others for the good rule of the City of London. From 1376, this assembly had regular meetings and was known as the Common Council. It gradually assumed greater responsibilities for the administration of the City, although to this day there remains a two chamber arrangement for issues affecting the City's constitution. The Court papers state that there must always be at least two Aldermen present, in addition to the Lord Mayor, at each Court of Common Council in order for its decisions to be legally **84** *Guildhall.*

binding. And, of course, it is the Court of Aldermen that produces a Sheriff and a Lord Mayor each year and it is the Aldermen who elect the Lord Mayor.

The Common Council is the principal operating arm and the executive, to which the statutory functions of local authority and police authority for the City and Port Health authority for the tidal Thames are attached. It operates on a non-party basis and all members of the City Corporation act as political independents.

The Court of Common Council comprises 100 Common Councilmen, who are elected by voters in the 25 wards for a term of four years, and 25 Aldermen, who are elected by each ward for six years. The Court meets once a month in Great Hall in Guildhall, with the 25 Aldermen seated on a dais above the seats of the 100 Common Councilmen. The Lord Mayor takes the chair, after processing up the aisle, led by the City Marshal and preceded by the sword and mace. It is a colourful affair, but the business is that appertaining to the administration of the kingdom's capital city.

THE LORD MAYOR AS HEAD OF THE CORPORATION OF THE CITY OF LONDON

The Lord Mayor is the constitutional head of the City of London Corporation. But he or she is much more than that. The Lord Mayor is the figurehead of the City's financial sector and is accorded the rank of Cabinet Minister. He has become respected as the leader of the business community and, for this reason, it is essential that the Court of Aldermen choose candidates who command the respect of the financial sector, as well as the Livery movement and, of course, the elected representatives and people of the City of London.

In his role as the head of the City Corporation, the Lord Mayor represents the activities of the organisation in all its capacities. In this he is helped by the Court of Aldermen and the chairmen of the various City Corporation committees. Foremost among these is the Chairman of the Policy & Resources Committee, who is elected annually and can serve a five year term. The Chief Commoner and officials of the City Corporation, including the Town Clerk (aka the Chief Executive), the Chamberlain, the Comptroller and City Solicitor, and the Remembrancer, also facilitate the achievement of the role of Lord Mayor.

THE CHAIRMAN OF THE POLICY & RESOURCES COMMITTEE

Because the City Corporation's members are apolitical, there is no 'Leader' as such. The Lord Mayor is the figurehead and also the champion of the businesses in the City. Working with the chairmen of the other City Corporation committees, the Chairman of the Policy & Resources Committee coordinates initiatives in the City Corporation's traditional roles of Planning, Transportation, Financial Policy, Police, Education and Environment (including Street Scenes and the Open Spaces of Hampstead, Epping Forest and Burnham Beeches, among others). He also works with the Lord Mayor in identifying and lobbying on business issues and there is a dedicated team (the Economic Development Office) in Guildhall to assist with this. The Chairman is elected for a maximum of five years, whereas the Lord Mayor is elected for just one year, so the best result is achieved when they are both working together with the former supporting the latter and the Lord Mayor supporting the City Corporation's strategy.

RELATIONSHIP WITH THE MAYOR OF LONDON

Elected by voters in the whole of London, the Mayor of London (for many years Ken Livingstone) focuses on Greater London as a whole, rather than on the financial sector and on the Square Mile. The constitution of the City, as described above, has been developed over the centuries and so is distinct from the London boroughs. The City has powers beyond those of the Greater London Assembly and of the Mayor of London. Typically, the Mayor is a politician whose concerns are transport, the community, education and, in recent years, the Olympic Games. This portfolio is enough to absorb anyone's time. So the Lord Mayor is accepted as the champion of the financial sector, about which most politicians aspiring to the Mayor's role know little. The two mayors complement each other, with the Mayor of London being more accepted as the champion of transportation, education and community integration. There is a natural synergy.

Most of the City of London Corporation's interface with the GLA is in relation to planning, transport and education. So I was pleased that, during my term as Lord Mayor, these issues were dealt with by Michael (now Sir Michael) Snyder, the Chairman of Policy & Resources. The decisions on Crossrail and its funding and the GLA Bill, which gave more planning powers to the Mayor, were matters for Michael, on which he had a history of experience and was superbly equipped to lead. The Chairman also spoke on many business issues, including the regulatory environment and the factors affecting London's success. When it came to international business issues, I found that my 30 years as a partner in PwC working for multinationals and in different countries meant that I was experienced and could speak knowledgeably in the international arena on the City's offerings and its role as the world's leading financial centre.

85 *Michael (now Sir Michael) Snyder with Ken Livingstone.*

THE CHIEF COMMONER

Each year a senior Common Councilman is elected to be the chairman of City Lands, the committee in the City Corporation that oversees the City's investment and corporate property interests which are its principal sources of private income.

The committee also deals with the City's grand events, such as State Visits. Its chairman also then becomes the Chief Commoner whose role is to act as an additional figurehead and also to counsel other elected Common Councilmen. He is sometimes referred to as 'leader of the house'. It is a valuable as well as an ancient role that is difficult to describe to foreigners – the officeholder was once introduced on a Mayoral visit to China as the 'Chief Peasant'. During my Mayoral year, Gerry Pulman was Chief Commoner for the first five months and Pauline Halliday for the remaining seven. They were both very supportive and helpful, offering advice to me at regular meetings at Mansion House.

THE RECORDER

Both before and during my Mayoralty, I met the City Corporation's High Officers, who were of tremendous help in ensuring that I was properly briefed on the matters for which they had responsibility.

The Recorder is, in terms of precedence, the City's senior law officer and provides wise counsel to the Court of Aldermen alongside his very important work as senior judge at the Central Criminal Court. The Recorder also has an important role in the elections of the Lord Mayor and the Sheriffs.

I had got to know Peter Beaumont, QC, the Recorder in my year, and his wife Annie, when I lived, as Sheriff for a year at the Old Bailey.

THE TOWN CLERK (OR CHIEF EXECUTIVE)

Chris Duffield was the Town Clerk during my year and visited Mansion House often to provide briefings on various matters and prior to each Court of Common Council. A well seasoned local government officer, Chris was always well prepared and utterly dependable. Issues discussed at our meetings included matters affecting members, particularly where elections were imminent; Cross Rail; the GLA Bill dealing with planning matters; discussions affecting the future of the City of London Police when there was a threat of amalgamation; preparation for terrorist incidents; impending planning applications and consents.

THE CHAMBERLAIN AND THE CITY'S FREEDOMS

The office of Chamberlain is a very ancient one and given to the person who is responsible for the administration and finances of a household associated with the sovereign, a monastery, a cathedral or a city. Today, the City of London Corporation's Chamberlain, Chris Bilsland, is the City of London's Finance Director, but he also continues a centuries old tradition of administering through the Chamberlain's Court the admission of individuals to the Freedom of the City. It is one of the oldest surviving traditional ceremonies still in existence and it is believed that the first Freedom was presented in 1237.

The medieval term 'freeman' meant someone who was not the property of a feudal lord, but enjoyed privileges such as the right to earn money and own land. Town dwellers who were protected by the charter of their town or city were often free – hence the term 'Freedom of the City'.

During my year as Lord Mayor I participated in a number of important Freedom ceremonies, some of which were performed by the Remembrancer, Paul Double, and some by the Clerk to the Chamberlain's Court, Murray Craig, who has a good patter and makes the event a real show. Those with whom I was pleased to be involved in connection with their Freedom included:

86 *The Lord Provost of Glasgow, Bob Winter, receives the Freedom of the City of London from the Chamberlain, Chris Bilsland.*

- Peter Ackroyd, the well known author
- Councillor Bob Winter, the Lord Provost of Glasgow
- Wang Qishan, the Mayor of Beijing
- Captain Tim Fraser of HMS Illustrious, the City of London's ship
- Pat Gallagher of Arthur J Gallagher & Co, Insurance Brokers
- Wang Jun, Vice-Minister Finance, People's Republic of China
- He Annan Cato, the Ghanaian High Commissioner

THE REMEMBRANCER

The City's Remembrancer, like The Queen's Remembrancer, is an office of great antiquity. As the City's (and the Irish Society's) Parliamentary agent, he is the guardian of the City's constitution and its heritage and ensures that its constitutional affairs and business are properly handled. It is a role separate from that of the local authority and he reports directly to the Court of Aldermen. His office is divided into two parts – the first dealing with legal and constitutional matters that stem from discussions in Parliament or prospective changes to legislation; the second dealing with ceremonial matters, such as State Visits, where his contact with Buckingham Palace, the Foreign Office and Number 10 are vital to the effectiveness of these activities. During my year, the City's Remembrancer was Paul Double, a clever, agreeable man with a fine sense of humour – with the interests of the City and the Mayoralty firmly stamped on his heart.

INTERFACE WITH THE CITY CORPORATION'S COMMITTEES

It would be a mistake for the Lord Mayor to spend too much of his time on the detail of each committee. This is the job of the chairman of each committee, the elected members and the officers of the City Corporation. Also, the Lord Mayor has other responsibilities, notably representing the financial sector and meeting the Livery companies. However, the success of the financial sector depends on the City of London Corporation being effective when it comes to ensuring security in the Square Mile, providing modern office space, facilitating an agreeable environment (with pleasant communal areas), interfacing with the other boroughs around the City and encouraging improvements in transport and education. The Lord Mayor must know what is going on in each of these areas and must speak on them from time to time. This requires contact with chairmen of the key committees and also interface with City Corporation staff, for example at meetings, lunches and dinners, where the Lord Mayor's presence and interest is appreciated. In addition, I attended the monthly meetings of the group of chairmen, to discuss current issues of importance affecting their committees and the City Corporation.

SUPPORT TO THE MAYORALTY ON BUSINESS ISSUES AND ON MEDIA MATTERS

The City of London has a first-class public relations team, headed by Tony Halmos and with some highly competent executive staff, foremost of whom was Greg Williams, Head of Press Relations. I have written a separate chapter on 'The Key Messages' and the excellent support I received from Greg. Tony also arranged for me to meet Lord (Jack) Cunningham on a regular basis to understand and appreciate the dynamics of Whitehall politics which might have a bearing on our work in the City. These meetings were most useful.

The City Corporation's Economic Development Office (EDO) commissions excellent reports on economic and social matters affecting London. I complemented their knowledge of the economic environment by using my own network of business expertise. For example, I relied heavily on personal contacts such as David Lascelles (former *FT* journalist and founder of CFSI), Peter Wyman and other partners at PwC, trade association directors, other Aldermen with specialist backgrounds, the No 1 Breakfast Group comprising senior City figures, visits to leading City companies and my own experience as a partner for 30 years at PwC working in many overseas countries.

It was for this reason that I concluded, perhaps not making myself universally popular in the process, that

> 'it is very difficult to perform the role of Lord Mayor unless you have experience in the financial sector'. I did however go on to clarify this by saying 'an understanding of the businesses of the City and an ability to act as advocate for them are essential to anyone undertaking this role. However, anyone who has had a successful career, for example running a business or a university or another institution, is likely to have come across bankers, insurers, accountants, lawyers, fund managers and the media in the course of their working life. The key characteristics are success in one's career, experience, credibility and the ability to represent and promote the Business City at home and abroad. And candidates must have confidence but also sufficient self-awareness to know where they have shortcomings and whether or not they can do the job'.

Support to the Arts

London has been judged the Number One city worldwide for arts and entertainment, with more theatres, museums and galleries than any other global city. The City of London has for many years supported the Arts, not least by providing the Barbican Centre.

During my year, the Barbican Centre celebrated its 25th anniversary and I was pleased to welcome The Queen, at the newly designed entrance in Silk Street, to a concert to mark this achievement. I presented to her Sir John Tusa, the Managing Director, and Graham Sheffield, the Artistic Director. Her Majesty had officially opened the Centre in 1982 when Sir Christopher Leaver, GBE was Lord Mayor. The Duke of Edinburgh made some quip, as he often does, about my not being dressed up in such finery as my predecessor had been 25 years earlier. Presumably he had seen the photos of the Opening in 1982 with the Lord Mayor dressed in formal Court Dress, as was customary in those days. I responded that we were trying to emphasise the modern City and that Lord Mayors were also representative of the Business City. He smiled.

I was also delighted to be able to attend a pantomime of Dick Whittington at the Barbican before Christmas 2006 as I had been using his story when promoting my theme for the year 'City of London – City of Learning'. During the performance, one of the actors called out the names of some of those in the audience and reported that 'the real Lord Mayor is with us in the audience tonight', to which some wag shouted out 'Oh, no, he isn't'.

During a Mayoral year there are many concerts and musical evenings which the Lord Mayor enjoys and supports. One series of events, which I was pleased to support, was the 'Sibelius and Beyond' Festival, the brainchild of Alderman Roger Gifford, Chairman of the English Chamber Orchestra and Music Society

87 *Alderman Roger Gifford marries Dr Clare Taylor at St Bartholomew The Great.*

and Head of SEB in the UK. The Finnish Ambassador to the UK, His Excellency Jaakko Laajava, and I were asked to be Honorary Patrons of this festival which was the largest and most impressive exploration and exposition of Finnish music that London has probably ever seen. At a recital and dinner in Mansion House over £50,000 was raised in one evening, so enabling the festival to be a financial success and increasing to 30 the number of concerts that could be enjoyed.

88 *Common Councillor Wendy Mead is a keen supporter of Bart's Hospital.*

SUPPORT TO BARTS

St Bartholomew's Hospital is the oldest hospital in London, having been founded in 1123, to care for the ill and the aged. Situated on the south side of Smithfield, it was reconstituted by Henry VIII in 1546 after the dissolution of the monasteries, following pleas from the City. The main building that dates from the 18th century was designed by James Gibbs and contains paintings by Hogarth. Barts is at the leading edge of medicine, as it has been over the centuries. William Harvey was physician between 1609 and 1645 and discovered the circulation of blood. Mozart had his tonsils removed at Barts in the 1770s and X-rays were first used at the hospital in 1896. Today it is one of the country's leading teaching hospitals as well as being a centre of excellence for oncology and cardiology.

Early in my Mayoralty I attended a fund-raising dinner, chaired by a former Lord Mayor Sir John Chalstrey, at The Old Brewery in Chiswell Street, for Stem Cell Research. Later, together with Sir John Ashworth, Chairman of the Barts and the London NHS Trust, I opened the new Coronary Care Unit and the new Linear Accelerator Unit. Then, in May, I returned to see the IVF unit and also to look down on the building site where the new Barts Hospital was being constructed.

In October, I was invited to visit the new PET/CT centre and the Stem Cells Unit, which has cost in total around £8 million. It was a most impressive facility, adding greatly to the oncology capabilities at Barts. Of nice coincidence was the fact that a contemporary of mine at Shrewsbury, Professor Andrew Lister, was the head of the Oncology Unit at Barts. It was a real pleasure to meet him again in a different environment, where he is at the forefront of thinking in his field.

THE CITY'S GREEN LUNGS

Municipal pride and civic vision in late Victorian England led to the creation of some wonderful parks and areas in the countryside where urban dwellers could escape the pollution of the towns and enjoy the fresh air, as well get some exercise.

This was not a new concept. Indeed, Epping Forest which was brought into the ownership of the City of London by Act of Parliament in 1878 had been used for Royal hunting parties since the 12th century. In Tudor times both Henry VIII and Elizabeth I hunted there and Henry commissioned a building, known as the Great Standing, from which Elizabeth used to watch the chase. Epping Forest, an area of 6,000 acres of ancient woodland, grassland, heath, bogs, ponds and streams, is a haven of green within the sprawl of Greater London. Since 1878, the City of London has acted as 'Conservators', keeping the Forest as 'an open space for the recreation and enjoyment of people'.

When I was first elected as an Alderman, I was assigned to the Epping Forest and Open Spaces Committee. On regular basis, before monthly committee meetings, the Superintendent would arrange a site visit on a Saturday morning. We would inspect a pond or the site of a new car park or the plan to modify a farm building in the Forest. It was a good way of getting acquainted with this jewel. Other visits were arranged to the City Corporation's other open spaces of Burnham Beeches, Hampstead Heath and Highgate Wood. These are costly to maintain and the fact that the City of London Corporation pays for their upkeep is not widely known.

Adjoining Epping Forest is Wanstead Park which was purchased by the City Corporation in 1881. I was delighted to be invited to attend an event at the Temple (a building left over from the 18th-century Palladian house) to celebrate the 125th anniversary of the City's association with this Grade II listed park. The Chairman of the committee, Wendy Mead, presented me with a large and attractive photo of bluebells in a clearing in the Forest.

Later in the year, in September, I visited Burnham Beeches to open the new Information & Visitor Centre, which had been built in a manner most sympathetic to its natural surroundings. This was followed by lunch at Dorneywood, the house that became well known when Deputy Prime Minister John Prescott's privacy was disturbed as he was photographed playing croquet on the lawn while the Prime Minister was away on holiday. Dorneywood was left to the nation for use by a Minister of the Crown, or by the US Ambassador or by the Lord Mayor of London. By tradition, the Lord Mayor lunches at Dorneywood once each year during his Mayoralty as part of a day's visit to Burnham Beeches.

The centenary of the foundation of Hampstead Garden Suburb occurred in 2007. My predecessors as Lord Mayor had visited the first house to be built,

89 *Burnham Beeches.*

Number 142 Hampstead Way, in 1907 and then again on the 50th anniversary in 1957. In those days, there was a procession in State from Mansion House with the all the works, including Sword and Mace and a brass band. These days, there is less ostentation but still the same commitment and respect for the achievements of those who developed and executed the idea. We were met by the Chairman of the Hampstead Garden Suburb Residents Association, David Lewis (a different one), Chairman of the Hampstead Heath Management Committee Alderman Bob Hall, and the Mayor of Barnet Maureen Braun. Our local Councillor from Totteridge Brian Coleman (who has also served as Chairman of the GLA Assembly), was also present. After a speech from the bandstand in a very wet Golders Hill Park I opened the Butterfly House and planted a tree, to commemorate the visit.

A final excursion into London's leafier boroughs took place at the end of September when I was invited to West Lodge Park to plant a tree. Starting with Sir Hugh Wontner in 1973, six other Lord Mayors of the City of London have planted trees at West Lodge Park, which is now a hotel, run by the Beale family, as well as a stunning arboretum. I planted a *quercus petraea purpurea* (a purple or sessile oak). I was pleased to continue the tradition.

OFFICE BUILDINGS AND THE STREET SCENE CHALLENGE PROGRAMME

The City Corporation's Street Scene Challenge initiative was established in 2003 to manage the appearance of the City's streets and to enhance the environment for pedestrians. Each scheme is different and is funded as a result of a partnership between the City Corporation and interested parties such as developers, owners of office buildings and occupiers. In 2006, as Sheriff, I had attended on the Lord Mayor when he opened a 'public space' comprising a terrace and water fountains in Old Bailey.

90 *London's famous 'wobbly' bridge.*

Early in my Mayoralty, I opened a seating area in a square in West Smithfield where a stone bench had been designed by two young architects and made by four stone masons from the Cathedral Works Organisation in Chichester. They joined in the opening ceremony chaired by Christine Cohen, Chairman of the City Corporation's Planning & Transportation Committee.

But the work of Christine's committee is far more than making the environment attractive. Without modern office buildings the City of London would not have developed in recent years as the world's prime international financial centre. Making planning applications and approvals simpler is a key ingredient for success. Attracting stunning new buildings such as the Swiss Re Tower, known as the 'Gherkin', designed by Lord Foster, is important.

PROTECTING THE PUBLIC

The City of London Police has an excellent reputation for preventing and solving crime and has become particularly adept in the area of financial crime and fraud. With its Ring of Steel and other security initiatives, such as Project Griffin, it is universally acclaimed in the field of prevention of terrorist atrocities.

During the early part of my Mayoralty, the Home Office had initiated a review, with the aim of amalgamating some of the Police Forces in England. Fortunately, as a result of pressure from business organisations in the City as well as the City Corporation, the Home Secretary decided that the City of London Police should remain independent and should also become the lead force in the country on financial crime. At a London Mayors' Dinner, at which both I and the Metropolitan Police Commissioner, Sir Ian Blair, spoke, I joked that there was a rumour going round in the City that the Met was about to be taken over by the City of London Police. I was pleased when Temporary Commissioner, Mike Bowron, QPM, was promoted to Commissioner of the City Police, which stabilised the Force and gave it a well qualified successor to his predecessor, the able Dr James Hart, CBE, QPM, who retired in June 2006.

Project Griffin is a programme of partnership between the Police and security guards at each building who are asked to look out for and report any suspicious people or cars and report these instances to the Police. It is known that prior to a terrorist attack, the perpetrators recce the scene some weeks beforehand. The City Police also have a bicycle squad which can move very fast through the City's streets.

The Binney Awards for Bravery are given each year in memory of Captain Ralph Binney who died in 1944 while trying to prevent smash and grab thieves from escaping, following a robbery in the City of London. Captain Binney's friends in the Royal Navy wanted to commemorate his bravery in some way and subscribed to a trust fund to found medals to be awarded each year. The awards are presented at Goldsmiths Hall by a selection committee comprising representatives of the City of London Police, the Metropolitan Police and the Lord Mayor.

A visit to the City's Fire Station at Dowgate Hill in May gave me the opportunity of thanking the brigade for the work they do in the City and also for protecting Mansion House. I was welcomed by the Commissioner for Fire & Emergency Planning, Sir Kenneth Knight, and the GLA Chairman of London Fire & Emergency Planning, Brian Coleman, together with the Station Manager, Peter Wolfenden, and Alderman for the Ward of Dowgate, Alison Gowman. I invited the firemen to pay a return visit to Mansion House.

JUSTICE IN THE CITY OF LONDON

To stand for election as an Alderman, one must be approved by the Lord Chancellor's Advisory Committee as being suitable to sit as a Magistrate. On becoming an Alderman one signs an undertaking agreeing to sit on the bench. I appreciated the periodic sittings as a magistrate and the discussions with colleagues on the bench as another way of keeping in touch with some of the issues which a city such as London faces.

From ancient times, the Lord Mayor becomes 'Chief Magistrate' of the City of London for the term of his or her office. The Aldermen are, by statute, members of the Central Criminal Court and their position in the constitutional hierarchy as judges is preserved by the Courts Act 1971. However, in practice the Aldermen have signed an undertaking not to sit in adjudication at the Old Bailey, except where the Lord Mayor occupies the bench at No 1 Court on the formal opening of the Sessions. He officiates at the opening of the courts at the Central Criminal Court in Old Bailey on the four quarter sessions and 'tries' a case, in his capacity as the senior judge. He does this by processing in grand style, with the Recorder, a High Court Judge and the two Sheriffs, into Court No 1. There, in consultation with the Recorder and the Judge, he 'considers' a case – usually something very straightforward such as an application for an adjournment.

It is also normal for the Lord Mayor to try a case in the Magistrates Court sitting as chairman but since I had not previously sat as bench chairman, the requirement was waived. I did however enjoy my periodic meetings on criminal justice issues relevant to the City with Simon Morrison, chairman of the City bench, and fulfilling my role by chairing the AGM and also attending the Magistrates Carol Service at St Mary Aldermary.

Interestingly, there is also in the City a Mayor's and City of London Court, which is the City's 'County Court', located next to Guildhall and presided over today by Judge William Birtles. An annual Mayoral visit is important to recognise the importance of these courts as a lower cost means of obtaining judgements on minor claims and disputes. Of historical note is the fact that Thomas More once presided over cases in this court.

THE CITY'S SCHOOLS

The City of London has always placed education close to the top of its list of priorities. In medieval times, the Livery companies took on youngsters as apprentices after initial schooling by the monasteries and by the City of London School (for boys) which has its origins in a foundation of 1442.

Indeed the origins of school education in the City go back even further than that and the first benefaction for education to St Dunstan-in-the-East, in the Ward of Tower, was by William Barrett in 1408. This makes the current year the 600th Anniversary of the founding of what is now St Dunstan's College in South London. Unfortunately St Dunstan-in-the-East was bombed in the Second World War but its shell still survives and surrounds a beautiful City garden. The College keeps its ancient links with the City with the Alderman of the Ward of Tower still being an ex officio member of the governing body (and the current Alderman, Sir Paul Judge, is the Chairman of the Governors) together with four people from the church of All Hallows by the Tower, the successor church to St Dunstan's.

After Henry VIII began his campaign of abolishing the monastic institutions, from 1536, basic education in England suffered enormously. So Mayors and Aldermen in each city around the country began to consider alternative ways of ensuring that the young did not loiter about the streets but instead were schooled. In 1552 and 1553 many petitions were made to the young King Edward VI. Charters were signed and very many King Edward VI schools were established in England including, in the City of London, Christ's Hospital and Bridewell Royal Hospital which later became King Edward's School Witley, south of Guildford.

91 *Tower and Tower Bridge – at the eastern end of the city.*

On election as an Alderman, I was appointed a member of the Court of the Bridewell Royal Hospital and a Governor of King Edward's School Witley. It was a lucky appointment. I developed great empathy for the school. First of all it was founded in 1553, at the same time as my alma mater, Shrewsbury. KES Witley has a foundation, largely built up by the Livery companies and other generous donors, to educate children from families who could not afford fee-paying education. Its origins lay in the gift, to the City of London, by King Edward VI, with encouragement from Bishop Ridley, of Bridewell Palace, south of St Bride's Church, Fleet Street, to educate the children of London. For centuries this has been a foundation school and, today, 40 per cent of its pupils are provided with bursaries to facilitate their education either as boarders or day pupils. It is ethnically very diverse, with pupils from many countries, with the Church of England its prime faith. For many years, the Chairman of the Governors, known as the Treasurer, has been Richard Abbott who has worked tirelessly to help build an amazing school. Led by the headmaster, Kerr Fulton-Peebles, a leader, with a great sense of humour and oratorial ability, the School has climbed the charts in the International Baccalaureate. Now, under the chairmanship of Peter Estlin, the new Treasurer, the school is flourishing. We were pleased when HRH The Duchess of Gloucester graciously accepted the role of President, following the death of her predecessor, Queen Elizabeth the Queen Mother. Former Lord Mayor, Alderman Sir Robert Finch, is the current Vice-President. I was pleased

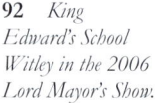

92 *King Edward's School Witley in the 2006 Lord Mayor's Show.*

to visit the school in my capacity as Lord Mayor and to present the prizes and make a speech on Speech Day – I referred, not surprisingly, to Dick Whittington as a role model for learning, hard work, success, public service and charitable giving. I was also pleased to make the School a beneficiary of my Lord Mayor's Appeal, to increase the bursarial funding available to enable pupils from poorer backgrounds to benefit from this School's amazing education.

The Sir John Cass Foundation Primary School was founded in 1710 by Sir John Cass, a great benefactor and an Alderman of the City of London. In 1834 the City of London School (for boys) was founded, although its origins can be traced back to 1442 when a provision was made in the will of John Carpenter to create an establishment for the maintenance and education of boys in the City. The City of London Freemen's Orphan School was opened by the City Corporation in Brixton in 1854 and moved to Ashtead Park in 1926 when the word Orphan was removed from its name. The Guildhall School of Music and Drama was formed in 1880. The City of London School for Girls was founded by the City Corporation in 1894. The latest school to be founded, with support from the City Corporation, is The City of London Academy (Southwark) which opened in September 2003 and moved to new premises in Bermondsey in September 2005.

Over the years, Aldermen and Common Councilmen have been appointed as governors of these schools and the Lord Mayor typically visits them during his Mayoralty, for prizegivings and Speech Days. Perhaps the most memorable is the visit to the Sir John Cass Foundation Primary School on Founder's Day when everyone is given and wears a red quill in memory of the founder who died while signing his will which made the school the beneficiary of his fortune. In my case, I was given a gold feather with a small ruby at one end, after which we toasted the pious memory of Sir John Cass.

While Mill Hill School and Brentwood School are not City schools, per se, their proximity to London means that they are closely involved with the affairs of the City and many of their old boys enjoy City careers. As Lord Mayor I was delighted to be invited to participate in the 200th and 450th anniversary celebrations of both schools at St Paul's and Mansion House, respectively, and to congratulate them on their achievements.

My old school, Shrewsbury, founded in 1552, was also far from being a City school, but it was a pleasure to welcome old Salopians to Mansion House for their annual dinner. About 350 turned up, with encouragement from the President, Tim Lewis. It was a jolly evening. Lord (Michael) Heseltine spoke about the awful aspects of teamwork that he had experienced at Shrewsbury and the importance of individualism and entrepreneurship. I kept my speech light with mythical letters from me, as a schoolboy at different ages, to my parents. It was wonderful to see some old school friends again. Michael Charlesworth, one of my old housemasters at School House, Lord (Richard) Best and Tim Butchard, as well as the Headmaster, Jeremy Goulding, and his wife Isobel, stayed the night at Mansion House.

Lesley and I were delighted to be asked to visit Shrewsbury for a weekend in May to be the house guests of the Headmaster and also to dine at Shirehall with the Chief Executive of the County, Brian Gillow, the Lord Lieutenant, Algy Heber-Percy, the High Sheriff, Meriel Afia, and the Mayors of Shrewsbury, Hereford and Worcester. It was nostalgic to be invited back to the School Chapel, where as a boy I had been Choregus (head of the Chapel Choir) and to read a lesson. We also enjoyed a visit to the nearby Coalbrookdale Museum of Iron at Ironbridge where we met the Chairman, Richard Clowes, and the President, Michael Lowe, whom I had met previously when he and I were both Sheriffs. For Lesley and me this visit was particularly interesting as we were shown, at Coalport, the influence on 19th-century British pottery of the porcelain from the Chinese town of Jing de Zhen in Jiangsu Province.

CITY AND OTHER UNIVERSITIES

93 *The Lord Mayor receives a D.Litt from City University London – seen here with Vice-Chancellor David Rhind, CBE.*

During his Mayoral year, the Lord Mayor becomes the Chancellor of City University London. Founded originally as the Northampton Institute by the City of London Parochial Charities Act, it became City University London in 1966 by Royal Charter, reflecting the close links which the institution had with the City of London. After being awarded an honorary doctorate (a D.Litt) at a ceremony in December 2006, I was installed as Chancellor before congratulating approximately 450 students who had passed their bachelor's or master's degrees or who were being awarded their doctorates.

My association with City University and its business school, the Cass Business School, had begun before my Mayoral year, as the then Vice-Chancellor, Professor David Rhind, CBE, had joined my Education, Training and Qualifications ('ETQ') Working Group to prepare for the campaign 'City of London – City of Learning'. Later, representatives of City University and Cass Business School were to join us on the overseas Mayoral visits and participate in seminars organised by the British Council and chaired by Sir Paul Judge.

In February 2007, together with the Dean, Lord Currie, and his successor, Richard Gillingwater (now CBE), I opened a Cass Executive Suite at Canary Wharf. I had known Richard for many years, having worked on a project together when he was at BZW. It was a pleasure to work with him again.

I had agreed to be chairman of a campaign to help Professor Costas Grammenos, Pro-Vice Chancellor of City University, raise funds for an Onassis Prize. This would be like a Nobel Prize to be given each year to someone for achievement in Shipping Trade & Finance, the field in which Costas had built up an incredible reputation at City. Costas' Shipping faculty is world class, perhaps the very best and, if you want to excel in this industry, this is the course to study.

In March 2007, the City University held its annual 'Chancellor's Dinner' at Mansion House at which Professor David Rhind and Lord Currie spoke. Sir Stelios Haji-Iannou, founder of EasyJet and a benefactor of City University, also spoke amusingly about packing passengers into a jet so tightly that, per passenger, his airline was the least polluting means of air transport. Another cherished benefactor, Maan Al-Sanea, founder of the Saad group, was also present as he was assisting in the refurbishment of City University's arts facility and the further enhancement of City's Saad Centre for Radiography Clinical Skills Education. I had the pleasure of meeting David Rhind's successor as Vice-Chancellor, Malcolm Gillies. In April, I chaired the annual meeting of City University's stakeholders who are representatives of the City Corporation and the Livery companies.

I was extremely pleased and greatly honoured to be asked formally, later in the year, if I would accept the position of Pro-Chancellor and Chairman of the Council at City University London, in succession to Sir David Howard who held that office since 2003 and would be retiring after five years in summer 2008.

But, during my year, I didn't forget the City's other university, London Metropolitan. Indeed the Vice-Chancellor, Professor Sir Roderick Floud, had also been a member of my ETQ Working Group and a former Master of the Guild of Educators. Although Roderick retired at the beginning of 2007, I met his successor, Professor Brian Roper, on a number of occasions, beginning with the Town & Gown Dinner at London Met's premises on the Holloway Road.

I was also pleased to present the degrees and other qualifications to students from the Guildhall School of Music and Drama (GSMD), one of Europe's leading music schools. There was a double personal connection, in that one of my daughters-in-law, Cori, had graduated from GSMD and then, in 2007, I handed out a degree certificate to the son of Shrewsbury's headmaster, Jeremy Goulding, before being made a member myself of the GSMD.

In September 2007, Imperial College celebrated the centenary of its foundation. The origins of the College go back 129 years when the City of London Corporation and 16 Livery companies came together to create the City & Guilds College. Twenty-nine years later this became the nucleus of Imperial College whose anniversary in 2007 was celebrated by a truly excellent speech by the Rector, Sir Richard Sykes, at an event at Guildhall.

In addition, I was delighted to be able to involve my old College – Churchill – from Cambridge University in various events. A reception at Mansion House was well attended and included the Master, Sir David Wallace, CBE, who spoke well. A special event was the award of the first David Stokes Bursary to two law students from Churchill. David and I were contemporaries at Churchill and we acted together in Churchill's embryo drama group, The Gods. We played two prisoners in Jean Genet's *Deathwatch* and, because we imagined that all criminals spoke with a Cockney accent, David and I learnt to speak as East Enders. We had a lot of fun. After I left Cambridge and then returned from teaching with VSO in Brunei in 1967, David contacted me. He was playing Don Adriano de Armado in *Love's Labour's Lost* for the Bar Theatrical Society at Lincoln's Inn. The barrister playing the part of Nathaniel, a curate, had dropped out. Since I had played the part of Holofernes at Cambridge many times, presumably I knew both parts since they were on stage together. Would I step in and play Nathaniel in this production, since they were desperate? Of course I would and I did, resulting in two wonderful years acting with the Bar Theatrical Society in Middle Temple.

But that was not the end. When I was elected as an Alderman, one of my first duties was to lunch with the judges at the Old Bailey, where David Stokes QC had been appointed as a judge. He looked very grand in his wig and judge's gown at lunch, something for which the Churchillian stage had equipped him well. My first lunch was disturbing to say the least. He and Judge Graham Boal QC welcomed me and then asked 'John, where's your hat?' 'What hat, I asked?' 'Well, you're wearing the right gown, but your hat is missing, you know the Alderman's hat, which you wear (and this is where they blew it) sideways like Napoleon on the first occasion and then lengthways like Nelson on subsequent occasions'. It was a spoof, which I thought merited a response. I had discovered that Graham Boal was a product of Eastbourne College and that, on Speech Day, monitors wore cornflowers in their lapels. I also found out that the Senior Alderman, Sir Christopher Leaver, GBE, had been the chairman of Eastbourne College. So I

94
Retirement card for Neill O'Connor, former Swordbearer.

asked the then Swordbearer, Brigadier Neill O'Connor, if he would write a letter to His Honour Graham Boal QC along the following lines, dated 12 July 2001:

> We are pleased that you are able to attend the Judges Dinner at Mansion House on Wednesday 18 July.
>
> Regrettably Sir Christopher Leaver is unable to be present at the dinner. I am writing, therefore, to ask you, as the most senior old boy of Eastbourne College, to continue the longstanding tradition of bringing a cornflower.
>
> City etiquette regarding flowers is not well defined. *Honours, Hats and Other Decorations* (second edition, 1921) provides that flowers should be carried in both hands. However, by tradition, this is confined to processions of City dignitaries and officials in certain ceremonies at the Guildhall. Ladies occasionally wear flowers at other City events and, in the case of a Lady Judge, this might be appropriate at Mansion House. For male judges, the dress of the day makes it difficult for flowers to be worn with decorum. I suggest, therefore, that you leave the cornflower with our attendant immediately on entry to the upper floor of Mansion House and before the line-up to be greeted by the Lord Mayor and the Lady Mayoress.
>
> You might feel however that the traditional gallantry, for which Her Majesty's Judges are rightly famed, is better served by presenting the cornflower to the Lady Mayoress as you are being received.
>
> If you have any questions regarding this unique etiquette, please contact me or the Junior Alderman. I know he would be pleased to advise you.

Graham was taken in, at least partially, and telephoned Sir Christopher Leaver to enquire what he should do. In the event, he took to Mansion House a bouquet of cornflowers for the then Lady Mayoress, Lady Howard. I wonder if a new City tradition had been created?

Very tragically David Stokes developed a brain tumour and, after surgery and an apparent recovery, he succumbed again. Together with his close friend and colleague from the East Anglian Circuit, The Hon Mr Justice David Penry-Davey, we established, with the agreement of Liz, David's widow, the David Stokes Memorial Fund to provide bursaries for law undergraduates from Churchill to encourage them to learn the skills of advocacy. On 17 January 2007, the first two bursaries were presented to Lucy Duane and Sahir Hamid who were standing in the dock of Number 1 Court at the Old Bailey. It is an experience that they will never forget.

THE TRADITIONAL SOCIETIES AND CLUBS

In times gone by the City was very clubbable. In many ways it is still is, but today's young executives work very long hours and barely have time for a breather at lunchtime when a sandwich is the normal fare. During my Mayoralty when I suggested a white tie dinner to either of my two sons, if they accepted, they would have to take a half day's holiday to be able to get dressed in time for an event starting at 19.30.

But this does not prevent the Ward Clubs and the traditional societies from continuing to hold lunches and dinners, to which the Lord Mayor is invited. With 24 ward clubs, it is physically not possible for the Lord Mayor to accept invitations from each, so one of the two Sheriffs or the Chief Commoner often deputises. The other societies – The Royal Society of St George, the United Wards Club, the Guild of Freemen, the City Livery Club and the Pickwick Club – all make invitations and I tried to go to each during my year. But the other commitments of the Lord Mayor make attendance increasingly difficult.

95   *The Lime Street Ward Club in a bus sponsored by Richard Walduck.*

However, one dinner that I was determined not to miss was the banquet on 30 May 2007 at Mansion House, arranged by Ann Benson and Wendy Kiernan of the Lime Street Ward Club of which I am the President. The Egyptian Hall was full to bursting with 340 people present, chaired by the Master, Robert Woodthorpe Brown, with his wife, Barbara.

FAITHS AND CULTURES

London is perhaps the only truly international city in the world. The immigration into the City over the centuries has enriched the capital and, without this, the finance sector would not have benefited. For example, Islamic finance would not have thrived in London without Muslims to support its development. But immigration has also created some tensions. During my year, I was keen to do whatever I could to demonstrate that the Lord Mayor stood for all cultures and religions. I was keen to emphasise the benefits of immigration and cross-border working. There were lots of opportunities.

Haifa Al Kaylani is a formidable, charming lady. A Lebanese graduate of Oxford University, she is the Founder Chairman of the Arab International Women's Forum which gathers together some able and distinguished ladies from the Arab world, including a banquet each year at Mansion House. At their annual event, I was pleased to welcome Sheikha Hanadi Nasser bin Khaled Al Thani from Qatar who spoke about globalisation. She finished with a vision of the future: 'I see the flourishes of my own country. I see the palm trees and the traditional arches. I see the wind towers and the narrow sleek walkways. I see unity through diversity, and in this I see strength.' Also speaking at the banquet was my old friend Hamid Jafar, a contemporary at Churchill College, and Willem Brocker, a former partner at PwC in Amsterdam.

The Chain Gang

At Mansion House, the Mayors of all the London Boroughs, including the Lord Mayors of Westminster and the City of London, are collectively and somewhat irreverently referred to as the Chain Gang. The Chain Gang meets on a number of occasions during the year. In the spring, the Mayors walked, fully robed and led by the Town Cryer, from the Whittington Stone on Highgate Hill to Mansion House, where we gave them a curry lunch and a glass of beer. Then in the summer, we all gathered together for a service at St Paul's. You've never seen so many Mayoral chains or Mayoral chauffeur-driven limousines.

We met the Lord Mayor of Westminster most often, for example at the State Opening of Parliament. We went to this twice during my Mayoralty – in November 2006 when we sat next to Councillor Alexander Nicoll and Mrs Grania Nicoll and then at the end of my year, in November 2007, when we were with Councillor Carolyn Keen and her brother Andrew. We were also part of the line up in Horseguards on the occasion of a State Visit.

We were also pleased to meet Tim Ahern, the Mayor of the Royal Borough of Kensington and Chelsea on several occasions, including a delightful lunch at Kensington Town Hall.

Regional Visits in the UK

Over the years, there have been visits by Lord Mayors to other regional cities in the UK. In return, Lord Mayors of major UK cities have visited London and attended many of the banquets at Mansion House. A special relationship has been built up with the Cutlers of Hallamshire by the Cutlers' Company in London and it has become a tradition that the Lord Mayor visits Sheffield each year, at the end of July. This is combined with a visit to Leeds and Manchester, which, after Edinburgh, have the largest concentration of financial sector companies in the country.

As Sheriff, I joined my predecessor as Lord Mayor on his visits to Leeds, Sheffield, Bradford and Edinburgh. The schedule during my Mayoralty was similar although we included Manchester, because of its growing contribution to the financial sector, and Burnley my home town.

Edinburgh is the UK's second largest financial centre. Visits to Scotland have, for some years, been arranged by Scott Dobbie, CBE, formerly with Wood McKenzie, stockbrokers, and now, among other roles, Chairman of the Securities & Investment Institute, with whom we cooperated in my year in the ETQ initiative. Scott arranged for us to meet Scottish Financial Enterprise, whose Chief Executive Amanda Harvie had been very active, and then Royal Bank of Scotland and Standard Life. All expressed an interest in the overseas Mayoral visits and I was joined by executives from Scotland on many of my foreign trips, particularly to the Far East. A roundtable on ETQ with, among others, the Principals of Glasgow and Edinburgh Universities, highlighted the cooperation in promoting the UK as a centre of excellence for business education and professional skills development.

Lord Mayors do not visit Glasgow every year but I was pleased when Glasgow was included in the diary in the light of the contribution made to the development of this city in the 18th century by the McCalls, from whom Lesley is descended.

Her great-great-great-great-great grandfather (yes, that's five greats grandfather) was a wealthy Glasgow merchant by the name of Samuel McCall. Born in Sanquhar, Dumfrieshire, in 1681, Samuel moved to Glasgow as a young man, was apprenticed and became a wealthy merchant, trading with Virginia and Maryland, in which he owned property. One of the tobacco barons, he was chosen a Baillie (or magistrate) of Glasgow in 1723. In 1736, the year that his ship, the Betty, plied between Glasgow and the United States, he was appointed Dean of the Guild, a position he declined to accept on account of ill health. For this he was imprisoned for some hours in the Tolbooth. Despite this discomfort, he continued to thrive and lived until he was seventy-seven. He was buried in Glasgow Cathedral Burial Ground in 1759. His son, John McCall, was also an eminent Glasgow merchant and a founder partner of the Thistle Bank. In 1760, John acquired 25 acres of land two miles east of Glasgow in an area called Bridgetown, together with fishing rights on the River Clyde. He built a house on the estate with the classic name the Belvidere. A keen supporter of the Royalist cause, John McCall lost all his lands in Virginia in 1783 following the American War of Independence. But the price of tobacco rose and his fortunes were regained, such that he built a house known, because of the colour of the stone, as the Black House, on the south-east corner of Queen Street and Argyle Street. He died there in 1790 and was also buried in Glasgow Cathedral. After this, like many Scottish families, the McCall descendants travelled to find business opportunities – initially to Liverpool and Penrith, and then to Essex, Brazil, Tasmania, Shropshire – and finally to London.

The Lord Provost of Glasgow, Councillor Bob Winter, gave us dinner in his parlour, attended by representatives of the Glasgow business community, including the Lord Dean of Guild John Chapman and the Deacon Convenor Malcolm Wishart. We later invited Bob to London and gave him the Freedom of the City of London and lunch at Mansion House. Subsequent to my Mayoral year, Lesley and I were invited to return to Glasgow by the Lord Provost to attend his Burns Supper Night, a grand event at the Glasgow Hilton, at which poems by Robert Burns were recited. Our visit to the Merchants House, the Glasgow home of the Guilds, proved to be fascinating. John Chapman showed us around and pointed out a mortification board dated 1704 of John Adam, a wealthy merchant and the father of Margaret Adam, who married Samuel McCall in 1714, and from whom Lesley is descended. Until this visit, I hadn't known what a mortification board was. It is a record of the amount left by someone in a will on death. In the case of John Adam, he 'left to the Poor of this House, One Hundred Pounds Scots. He deceased the 19 Day of November 1704 in the 50 year of his Age'.

Our visit to the North of England at the end of July 2007 was equally interesting. Our 24 hours in Leeds was organised by John Ansbro, Chief Executive of Leeds Financial Services Initiative, and included a roundtable at Leeds University Business School and visits to the Headingley Carnegie Stadium, Leeds Metropolitan University, the Bank of England Agency and Gordons, a local firm of solicitors whose Senior Partner, Paul Ayre, was Chairman of Leeds Legal. We were impressed by the developments that had taken place in Leeds, with the rise of the financial sector, replacing the woollen industry.

After another stunning dinner, known as the Forfeit Feast, at the Cutlers' Hall, Sheffield, hosted by the Master Alan Reid and his wife Ellen, and a brief meeting with the organisation Pro-South Yorkshire, we drove to the Devonshire Arms in Wharfedale for the weekend.

Wharfedale is one of the most attractive Yorkshire Dales with the wide River Wharfe a magnet to fishermen as well as to ramblers and painters. The ruined Bolton Abbey is a popular tourist spot. Bolton Woods and the menacing Strid, where the river narrows, and the pretty village of Grassington are also worth a visit.

Together with Sheriff Richard Regan, and his wife Anne, we began our visit to Burnley on a Saturday with a call on the Burnley Catenians, a Roman Catholic community centre, and then a match at Turf Moor, the home of Burnley Football Club. I hadn't been back to Turf Moor since my father died. He was the accountant and auditor of the Club for many years before becoming a director. As such, he had two seats in the Directors' Box and I watched with him some of the great matches during Burnley FC's glory days of 1959 and 1960. Watching Burnley play Leeds a half century later was combined with meeting Kitty Ussher, the MP for Burnley and the new Economic Secretary to the Treasury. It was a happy chance coincidence and meeting, as there was plenty to discuss. The club Chairman, Barry Kilby, gave us lunch in the board room, where we met the former manager Dave Edmundson and the Burnley Council Leader Gordon Bertwistle who was to be our host on the Monday morning and who showed us an area of Burnley about to be redeveloped, the Weavers' Triangle, which sits beside the Leeds-Liverpool Canal and dates from the 18th century.

96 *Visit to Burnley FC (Turf Moor) with Economic Secretary Kitty Ussher MP, Council Leader Gordon Bertwistle and Sheriff Richard Regan.*

Burnley has suffered enormously in the last 50 years with the decline of the textile industry and nothing to replace it. Racial tensions between the Bangladeshi, Pakistani and poorer white community have thereby been exacerbated. But Burnley has been earmarked for regional development funds and we saw evidence of this at the new Lancashire Digital Technology Centre, the site of the new Burnley College and site of a new school. This hope for the future was echoed by the Mayor Councillor Peter McCann and local historian Councillor Roger Frost, MBE at our meeting at Burnley Town Hall.

By contrast, Manchester has recovered much of its 19th-century glory with the development of the financial sector and, physically, after the destruction of the Arndale Centre by the IRA which enabled the heart of Manchester to be replanned. The City Hall, designed by Waterhouse and built in 1879, is a stunning example of late Victorian Venetian Gothic. It is evidence of a major textile and trading city that was extraordinarily confident about its future. We were welcomed by the Lord Mayor Councillor Glynn Evans prior to a banquet in the grand main banqueting hall. Our meetings with the Greater Manchester Strategic Alliance, the Pro-Manchester Young Professionals and the main Pro-Manchester group, led by Daniel Mouaward, gave us a good impression of the growth of the financial sector and its contribution to, among other things, the AIM market. We were able to complete our visit by some sightseeing, to the John Rylands University Library, a must if you have an hour to spare in the vicinity of Deansgate. It has wonderful stained glass and an amazing collection of ancient books, all housed in a Victorian building that matches the Town Hall.

THE CITY'S MARKETS

Back at home, the Lord Mayor visits each year the City's three main markets of Smithfield, Billingsgate and Spitalfields, only the first of which is still in the City.

97 *The Lord Mayor visits the Lord Mayor of Manchester.*

Markets start early in the morning and are finished by around 08.00 hours. So this requires an early start, a visit to each market before it ends and then a breakfast with the superintendents and some of the market executives and traders. These are fun outings but also demonstrate the importance of the meat, fish, fruit and vegetable markets to the City of London, complementing its pre-eminent position as a financial market. I was grateful to the Chairman of the Markets Committee Stanley Ginsburg and to the Director of Markets David Smith for escorting us on these visits.

MARITIME CONNECTIONS

Even before my Mayoralty began I had developed contact with the Maritime sector. In 2005, the 200th anniversary of the Battle of Trafalgar, I organised at Greenwich, for the Finnish-British Chamber of Commerce, a conference entitled 'Shipping in the Baltic and London as a Maritime Centre'. I had enjoyed discussions with many of the leading players and organisations, Thomas Tune Andersen from Mærsk, Slin Yeh and Maurice Storey, CB from Evergreen, Executive Chairman of Lloyd's Register David Moorhouse, The Baltic Exchange with its Chief Executive Jeremy Penn and the Chamber of Shipping with its Director General Mark Brownrigg. I was extremely honoured when the grand old man of world shipping, 95-year-old Mr Mærsk Mc-Kinney Møller, the Danish shipping magnate, visited me at Mansion House. I was also pleased when Anthony Cooke, then Chairman of the Baltic Exchange, joined me on my Mayoral visit to Mumbai.

I was a frequent visitor to HQS Wellington and on 27 September welcomed HRH Prince Andrew on the occasion of World Maritime Day. I enjoyed my visits to Trinity House, the home of the City Corporation by the same name, which owns and runs the lighthouses around the coast of the British Isles and also manages the Deep Sea Pilotage Authority. I had met Rear-Admiral Jeremy

98 *Smithfield is still a thriving meat market in the heart of the City of London.*

de Halpert, CB on many occasions – in fact we lay a wreath together each year at Lloyd's of London. My final lunch invitation of the year was from the Master, HRH The Duke of Edinburgh, and the Elder Brethren, as they are known, of Trinity House. The UK's development as the world's prime international financial centre owes everything to its seafaring and trading history. It was most appropriate that I should finish my year as Lord Mayor with a bunch of sailors.

99 *The Lord Mayor receives the Loving Cup of England.*

Part IV

THE LORD MAYOR AND THE LIVERY COMPANIES OF THE CITY OF LONDON

100   *The Thames on Lord Mayor's Day (Canaletto).*

The Lord Mayor and the
Livery Companies of the City of London

For centuries, the Livery companies were the all-powerful institutions of the City of London. They supported schools which provided recruits for their craft. They had well defined systems of apprenticeship. They ensured quality among their members (known as Liverymen). They would penalise the baker who sold stale bread and the fletcher who made arrows that did not fly straight. Without their support, in London at least, you could not learn a craft. If you were not a Liveryman you could not trade and you would not be considered for election as a Sheriff. You would certainly never become Lord Mayor. The Livery companies were closed shops and they were protectionist. While this has changed, and trades are now open to everyone, they were, and still are, the backbone of the constitutional make up of the City.

In the 19th century new professional institutes and trade associations were established which operated on a national basis, some with Royal Charters. With new nationwide exams and certification procedures, they gradually assumed the role of Livery companies in terms of training, quality control and ethical behaviour. In the late 20th century, deregulation was introduced such that there are now no barriers to entry into any trade or profession. If you can pass the relevant exam, you can use the initials of the certifying organisation and you can then trade or practise, subject to external independent regulation.

Today, the Livery companies still support their crafts. Their links with their trades and professions are very strong. But this role is focused, in most instances, on encouraging young trainees, through prizes and bursaries, and on providing a forum for discussion of major issues affecting their area of interest. The charitable role of Livery companies is significant and it is calculated that their donations total around £40 million each year. Many support schools and colleges, which in some cases they founded, and they offer many prizes and awards. They generously support the Lord Mayor's annual charitable appeal and they are great supporters of the cadet movement and the Reserve Armed Forces.

Today's 35,000 Liverymen are the only franchisees entitled to vote each year in the Shrieval elections and around 1,000 gather together in Guildhall on Michaelmas Day to be invited to express their support for the Court of Aldermen's candidate for Lord Mayor. They also contribute to the collegiality of the City and maintain the customs and ceremonies, some of which are centuries old. They are the bedrock of the Civic City. In addition to adding colour and tradition, they represent the continuity of the values of the City, as evidenced in a unique culture that makes the financial sector successful today. They cherish values such as honesty, integrity, equity and fairness, where one's word is one's bond.

I should add a word of thanks not just to the Masters who supported me in my year, but also the Clerks of the Livery companies who provide continuity from one year to the next.

Many books have been written about the Livery companies – both individual histories and general works about their contribution to trade, education and charity. It is not my intention here to repeat these. Rather I will describe the interface which the Lord Mayor has with the Livery movement after he has assumed office.

THE CHAMPION OF THE LIVERY COMPANIES

I have described the role of the Livery companies in the election of Sheriffs and of the Lord Mayor. The approbation by the Livery movement of the choice of candidate for Lord Mayor is clearly important, even if the Lord Mayor's main role is head of the City of London Corporation, supporting and promoting the businesses of the City. The Livery companies regard each Lord Mayor as theirs. And it is important that he, or she, understands and respects this.

The interface with the Livery movement is extensive, as there are 108 Livery companies, each of whom expects to see the Lord Mayor at some function or event during the year. While it is physically impossible for the Lord Mayor to accept an invitation to lunch or dine with every company, there are many other Livery activities, described below, in which he can participate and which are enjoyable as well as having enormous historical significance.

Additionally, the Lord Mayor is in an excellent position to influence the thinking of Liverymen, to help Livery companies respond to the changing needs of society. He also needs to keep abreast of changes taking place in the Livery companies and to listen to their opinions and views.

The organisation which can be very effective in ensuring effective contact is the Livery Committee, which exists to form a channel of communication between the Livery movement, the City of London Corporation and the Lord Mayor. I was fortunate in having, during my year, Geoffrey Bond, OBE as the Chairman of the Livery Committee. As fellow Glaziers we knew each other well. Together with his Deputy, Ken Ayers, a fellow member of the Court of Common Council, whom I had also met often, we had a head start.

THE MAJOR MEETINGS WITH THE LIVERY COMPANIES

It has become traditional for the Lord Mayor to address the Masters and Clerks of all the Livery companies at Mansion House soon after taking office. So a meeting was arranged on 29 November 2006.

After words of welcome, I thanked them for their support in the Lord Mayor's Show, in which no fewer than 50 Livery companies were involved. I spoke about the changing nature of the Livery companies – from traditional trades to modern professions. In medieval times, the predominant businesses were those associated with everyday life – bakers, butchers, carpenters, fishmongers, vintners – and also with defence of the realm – armourers, bowyers and fletchers. Today, the City's businesses comprised bankers, insurers and fund managers as well as actuaries, arbitrators, accountants, management consultants, shipbrokers, solicitors, tax advisers and valuers. In the last 30 years, stimulated initially by Sir Kenneth Cork who was Lord Mayor in 1978, 20 new Livery companies have been formed, representing these modern trades. The occupations of Liverymen have also changed as older businesses (such as textiles) have declined and newer ones have developed. In the same way, fan makers are now more likely to make air-conditioning units than ladies' fans and plumbers are more likely to install central heating in houses than cold water lead pipes.

I explained that the City today needed individuals as Sheriffs and Lord Mayor who had the appropriate experience, background and capabilities to hold their own when representing their constituents and their businesses – which, these days, reflecting the changing City, were now predominantly in the financial sector. For this reason, the Court of Aldermen had introduced a rigorous appraisal system, with independent members, and had done away with 'Buggins' Turn'. The City of London Corporation needed Liverymen who could become Common Councilmen and Aldermen who have achieved a measure of success in their business careers and who could contribute to the promotion of the City and to the work needed to keep London ahead of the game.

I also spoke about the need to expand the Lord Mayor's overseas travel programme, reflecting the growing international nature of the City's businesses and the changes in staffing at Mansion House necessary to ensure a greater business focus and understanding.

I thanked them in advance for their involvement with my Lord Mayor's Appeal 'Sharing Skills, Changing Lives' and encouraged them to form links, if they hadn't already, with cadet groups of the Armed Forces.

The meeting in November went well and Livery masters and clerks seemed content with the observations made and with the direction of travel. Things changed a bit in the early part of 2007 when some Livery companies were upset as a result of communications sent to them. These communications suggested that the appraisal process for Sheriffs and Lord Mayor was undemocratic and that a small group was trying to promote candidates who fitted a certain specification and to exclude others.

At the banquet for Masters, Prime Wardens and Upper Bailiff at Mansion House on 22 March 2007, after being in office for four months, I offered the following observations:

- First, in addition to being the head of the City Corporation, the Lord Mayor speaks on behalf of the financial community and promotes the

101 *The Mercers and the Grocers are numbers 1 & 2 respectively in the City Livery Companies pecking order. They process with the Lord Mayor and the Sheriffs at the Banquet for Masters, Prime Wardens and Upper Bailiff at the Mansion House.*

financial, maritime and other business services industry. The other Mayor focuses on other things, such as the Underground and buses – and the Olympics. The Governor of the Bank of England has his eye primarily on the money supply, inflation and interest rates. The City's businesses in the 21st Century are in the financial sector and they need a champion. This is the role of the Lord Mayor today – and, what's more, both the financial community and the Government recognise and welcome this.

- Second, it is very difficult to perform this role unless you have experience in the sector. This is sometimes misinterpreted – as ruling out someone who is a Liveryman of the Poulters, Merchant Taylors or Glaziers. But then, as you know, the last three Lord Mayors (coming from these Mother Livery companies) have also been a stockbroker, an insurer and an accountant respectively. The important criterion is that you have to be credible when speaking to Prime Ministers or Finance Ministers and no amount of briefing can make up for lack of relevant experience. It was therefore both essential as well as forward looking of the Court of Aldermen to adopt a system of objective assessment and open competition. By doing this, the Mayoralty has a very good chance of surviving and thriving for another 800 years. It is necessary therefore to ensure that we have a pipeline of talented Aldermen who can be considered for the Office of Lord Mayor.

- But the third and perhaps most important observation that I want to make this evening concerns the Livery movement. It is as relevant today as it was in the Middle Ages. New companies are being formed every year. Training and charity are at the heart of what Livery companies do. There is nothing more vital to our future than training and the development of skills. And there is nothing more vital to a civilised society than charity. At a time when some politically motivated individuals are questioning City remuneration packages, one has to remember the benefits of an open market economy and how much is given away by wealthy people. We have a tradition of giving in the City – John Cass, Thomas Gresham and, of course, Dick Whittington. It's great to receive, but it is even better to give. And the Livery movement does that so well.'

My comment about it being difficult to perform the role of Lord Mayor unless 'you have experience in the sector' was seized upon by some. A storm was whipped up among some Livery companies, who complained that this might exclude doctors and teachers, as well as musicians. Some believed that the power to elect the Lord Mayor had been removed from the hands of the Livery companies.

It was necessary, therefore, for me to set the record straight – to dispel doubts and to restate the procedures and the *real politik*. I sought the advice of the then Senior Alderman, Sir Richard Nichols, and also two other Senior Aldermen, Lord (Peter) Levene, KBE and Sir David Howard Bt. A further meeting of the masters and clerks was held at Mansion House on 19 July 2007.

I reminded them of the existence of the Appraisal Panel, with independent members, which examined and interviewed Aldermen who had ambitions to become Sheriff and Lord Mayor. I reminded them that the Court of Aldermen decides which Aldermen to support for the office of Sheriff and Lord Mayor. I also used the following words when it comes to deciding whom to choose:

- It has been suggested that the Lord Mayor must have a financial background and that no-one can become Lord Mayor if he or she doesn't come from the financial sector. I want to dispel this myth.
- It is certainly true that nearly all of the last 10 Lord Mayors have come from the Business City. An understanding of the businesses of the City and an ability to act as advocate for them are essential to anyone undertaking this role. However, anyone who has had a successful career, for example running a business or a university or another institution, is likely to have come across bankers, insurers, accountants, lawyers, fund managers and the media in the course of their working life. The key characteristics are success in one's career, experience, credibility and the ability to represent and promote the Business City at home and abroad. And candidates must

have confidence but also sufficient self-awareness to know where they have shortcomings and whether or not they can do the job.

- The City of London Corporation needs Liverymen who can become Common Councilmen and Aldermen who have achieved a measure of success in their business careers and who can contribute to the promotion of the City and to the work needed to keep London ahead of the game. If you are aware of talented individuals who have achieved something in their careers and are interested in becoming Common Councilmen or Aldermen, please ask them to contact the Town Clerk's Office.

I also dealt with further myths that had developed, as follows:

- Some have suggested that the Mayoralty responds too much to the demands of the Government and that Lord Mayors are somehow beholden to and take instructions from Ministers. I can tell you that this is not true.
- The Lord Mayor and the City Corporation listen to the City's business leaders. Problems are identified and these are communicated to Government. Recent issues which we have highlighted to Ministers and Officials include visas for young executives from abroad, the need to keep the City of London Police independent, the dire state of Heathrow airport, planning policy and, of course, the need for Crossrail. No punches are pulled. But we are communicating in an open, sensible way that encourages dialogue and mutual respect. I can tell you that relations between the City and the Government are extremely good. And that is because both we and Ministers are listening and because we have an excellent relationship. It is a case of listening, not being subservient.
- We also have a complementary relationship with the Mayor of London, Ken Livingstone. He is responsible for matters such strategic planning, transport and the Fire Service across the whole of London, whereas the Lord Mayor is focused on representing the Business City, as well as the Livery and the City Corporation and its objectives. There is some, but little, overlap and we support each other wherever possible.
- It has been further rumoured that the Foreign Office tell us which countries the Lord Mayor should go to. This is also not true. About six months before the start of each Mayoralty, Kay Brock, the Chief of Staff at Mansion House, contacts City businesses and seeks their views on where they would most like the next Lord Mayor to visit. The responses are then discussed with the next Lord Mayor and within the City Corporation before a roundtable with UKTI, which supports the Mayoral overseas visits. It is the City that decides where the LM should go and the FCO and UKTI seek to accommodate this. I should add that the City Corporation pays for the costs of the Lord Mayor's overseas programme. However, we need the FCO and the UKTI to help arrange the visits. The Foreign Office also relies heavily on us – after all, the Lord Mayor travels as

much as, if not more than, many Ministers, to represent and promote the Business City in a most important and effective way.'

I was joined at this meeting by Geoffrey Bond and Ken Ayers of the Livery Committee, who responded well to questions. My speech seemed to calm the situation. The messages described above do, however, need repeating since masters of Livery companies change each year.

The Livery companies were, throughout my Mayoralty, supportive of the changes to make the Court of Aldermen adhere to best corporate governance

102 *Lord Mayor processes into the Egyptian Hall with Ken Livingstone at the London Government Dinner.*

practice and to move towards a position of choosing the right person for the job, rather than 'Buggins' Turn' based on length of service. They accepted that, being elected an Alderman is a necessary but not a sufficient condition for becoming Lord Mayor.

The Masters of the Livery companies in my year also became great friends and I was delighted when they formed a Past Masters Association, known as the 007 Masters, with me as their President in the title role. Thanks for this go, in particular, to the first Chairman of the Association, Tim Piper (Past Master Tallow Chandler, aka the Minister), Jonathan Munday (Past Master Wax Chandler, aka M), Dennis Tapper (Past Master Tin Plate Worker, aka Miss Moneypenny) and Peter Dowling (Past Master Innholder, aka Q). I was also grateful to the Past Master of the Playing Card Makers, James Madden, for designing and producing a set of playing cards with me on the reverse as James Bond, holding a gun, and with Lesley wearing her tiara as The Queen of Hearts.

THE UNITED GUILDS SERVICE

The day after the banquet for 'Masters, Prime Wardens and Upper Bailiff' there is a most colourful service at St Paul's Cathedral for the Livery companies. Dressed in their fine gowns, the masters and their clerks fill the nave and the Lord Mayor and Sheriffs process in, preceded by the City Marshal, the Swordbearer and the Common Cryer & Serjeant-at-Arms. This is normally followed by a lunch at the

103 *St Paul's Cathedral from the south.*

Livery halls for those involved. It is a demonstration of the attractive, centuries old pageantry of the City.

THE COOPERS BANQUET AT MANSION HOUSE

I attended many Livery company lunches and dinners during the year at Mansion House and at Livery halls. One stands out for very special personal reasons. Fellow Alderman John Hughesdon presided over the banquet on 17 November 2006 as Master of the Worshipful Company of Coopers. Our daughter-in-law Cori's baby was now a week overdue. After the main course, Lesley was called away from the table to take a call and she came back beaming, with the news that Cassia Rebecca Elisabeth Stuttard had been born at 19.48. John Hughesdon kindly referred to this in his speech and Cassia's birth was toasted in Mansion House by Liverymen of the Coopers' Company.

104 *Grand-daughter Cassia cutting her teeth on the Lord Mayor's diamond badge.*

105 *Theresa Lewis, Lesley Stuttard and Averil Watson at Glaziers' Hall.*

MY OWN LIVERY COMPANIES

It is always very special when the Lord Mayor has an event with his own Livery companies during the year.

My Mother Livery company, the Glaziers, formed a special committee, chaired by Past Master Phillida Shaw, to plan for and celebrate my Mayoral year. Apart from the magical entry in the Lord Mayor's Show, the Glaziers came to Mansion House on two separate occasions, first for a fund-raising event, the Summer Extravaganza. This was organised by Mary Lou Carrington, who tragically died of cancer in early 2008, and Susan Fey. It raised over £40,000 towards my Appeal and the Glaziers Trust. Then the Glaziers came for their annual banquet. I am enormously grateful to the Company, in particular the then Master, John Watson, and the Court including Brian Harris, David Ball, John Vartan, Steve Graham and Peter Doe for their support during the year.

106 *The Glaziers' Carriage in the Lord Mayor's Show – Peter Beesley (Master), John Watson (Upper Warden) and David Ball (Renter Warden).*

However, a very special event for me was the unveiling of a portrait of me at Glaziers Hall commissioned by artist Petri Anderson. It was special because it was in stained glass. Petri had come to Mansion House soon after I became Lord Mayor. He had photographed me wearing the State robes, with an ermine cloak in red velvet, over the black velvet Court Dress, holding the Lord Mayor's sword. The finished result was spectacular and much admired by the Liverymen of the Glaziers, as well as by Lesley and me.

The Chartered Accountants' Ladies Banquet at Mansion House in July 2007 was another occasion when I could wear the original Lord Mayor's Chain, allegedly worn by Thomas More. My erstwhile PwC partner, Peter Wyman, was the Master and my host, together with Joy, his wife. Ed Balls was due to be the guest speaker but could not be present because of discussions over Cabinet reshuffles in the wake of Tony Blair stepping down and Gordon Brown taking over. So, the Hon Sarah Morrison, a real character, stepped in and made fun of being the stand in. Other guests included some old chums from the past – The Rt Hon Sir Jeremy Hanley, KCMG and Kerry Hawkins.

I became an Honorary Member of the Court of the Plumbers in 2005 and was delighted with their support at the Lord Mayor's Show and in connection with

107 *Stained glass portrait of the Lord Mayor by Petri Anderson in Glaziers' Hall.*

my Lord Mayor's Appeal. Apart from holding their annual banquet at Mansion House, they also organised a Summer Extravaganza Appeal at Goldsmiths' Hall in stunning surroundings. All 196 candles, in the four chandeliers, were lit which illuminated the magnificent hall so beautifully. The Master, Mike Swallow, and others including David Alexander, Steve Hodkinson, Mike Samuel and David Hamilton contributed greatly to organising a great evening which raised £47,000.

The Guild of Educators is a relatively young organisation, having been approved by the Court of Aldermen in 2000 and of which I am Sponsoring

Alderman and now Honorary Freeman and member of the Court. It comprises around 150 Freemen involved in the field of education as teachers, lecturers or administrators, with help from an excellent Clerk, Keith Lawrey. It aspires to be a City company and, later, a Livery company. To achieve this end, it must have a charitable fund of £300,000. Part of my Lord Mayor's Appeal went to the Educators to help them meet this target.

It was a pleasure to receive the Master (Dr Peter Warren, CBE) and Freemen of the Guild of Educators at Mansion House for a joint dinner with the Guild of Public Relations Practitioners, another aspiring Livery company. I drew attention to two stained glass windows in the Egyptian Hall which made a connection with the two guilds. The signing of the Magna Carta was a great moment in our history, a stunning PR achievement, while the image of Edward VI entering the City at the time of his Coronation reminded one of the contribution he made to education by the number of schools founded in his name.

PRESENTATION OF THE BOAR'S HEAD

During the year, many Livery companies bring a gift for the Lord Mayor. The Butchers Company excelled by bringing a boar's head, in a time honoured tradition, before Christmas. On 5 December 2006, a procession began at Butchers' Hall comprising the Master and Wardens, four policemen on horseback and police outriders, escorting a boar's head on a bier carried by Liverymen of the Company. Needless to say, in these days of Food Standards Agency regulations, it was not possible for the Butchers to bear a real boar's head through the streets of London, So, a papier mâché look-a-like boar's head was carried aloft. At a suitable moment as it entered the Walbrook Hall Entrance of Mansion House it was quickly exchanged for the real thing, a boar's head carefully cooked by members of the Army Catering Corps. After a suitable ceremony of welcome and thanks, the Boar's Head was carefully carved and it tasted simply fantastic. Mansion House staff enjoyed it enormously. So did we.

THE CUTLERS BOAR'S HEAD FEAST

Another pre-Christmas extravaganza is the Boar's Head Feast at Cutlers' Hall. It is based around the medieval tradition of sacrificing a boar and presenting its head at a feast at Yuletide. The origins of this may be Norse. A bier bearing the boar's head is brought into the hall, accompanied by choristers singing the ancient boar's head carol, with the following words:

> The boar's head in hand bear I
> Bedecked with bays and rosemary
> I pray you, my masters, be merry
> *Quot estis in convivio* [as many are as at the feast]
> *Caput apri defero* [I bring in the boar's head]
> *Reddens laudes Domino* [giving praises to the Lord]

The boar's head, as I understand,
Is the rarest dish in all the land,
Which thus bedecked with a gay garland
Let us *servire cantico* [serve it with a song]
Caput apri defero
Reddens laudes Domino

Our steward hath provided this
In honor of the King of Bliss
Which, on this day to be served, is
In Reginensi atrio [in the Queen's hall]
Caput apri defero
Reddens laudes Domino

After this, the apple or orange which has been stuck in the mouth of the boar is given to the Master (on this occasion, Peter Roberts) who presents it to the youngest chorister. Slivers of boar's head are then cut and given to each person present. It is delicious.

In what is, these days, a somewhat politically incorrect arrangement, the dinner is for men only, while the ladies of the Lord Mayor, Sheriffs, Master and Wardens dine separately in an upstairs room and then appear on the balcony to watch the ceremony and listen to the speeches. We were informed, rather apologetically, that this was due to a shortage of space in the main hall. Lesley was not at all unhappy to dine with the ladies.

On the date of the Boar's Head Feast in my Mayoral year, 13 December 2006, an Aldermanic by-election was held in the ward of Broad Street. Sheriff David Lewis had tendered his resignation as an Alderman as he approached the end of five years during a maximum, renewable, term of six years. He had been chosen as Lord Mayor by the Court of Aldermen but needed to be an Alderman during his Mayoralty in order to qualify. He therefore needed to be re-elected for a second term. As Lord Mayor, I was obliged to leave the Boar's Head Feast in order to preside over the ward mote. It was contested and after the count I announced the result, namely that he had polled 139 votes while his opponent, John Scott, a Common Councilman in his ward, had polled 40 votes. This gave David the democratic mandate he needed and he was later elected my successor as Lord Mayor. After the ward mote, we both returned to Cutlers' Hall, where he received a rapturous welcome.

Gifts from the Livery Companies

It has become traditional for many Livery companies to present gifts to the Lord Mayor and Lady Mayoress as a token of their esteem and in return for hospitality received and gifts presented by the Lord Mayor. Some of these are presented on the day of the Lord Mayor's Show at the Presentation Ceremony in Guildhall and have been mentioned above. Others are the subject of separate events at

Mansion House and are summarised below. I must apologise to any that I have inadvertently omitted:

- The Bakers provided an enormous cake which was enjoyed by the lucky few who came to tea with the Lady Mayoress and was finished off at Mansion House staff Christmas lunch.
- The Basketmakers ask the Lady Mayoress to choose an object to be made out of woven wicker. Lesley asked for two wicker pigs to be placed in her garden and these were christened 'Hog' and 'Mahog' after the City's protective Gods 'Gog' and 'Magog'. Presented to her at the Basketmakers Banquet at Mansion House on 26 September 2007 (our wedding anniversary), for some days afterwards they sat upright in chairs in my office, the Venetian Parlour.
- The Brewers provided some beer which was consumed by Mansion House staff at their Christmas Party.
- The Coopers present a barrel of rum.
- The Cordwainers arrange for the Lord Mayor to be given a pair of shoes.
- The Distillers bring much appreciated whisky.
- The Feltmakers arrange for the Lord Mayor to be measured for his Mayoral hat, which is a black tricorne with black feathers which he wears on ceremonial occasions including, of course, the Lord Mayor's Show.
- The Spectacle Makers gave me two pairs of prescription glasses – one for reading and the other for general use.
- In former times, a levy was charged annually to the Fruiterers for selling fruit in the City. More recently, when the levy was removed, the tradition was kept alive by the Fruiterers bringing a gift of fruit to Mansion House. Some years ago it was suggested that the fruit should instead be taken to hospices and community centres. However, the Fruiterers still come to Mansion House each year to announce that they have fulfilled their traditional obligation and, in addition, bring some exotic fruit as a gift to the Lord Mayor and Lady Mayoress.
- The Gardeners bring a huge basket of fruit and vegetables which is a very welcome addition to the Mayoral diet.
- The Glovers' Company presents the Lord Mayor with a gift of white (calf's leather) gloves for use with Court dress and on ceremonial occasions. This is complemented with gloves for day wear. The Lady Mayoress also receives some gloves.
- The Leathersellers gave a large leather bag, most appropriate for the many overnight stays abroad as Lord Mayor.
- The Makers of Playing Cards give everyone a present at their Banquet – a set of playing cards bearing the image of their Master.
- The Pattenmakers brought a pair of 'pattens' in a glass case, as an example of what was worn in muddy London streets in Medieval times to protect one's shoes.

108 *Master Gardener, Bill Fraser, in the Lord Mayor's Show.*

- The Scriveners give a quill pen, which is used for the Lord Mayor to sign his declaration at the Silent Ceremony, and also a Parker pen for the Lady Mayoress.
- The Turners gave a beautifully turned wooden box, with a silver band and inscription, for keeping collar studs and cufflinks.

THE WORLD TRADERS' TACITUS LECTURE

One of the City's notable annual events is the Tacitus Lecture organised by the World Traders and held in Great Hall, Guildhall. Attended by over 600 people, the speakers are chosen from a distinguished list and have included Lord Owen, Sir Richard Sykes, Sir (now Lord) Digby Jones, Philip Lader, Peter Sutherland, Sir Howard Davies and Sir Mark Moody-Stuart.

In my year, on 22 February 2007, the Master of the World Traders, our old friend Jack Wigglesworth, introduced Antony Burgmans, the Chairman of Unilever, who spoke on 'The Role of Business in Society'. He described the contribution of the multinational City Corporations to economic growth, the emancipation of women, the environment and the 'vitality of life'. In an amusing speech, he quoted President Reagan's characterisation of the role of government in the economy as 'If it moves, tax it. If it keeps moving, regulate it. If it stops moving, subsidise it' and he repeated the words of his father, namely 'Success comes before work only in the dictionary'.

THE BILLESDON GAVEL EXCHANGE

In medieval times the Livery companies jealously guarded their privileges and their trades. They were also very status conscious about their ranking in City processions. In 1484, a violent fight occurred between the Skinners and the Merchant Taylors as to which should be number 6 and which number 7 in the pecking order. The Lord Mayor of the day, Robert Billesdon, summoned them to see him and arbitrated between the warring Livery companies. He decreed that from then on, they should rotate annually between sixth and seventh in order of precedence and that each should hold an open dinner at which it would feast its former rivals.

Since that time, each year, the Masters and Wardens of both companies have appeared before the Lord Mayor so that they can surrender their gavels, which are then returned to the other party. By tradition the Lord Mayor asks the two delegations the question, 'Is there anything which has come to your attention which prevents me from continuing the age old tradition of accepting from you the Skinners gavel number 6 and giving it to you the Merchant Taylors and of accepting from you the Merchant Taylors gavel number 7 and giving it to you the Skinners?' After a moment's silence the exchange takes place.

On this occasion, having consulted the City Marshal, Billy King-Harman, if he thought the two companies would be open to a bit of fun, I asked the traditional question. Then I paused before saying, 'Masters, something has come to my attention which prevents me from continuing the age old tradition of accepting from you the Skinners gavel number 6 and giving it to you the Merchant Taylors and of accepting from you the Merchant Taylors gavel number 7 and giving it to you the Skinners. I therefore make my own Livery companies, the Glaziers who are number 53 and the Plumbers who are number 31, numbers 6 and 7 respectively and you are hereby demoted to numbers 53 and 31'. There was a stunned silence before they realised it was a spoof and burst out laughing. I continued 'Oh, I'm very sorry, Masters, I seem to have the wrong text'. For one magical moment, I could have changed the course of history.

The Water Conservators

In 1197, after spending the kingdom's wealth on the Third Crusade and being ransomed by the German Emperor, King Richard I, the Lionheart, was broke. He looked at all possibilities to raise money for the country's exchequer. An idea came to him. He would sell to the City of London the rights of the Thames Conservancy, the rights to the River Thames. The Worshipful Company of Water Conservators are the guardians and, each year, bring a jug of water to the Lord Mayor to commemorate the purchase of the water of the River Thames on 14 July 1197. Apparently this is referred to as 'The Ceremony of Passing Water'.

The Feast of St Cecilia

St Cecilia is the patron saint of musicians. Her feast day is celebrated on 22 November, the birthday of one of my daughters-in-law, Cori, who graduated from the Guildhall School of Music and Drama. For over 300 years, this feast has been marked each year by the Stationers' Company who have mounted concerts of outstanding quality at their stunning hall which dates from 1673.

We had enjoyed hearing many concerts during the festival of St Cecilia and were royally entertained at their hall during my year, when we met many old friends who are Liverymen of the Company.

CART MARKING

For centuries the City of London Corporation has exercised rights over carts, which are plied for hire, and their carriers. It was an excellent method of raising taxes as today's Chancellor of the Exchequer knows when charging an annual fee for cars to be driven on public roads. It was also an excellent way of ensuring that the carts were roadworthy – a precursor of today's MOT. An Act of 1838 vested the licensing in the Keeper of Guildhall. Owners of carts had to be Freemen of the City of London and also members of the Worshipful Company of Carmen. The traditional ceremony of cart marking takes place in Guildhall Yard each year when carts to be marked are driven into the yard and branded with a red hot iron denoting a letter of the alphabet. It is a very colourful event, attended by Masters of many Livery companies, dressed in their gowns and hats, with the 'carts' being a variety of vehicles used over the last century, from

109 *Cart marking ceremony in Guildhall Yard – Master Carmen, Gerry Pulman, marks the Lord Mayor's Silver Ghost.*

ancient steamrollers to vintage buses to modern articulated lorries. The Master Glover provides special padded gloves to the Lord Mayor, Sheriffs and Masters who are involved in the cart marking. It is a popular event which attracts large crowds and is part of the pageantry of the ancient City.

During my year as Lord Mayor, the Master Carmen, Gerry Pulman, suggested that my 1921 Rolls-Royce Silver Ghost, which he once owned, should be marked. So I drove it to Guildhall on the day before the cart marking ceremony and Gerry duly marked a piece of oak hung from the side with a letter 'Q' also containing the City's shield and the Carmen's arms.

INAUGURATION OF THE NEWGATE STREET CLOCK

To celebrate the 375th Anniversary of the Worshipful Company of Clockmakers, on 31 May I unveiled a new public clock which had been erected in Newgate Street close to St Paul's tube station. The clock, designed by Joanna Migdal and made by Smith of Derby, uses an unusual 'wandering hour' mechanism, with GPS satellite time synchronisation. The unveiling ceremony was preceded by a reception at Cutlers' Hall hosted by Master Cutler Peter Roberts and Master Clockmaker David Poole. The assembled company was then escorted by a detachment of Pikemen & Musketeers from the HAC. Many Liverymen joined in the procession and the ceremony was watched by a large contingent from the City, including Deputy Ann Pembroke, a Common Councilman, whose idea it was to mark the anniversary with this most unusual clock.

FLOWERS IN THE CITY AWARDS

As an example of the modern day relevance of an ancient Livery company, the Gardeners' Company holds an annual competition for the best floral displays, including gardens, window boxes and atrium floral decoration, in the Square Mile. Chaired by Edward Wright, MBE, there are some 20 judges who make as many as 10 awards and the winners come to Mansion House to receive their certificates and cups. As a result of this and other campaigns, for example the City Corporation's own Street Improvement Campaign, the City of London is a very pleasant place in which to live and work.

110 *The Lord Mayor on a visit to a village in Ghana with VSO.*

Part V

VOLUNTEERING, CHARITY AND THE LORD MAYOR'S APPEAL

The Spirit of Service
My Missionary Ancestor

When I was a young boy, I used to visit my great aunt, Emily Whitehead, in Todmorden, Yorkshire, where my mother was born. Actually the postal address is Lancashire which often confuses. Aunt Emily subscribed for many years to the National Geographical magazine. With dramatic photographs and stories of exotic places and people, this periodical inspired and whetted my appetite for travel. But the origin of her interest in foreign lands is also worth recording. Born in 1882, she never married, but managed the family home, including caring for her great uncle James Midgley, who had been a missionary in East Africa, with Livingstone, and later in Brazil.

James was born in 1832 into a farming family on the Lancashire/Yorkshire border. After a grammar school education at Hepstonstall, an attractive hill top village near Todmorden, he won a scholarship to St John's College Cambridge to read moral science, graduating in 1858 with a First. While at Cambridge in December 1857 he heard David Livingstone speak at the Senate House about his first expedition to Africa between 1852 and 1856, along the Zambezi River. James was inspired by missionary zeal and entered the church.

I, too, was taken by a paragraph in Livingstone's speech and I have reproduced it for others to read:

> For my own part, I have never ceased to rejoice that God has appointed me to such an office. People talk of the sacrifice I have made in spending so much of my life in Africa. Can that be called a sacrifice which is simply paid back as a small part of a great debt owing to our God, which we can never repay? – Is that a sacrifice which brings its own blest reward in healthful activity, the consciousness of doing good, peace of mind, and a bright hope of a glorious destiny hereafter? – Away with the word in such a view, and with such a thought! It is emphatically no sacrifice. Say rather it is a privilege. Anxiety, sickness, suffering, or danger, now and then, with a foregoing of the common conveniences and charities of this life, may make us pause, and cause the spirit to waver, and the soul to sink, but let this only be for a moment. All these are nothing when compared with the glory which shall hereafter be revealed in, and for, us. I never made a sacrifice. Of this we ought not to talk, when we remember the great sacrifice which He made who left His Father's throne on high to give Himself for us.

111 *The Reverend James Midgley (in retirement).*

He ended his speech with the exhortation: 'I go back to Africa to make an open path for commerce and Christianity. Do you carry out the work I have begun? I leave it with you.'

Livingstone returned to Africa, taking with him six missionaries, four of whom died while on service. Not to be dissuaded from his purpose, he journeyed forth again, having signed up another six missionaries. One of these was James Midgley, who set sail for Zanzibar in 1873. From there, he was sent to Magila (now Msalabani) on the mainland, in what was then German East Africa and is now Tanzania. The Reverend Midgley had a material effect at Magila. He was responsible for building a small hospital surgery and a series of rooms for villagers and travellers. He did not build a church, but probably erected a small portable altar in one of the rooms or outdoors for church services. Most of his time was spent travelling through nearby villages preaching. Unfortunately a disastrous fire in 1885 destroyed most of Magila and with it all of the Reverend Midgley's buildings. However, two early sepia photographs have survived of the hospital and the two rooms that he had built. The originals are in the possession of The United Society for the Propagation of the Gospel (USPG), after its merger with The Universities Mission to Central Africa (UMCA), and I have copies of these.

While at Magila, the Reverend Midgley suffered repeated attacks of malaria and, in his words, it was 'with regret and after heart felt searching that I decided

112 *The Reverend James Midgley.*

113 *Mission, Magila, German East Africa.*

114 *Mission, Magila, German East Africa.*

to leave the mission field'. He resigned from his post at Magila in April 1874, returning to Zanzibar and immediately to England. During the voyage home, two members of the mission died from malaria.

After recovering from his illness and regaining his strength, he was posted to Recife in north east Brazil where he spent 17 years as consular chaplain, before retiring to England, to be cared for by my great aunt Emily. He never married and, when he died in 1922, he left all his money to endow honorary canonries of Wakefield Cathedral and to increase the stipends of the poor clergy in the Deanery of Halifax. He is buried in Todmorden and there is a memorial to him in Halifax Parish Church.

His personal effects, which are now in my possession, include his black top hat, in a large leather hat box, and his military style travelling desk.

THE SPIRIT OF SERVICE – MY EVANGELICAL ANCESTOR

This story of ecclesiastical and charitable endeavour was matched on the other side of my family by a distant ancestor of the same name as me. John Stuttard lived between 1748 and 1818 in Burnley, Lancashire – a few miles from where James Midgley was born. A founder of Haggate Baptist Chapel, near Burnley, in 1767, he established Colne Baptist Chapel in 1769 which was formally opened by John Wesley in 1777. He was noted for his baptisms, through total immersion, in the cold waters of the River Calder that passes through Colne. I can't help thinking of the souls saved one moment who might have succumbed to pneumonia the next. In the Baptist Quarterly, he is recorded as preaching no fewer than 7,937 sermons.

The Spirit of Service – A Family of Teachers

When I was young it seemed that half my family were teachers – aunts, cousins and even my brother. As I have related elsewhere, this gave me an interest in education as a means of enriching people's lives, both intellectually and economically.

The Benefits of Volunteering

At the time I left university, National Service had been abolished. There was a widespread view that, to replace it and to bring similar benefits, it would be a good idea to take a gap year, as it has now come to be known. Voluntary Service Overseas had been founded in 1958 as way of matching school-leaving 18-year-olds with an African or Asian country that would benefit from a pair of hands and a year of enthusiasm. They would build things or teach or help run organisations. By the early 1960s, VSO was recruiting graduates to go to an 'underdeveloped country' for a year or two, typically teaching at a secondary school. I applied, was accepted and signed up, and was sent to Brunei for a year. Although it was a rich oil state, this had not yet fully evidenced itself in the economy and society. Brunei in 1966 was primitive and colonial in many ways, and could be correctly described as 'underdeveloped'. All that was to change and I was part of that change process, bringing western ideas, English language training and a glimpse of the outside world which has brought technology, consumer luxuries and other benefits to Malays, Chinese, Indians and the indigenous people. During my year at Sultan Omar Ali Saifuddin College, Brunei Town, I taught English and English Literature, edited the School magazine, built an all-weather cricket net and directed a school cast in *The Importance of Being Earnest*.

The Oscar Wilde classic stands out. I had a Brunei Malay Lady Bracknell, an Indian Canon Chasuble, a Chinese Miss Prism and my Algernon was the son of a head hunter. We began with a run-through, where the full meaning of the 'unfashionable side of the street' could be understood and the cynical wit of the playwright might be appreciated in the words 'To be born, or at any rate bred, in a hand-bag, whether it had handles or not, seems to me to display a contempt for the ordinary decencies of family life that reminds one of the worst excesses of the French Revolution.' Can you imagine Brunei Malays, Indians, Chinese and sons of head hunters understanding all this? But they did. They also learnt how to act, to project their voices and to enjoy being involved with the theatre.

It was therefore pleasing for me to hear, some years later, that my Lady Bracknell had been appointed the headmistress of the Girls' School in Brunei and that others had gone on to jobs in the civil service, in some cases reaching the ranks of Minister. I was also pleased to welcome my Canon Chasuble to Mansion House while I was Lord Mayor and to learn that the cast had organised a 40th-anniversary reunion in Brunei in 2007.

During my year in Brunei, I was asked if I would read the English language News on Radio Brunei. Having an Oxford, or vaguely Oxford, accent, with an ability to speak clearly, meant that I was a candidate for this prestigious job. Turning up at the radio studios at nine o'clock in the evening, after dinner, required a discipline that ruled out too much evening alcohol at the OK Bar or the Brunei Sports Club – and in those days, Brunei wasn't dry. Indeed the expatriate Brits behaved in a manner that Evelyn Waugh would have recognised. It was here that I made a lifelong friend, Peter Berry, later to become Chief Executive of the Crown Agents and be honoured with the CMG. But the experience at Radio Brunei did teach me an added sense of timing when it came to giving speeches. This was to prove helpful some 40 years later when, as Lord Mayor, I gave 764 speeches in 12 months. Another 10 years at it and I might have beaten my Baptist clerical ancestor.

But I learnt important things about race, religion and culture. When one is a teacher one tries to understand the way pupils think. Individuals with a different background think in different ways. Being immersed in a multiracial environment was a great experience.

So volunteering was beneficial – to those one was helping and to those who volunteered. Voluntary Service Overseas now has the strap line 'Sharing Skills – Changing Lives'. That sums it up nicely. It changed my life significantly.

On my return to the UK, I felt more at ease with people of different nationalities and religions. I had begun to understand that they thought and behaved differently. The world is an increasingly international place and the need to understand other people has never been more important in optimising opportunities and in reducing tensions.

My year in Brunei made me a lifelong convert to the benefits of volunteering and of cross-border learning. For this reason I chose as my charitable appeal for the year a cause and a theme which emphasised this.

THE LORD MAYOR'S APPEAL

The City of London has always been associated with public service, through volunteering and charity. There have been some outstanding and well known examples. Richard Whittington, Sir Thomas Gresham and Sir John Cass stand out.

Lord Mayors have also normally had a charitable cause, particularly when times and circumstances demanded it. After the disastrous storms and floods of 1953, when 307 people lost their lives and 24,500 homes were damaged on the East Anglian coast, the Lord Mayor of the day established 'The Mayor of London's Disaster Relief Appeal'. Another charity, established by Sir Christopher Collett, GBE, is the Lord Mayor's 800th Anniversary Awards Scheme. I was pleased to have been involved with both of these.

In recent years, each Lord Mayor has had his own chosen charitable appeal and has identified a theme based on his or her own interests and the needs of the moment.

At the G8 summit at Gleneagles in July 2005, the issues of eliminating global poverty and of encouraging international understanding were very much back on the agenda. The bombings of the earlier 9/11 and of 7/7, which actually occurred during the Summit, emphasised the need for greater cross-border contact and understanding.

115 *King Edward's School Witley.*

The political momentum married up very much with my own desire to focus on this subject as one worth promoting during my year. From my previous experience and current contact, VSO was the obvious organisation to manage the Lord Mayor's Charitable Appeal. I had discussions with Mark Goldring, VSO's Chief Executive, and a plan was hatched, with VSO leading the project.

But I also wanted some funds to go to three other charities that would participate in this programme:

> 1. King Edward's School Witley. Each year the School sends pupils to Malawi to learn about Africa and to help with community projects.
> 2. Mansion House Scholarship Scheme, established by Sir Richard Nichols during his Mayoral year, to provide bursaries to bright young people from overseas that would benefit from training and work experience with a leading organisation (eg a university or the Financial Services Authority or the London Stock Exchange) in London.
> 3. The Guild of Educators, an aspirant Livery company made up of teachers, lecturers, professors and others interested in education. I am the Sponsoring Aldermen, helping the Guild progress to full Livery status within the City of London.

So the basic concept was determined. However I knew that, once I became Lord Mayor, I could not direct or manage this programme myself. I bumped into Sir Paul Judge, whom I had known from the time when Coopers & Lybrand were auditors to Cadbury Schweppes plc, where he had been Deputy Finance Director and then Group Planning Director.

Paul, an accomplished businessman and philanthropist, was committed to business and skills education. He had inspired, and was the key benefactor of,

116 *Lord Mayor with Mansion House scholar, Bilyana Apostolova from Bulgaria.*

the Cambridge University Judge Business School and was a recent President of the Chartered Management Institute as well as the current President of the Association of MBAs. He also had excellent City connections as a recent Master of the Marketors' Livery Company and as Chairman of a Schroder investment trust. We discussed the objectives and the action programme. Paul was enthusiastic and agreed to chair my Lord Mayor's Appeal with the slogan 'Sharing Skills – Changing Lives'. His leadership was invaluable.

The next step was to find an Appeal Manager, who would be full time directing and managing the detailed appeal. VSO advertised and found an exceptional person, Anne-Marie Jubber, who was known to a former partner of mine at Coopers & Lybrand, Adrian Lamb, OBE, the Treasurer of Chatham House. Anne-Marie proved to be a real star.

VSO's Programme for the Year

Our aim was to raise £2million (gross) from donations and events. We got off to a really good start with three organisations, HSBC, the Government of Kuwait and PricewaterhouseCoopers each donating £100,000 to become Appeal Benefactors.

As part of the Mayoral overseas visits programme, we visited VSO projects in a number of countries, including Ghana, Pakistan, South Africa and Vietnam. These included a number of projects for AIDS sufferers or those with disabilities, where volunteers were working in extremely heartrending but rewarding circumstances. It made it easier when giving speeches at Appeal events to have seen VSO in action and to be able to refer to the good work VSO does.

In Ghana, for example, VSO had worked with the Ghanaian Government to develop a national volunteering programme. From a start in 2003, this had grown from 53 Ghanaian volunteers to a staggering 8,500 volunteer teachers in both primary and secondary schools. Another VSO scheme involved British volunteers working with the Ghana Department of Social Welfare to help disabled people identify work opportunities, thus providing a real role for them and thereby giving them dignity and self-esteem. These projects showed the caring nature of Ghanaian society and are an excellent example of capacity building.

In Vietnam, we met one British VSO volunteer who had retired at the age of 52, sold all his possessions, and moved to Ho Chi Minh City, where he was helping children with disabilities benefit from main-stream schooling.

In Pakistan we saw two AIDS-related projects where volunteers were helping manage two care centres. AIDS sufferers are stigmatised and shunned by Islamic society in Pakistan. At these two community centres they were welcomed in and looked after. Slowly they have gained back their self-esteem and dignity. It is a wonderful example of what volunteering can do.

One of the first few fundraising events was a poetry reading at Mansion House involving Harold Pinter, Lord (Grey) Gowrie and Benjie Fraser, Harold's stepson and organiser. Well attended by over 250 people, the first two poets read some of their poems about near death experiences.

Mirroring my message that London is a truly international city and that foreign nationals contribute greatly to it success, the VSO fund-raising programme of events for the year had an international theme. The first of these was the Africa Gala at Guildhall in March 2007, the week after the State Visit of the President of Ghana. Africa was on everyone's minds and we had great support from the 400 people who attended and the evening's sponsors:

117　*The Lord Mayor and Lady Mayoress greet the High Commissioner from South Africa, Ms Lindiwe Mabuza, at the Mansion House Easter Banquet.*

Standard Bank, Rio Tinto, Berwin Leighton Paisner and SAB Miller. The Great Hall looked marvellously luxuriant with palm plants and African flowers, with African music to create the right atmosphere. A number of ambassadors attended from African countries and other guests included our friend the Kuwaiti Ambassador His Excellency Mr Khaled Al-Duwaisan, GCVO, as well as Jon Snow and Nick Bonham, who raised £78,000 as the auctioneer of items including a painting of a cheetah by David Shepherd who also attended. The evening raised over £200,000.

Other events during the year followed the pattern of previous years – the City Dip, involving many City schools, the British 10K Road Race in London, a Concert at Canary Wharf, sponsored by Citi, and the Three Peaks Challenge. Then, Alderman Roger Gifford kindly donated the charitable proceeds of SEB's annual day at Bisley. Following some enjoyable shooting (at targets and clays) the guests were generous when it came to the auction.

Her Royal Highness The Princess Royal is VSO's Patron and kindly attended and spoke at a dinner at St James's Palace in June, sponsored by KPMG. We were wonderfully entertained by a children's choir of seven to 11-year-olds from East Africa who had been orphaned or had come from single parent families. Older children who had participated in VSO's Global Xchange also spoke about their experience of an exchange between London and Mongolia.

I was also delighted to be able to include a large number of donors to be invited to a Reception at Number 10 Downing Street hosted by the Prime Minister's wife, Cherie Booth. She was very gracious and I was most impressed that she held such events each week for those who contributed to charity. She spoke very warmly of VSO and the work that we had been doing.

118 *The City Dip raises funds for the Lord Mayor's Appeal.*

119 *Cherie Blair hosts a reception for the Lord Mayor's Appeal at Downing Street.*

In the autumn, the first major event was the South Asia Evening organised by Mike and Sonal Jatania, with support from Lord (Karan) Bilimoria who provided the Cobra beer. Fitting the occasion, the décor looked more out of a Bollywood Awards ceremony and our guests included ladies dressed in wonderfully colourful saris. The Indian food was delicious. For entertainment there was dancing, including the delightful Payal Patel. We raised over £130,000.

The second major event of the autumn was the Oriental Court Dinner, held at Mansion House in the Egyptian Hall, which was beautifully lit and decorated with exotic oriental flowers. Organised by a team led by Hugh Davies, CMG, the sponsors were UBS, Evergreen, Citi and Ty Nant Spring Water. Distinguished guests included Lord and Lady Brittan, the Chinese Ambassador Madame Fu and Keith Vaz MP. The entertainment was suitably eastern, with sword dancing in the Chinese operatic tradition and Chinese music by a talented flautist, Guo Yue. Around £150,000 was raised.

Throughout the year, we received some generous donations and a lot of support. The four charities were highlighted and, in the run-up to VSO's 50th year, it helped put this wonderful organisation well and truly on the map.

And the result? Well we raised just over our target of £2 million, raising the profile of all four organisations. Grateful thanks go to Sir Paul Judge and Anne-Marie Jubber and, indeed, to all those who contributed.

THE RESERVE FORCES AND THE CADETS

Each Lord Mayor, in his year of office, becomes the President of the City of London Reserve Forces and Cadets Association. In this capacity, he welcomes to Mansion House the Association itself and many cadet groups, including St John Ambulance and the Red Cross.

At the beginning of the year, the Lord Mayor's Speechwriter, Bill Beaver, persuaded me to encourage the involvement of the Livery companies with cadet groups, on the grounds that this would fit in well with my theme for the year of encouraging volunteering. I'm pleased that Bill came up with this suggestion as it was taken up with enthusiasm by the Livery companies which literally doubled, in the year, the number of groups with which they were associated.

For each county in England and Wales, Her Majesty The Queen appoints a Lord Lieutenant, to represent her in that county. For London, the Lord Lieutenant's responsibilities do not extend, constitutionally, to the City of London, although we were always pleased to welcome Lord (Peter) Imbert, CVO, QPM and his wife, Iris, to the City and we saw them often during our year. For the City of London, the Lord Mayor is The Queen's representative and is head of an organisation known as Her Majesty's Commission of Lieutenancy for the City of London. Under the watchful eye of its Clerk, Major William Hunt, who is also a Common Councilman and Windsor Herald at the College of Arms, the Commission meets annually and holds a dinner to thank those colonels and commanding officers of reserve forces and cadets in the London area. At the dinner I hosted during my year, I had the pleasure of sitting next to Colonel Mark Bryant who ran the Armed Forces cadet groups in the north and east of London and heard of the contribution that the units make to young boys and girls, often from disadvantaged or poor backgrounds. Those teenagers who drop out of school and later join the cadets often find a sense of belonging and purpose. They are motivated, learn life skills and, sometimes, start to study again and can take their GCSEs in the cadets. I was inspired.

In the last week of my Mayoralty in November 2007, I was pleased to welcome to Mansion House, Sir Brian Jenkins, GBE, former Lord Mayor, as Prior of the Order of St John for England and the Islands together with around 300 cadets and friends of the St John Ambulance. The Egyptian Hall and surrounding rooms were filled with displays and young cadets (as well as Badgers – the little ones) doing things – tying bandages, ascending a climbing frame and learning about the City. Each year, someone is selected to be the Lord Mayor's cadet and Alice Barrett, my cadet, showed me round the displays.

DRAGON AWARDS DINNER

One of the major events in the Lord Mayor's calendar is the annual Dragon Awards, where awards are presented to organisations and individuals who have

120 *Dragon Awards at Mansion House – on the left is Sir David Rowe-Ham, originator of the awards in 1986, together with chief guests Lord George and Martyn Lewis.*

demonstrated a special contribution to the community by helping in schools, community projects and where there are people in need. Established 20 years ago by a former Lord Mayor, Sir David Rowe-Ham, GBE, it is extremely prestigious to win a Dragon Award and the dinner is well attended. It is also extremely well compered by Martyn Lewis, CBE, the former broadcaster.

This year's Dragon Awards dinner was the 20th and I was pleased to welcome David Rowe-Ham, as well as Lord (Eddie) George and Gerry Acher, CBE, LVO, Co-President and Chairman, respectively, of Heart of the City, which supports companies considering a community programme.

NEW HORIZON YOUTH CENTRE

In 1972, a Cambridge friend, Bernard Simons who was a well known human rights lawyer, introduced me to New Horizon, founded by Lord Longford,

121 *Bernard Sullivan, MBE, Chief Toastmaster for many years, shares a memory with Lord George.*

which helped young people homeless in London. It did not provide shelter or food but advised youngsters, who had left home in Glasgow or Newcastle and who now found themselves unemployed and adrift on the streets of London. Its first director was Jon Snow, who became a well known broadcaster, then a trustee (and now some 35 years later the chairman), and Jack Profumo who did such a wonderful job at Toynbee Hall after his fall from grace as Minister of War during the Macmillan years.

New Horizon has thrived over the years, complementing the work of Centrepoint and Shelter. It seeks to advise youngsters and get them on a track which will lead to employment and a stable life. A former colleague at Coopers & Lybrand, Robert Barnes, took over as treasurer from me in 1977 and is still involved.

Jon Snow was a stalwart at VSO and I was pleased to attend a fundraising breakfast in support of New Horizon at the Savoy, before it closed for refurbishment. New Horizon is such a worthwhile charity, ably run and playing a vital role in meeting social needs in the capital today.

THE BRITISH RED CROSS

The links between the City and the British Red Cross are very close. Before I was Sheriff, Lesley and I were co-chairmen of the City of London British Red Cross Christmas Market at Guildhall. This takes place every two years and is a wonderful way of organising a village fête in the City with the funds going to a great cause. We raised £100,000 net of costs and got to know a lot of people and raised the profile of the British Red Cross. We also became acquainted with a number of the Red Cross staff in the City who do so much good work: Sue Dowell, Rebecca Payne and Dan Windross.

Each year there is a street collection which is well supported by Aldermen's wives and makes a great contribution to the Red Cross. It was a pleasure to see Lady Newall receive an MBE for services to the British Red Cross Society in London and, on her retirement, to see Lady (Tessa) Brewer take over.

122 *Visit to India – Lady Mayoress at a Red Cross Depot in Delhi.*

CHARITIES AID FOUNDATION

I had been introduced to Charities Aid Foundation (CAF for short) by Sir Brian Jenkins, who had been Chairman for many years. CAF is committed to increasing charitable giving in the UK (and increasingly overseas) through providing tax efficient products and services for individuals, charities and trusts. Now, under the leadership of Lord (Simon) Cairns, CVO and Deputy Chairman Peter Berry, CMG, I was pleased to act as Chairman of its Audit, Risk and Compliance Committee and to involve CAF's executive team in fund raising discussions in Mansion House, led by Tony Rogers, CAF's former Finance Director and Acting Chief Executive.

MORDEN COLLEGE

I couldn't possibly finish this chapter without a word about Morden College. Over the years, London has produced some great benefactors. Sir John Morden was one.

Born in London in 1623 and baptised at St Bride's Fleet Street, John Morden was an English merchant who traded with Turkey and, allegedly, after his ships went missing, worked as a butcher and was lodged in a poor house. The ships returned to England and, thanking God, he vowed that he would build an asylum for 'decayed merchants' so that none would have to endure what he had. He acquired 250 acres of land in the area of Greenwich and had Morden College built in 1700 in Blackheath, to house 40 single or widowed men. It was designed as a home for 'poor Merchants ... and such as have lost their Estates by accidents, dangers and perils of the seas or by other accidents ways or means in their honest endeavours to get their living by means of Merchandizing'. College trustees were drawn from the Turkey Company, then the East India Company and now the Court of Aldermen. Today, the College is home to 330 elderly people, of both sexes, who have to prove a certain amount of hardship and limited income. It is a very happy place. Its trustees are Aldermen, or former Aldermen, of the City of London – today chaired by Sir Alexander Graham, GBE, Lord Mayor in 1990, with a first-class Clerk to the Trustees and Chief Executive, Sir Iain Mackay-Dick, KCVO, MBE.

I was fortunate to be asked to be a trustee and, during my Mayoral year, visited Morden College on 16 July 2007 for the annual garden party. In a marquee on the lawn, with the HAC band playing, one could be forgiven for thinking that the clock had been turned back many years. It was such a delight to be there and to see so many happy people.

123 *The Lord Mayor of London in business attire.*

Part VI

THE MODERN ROLE
OF THE LORD MAYOR

The Key Messages –
764 Speeches and 133 Media Interviews

In addition to his work at the head of the City of London Corporation, the Lord Mayor has a much wider business role. This includes representing, supporting and promoting the country's financial and business services industry (referred to as 'The City') both at home and abroad.

The fact that the Lord Mayor's office is of an apolitical nature enhances his position greatly as a trusted spokesman for the business community. With the prospect of hundreds of speeches and media interviews, a lot of work necessarily goes into understanding the business issues and into getting the messages right.

A Period of Preparation

Before my year began, I spent a great deal of time reading, meeting people and preparing. I prepared an overall promotional plan which included the following elements:

- Promoting the financial services industry in the UK and the City of London as the world's leading financial, maritime and business services centre, with access to capital markets, fund management, insurance services, shipping services, legal services, accounting, auditing and business advisory services.
- Promoting London as the only truly international city and a city that welcomes people from all around the world.
- Promoting the UK as the centre of excellence for professional education, training and qualification under the banner 'City of London – City of Learning'. Encouraging cross-border transfers of personnel and extolling the virtues of working in other countries as part of one's career development.
- Promoting the 'Risk' based approach to financial regulation, rather than the 'Rules' based approach that is adopted in other jurisdictions, such as the US.
- Promoting London as a place of high integrity, corporate governance, open access and fair reporting where 'my word is my bond'.

124   Lord Mayor's speech at the Lord Mayor's Banquet on 13 November 2006, with the Prime Minister and the Toastmaster.

157

- Promoting the City of London Corporation's Community Strategy, embracing education and skills based training in the City Fringe, City Academies and CSR.
- Supporting the City Corporation's strategies in the areas of security, transport and the prevention and detection of financial crime.
- Supporting the City Corporation's strategy of protecting the business environment through measures aimed at better regulation and preventing the corporate and fiscal regime in the UK from making 'the City' less attractive and less competitive.
- Encouraging volunteering and charitable giving by companies and individuals working in the City using the Lord Mayor's Appeal 'Sharing Skills, Changing Lives' managed by Voluntary Service Overseas (VSO).
- Encouraging the contribution that the City of London can make to global prosperity and the elimination of poverty through the encouragement of free trade, the removal of trade barriers, sharing of skills and cross border learning.

Using statistics and other information produced by International Financial Services, London (IFSL) and the City of London Corporation's Economic Development Office (EDO), I drafted standard paragraphs that could be inserted into speeches relaying the above key messages. Over the years, I had gathered together around 14 pages of jokes on different subjects. These were then passed to the Lord Mayor's Speechwriter, Bill Beaver, who has the enormous but fascinating task of researching and preparing almost 800 speeches each year, with the help of an assistant – Ruth Smith for the first 10 months, and Lucia Graves for the remaining two months, of my Mayoralty.

THE CORE SPEECH

I have reproduced the core speech, which developed as the year progressed, based on some of the above key messages:

> During the past decade, the City of London, which is the brand name for all UK-based financial services, has become Britain's great success story. With funds managed of over £3.5 trillion, with over 600 foreign companies listed on the London Stock Exchange and with 32 per cent of global currency trading, London is the most international of all the world's financial centres.
>
> Within the City of London, a stunning 90 per cent of the world's trade in metals takes place, 25 per cent of the world's aviation and marine insurance and almost 50 per cent of all ship brokering. And in the ever expanding area of derivatives trading, London has 43 per cent of the Over the Counter market. The London Stock Exchange lists more companies in any one year than the New York Stock Exchange, NASDAQ and Hong Kong combined. Today the UK-based financial sector accounts for 12 per cent of Britain's

GDP and employs over one million people. With a contribution of £20 billion to the UK balance of payments and a staggering quarter of the Treasury's corporate tax take, this industry is hugely important to the EU economy.

It is, in short, a staggering success story. But how did it all happen? 20 years ago, we were all fearful that London might be outflanked by Paris or Frankfurt and we never dreamt that we would outpace New York. 'But Big Bang' in 1986 led to the removal of restrictive practices and a deregulation of the market. Now foreign companies can enter the market freely. Foreign companies can buy anything. Foreign capital and foreign nationals have contributed enormously to the success of the financial sector. Citigroup is now larger in London than they are in New York. Morgan Stanley has shifted its key global roles to London. And foreign nationals are welcomed in the City. Indeed a large proportion of our talented people come from abroad. More than half our workforce is under 30 years of age and they are hard working and innovative. They relish change and they believe that nothing is impossible. These young people from all over the globe add greatly to the success of our financial economy. Some stay in London, but many return, having seen what a truly open economy can do to promote prosperity. So openness of market entry and competition are the prime factors in London's success.

But there are others. First, the fiscal environment. The financial services industry is geographically very mobile. Money can flow from one country another very easily. And the key assets walk out of the office every evening. So, to be attractive, the fiscal environment has to be competitive. And the UK has a particularly generous regime for foreign nationals working in the UK – in that they are not taxed on income arising outside the UK. Then, just recently, corporate tax rates were reduced. But we have to keep an eye on the fiscal environment, to simplify it and to keep it competitive. Then the independence which Gordon Brown gave to the Bank of England ten years ago when he was Chancellor of the Exchequer, with its focus on monetary policy, has also helped to ensure a stable and successful macro-economy.

But one of the most important success factors has been the regulatory environment. Our Government created a single, business-friendly regulator for all financial services: the Financial Services Authority. The FSA does not act like the SEC. Instead, it relies on a principles, risk-based approach. This is very different from the line-by-line rules-based approach, with its box-ticking mentality. The FSA puts the responsibility on companies to manage their own affairs and to regulate their own business. This self-regulation requires companies to identify the risks of entering new business areas and then to manage these risks. This necessitates good corporate governance where the company itself has its own checks and balances via non-executives on the board of directors. Companies that fail rarely do so because of poor internal systems. They usually fail because the wrong strategy has been chosen or because it has been badly implemented. We in the UK have put the emphasis on improving corporate governance rather than on introducing detailed rules. And the better the corporate governance in the business community the less need there is for detailed regulation. The Sarbanes-Oxley legislation in the US was the wrong solution. It was a political reaction to the Enron and WorldCom failures. The UK model, unlike that adopted in the US, reduces the cost to global businesses of complying with detailed onerous regulations, such as Sarbanes-Oxley which has had a demonstrably detrimental effect on New York's competitiveness. The Sarbanes-Oxley legislation did not address the core problem of poor corporate governance, yet it increased the burden of compliance and regulation. By adopting this business-friendly approach, the FSA has given the UK-based financial services a framework within which businesses can innovate and prosper.

And there are many examples of new financial instruments and new areas of business that have been created in London in recent years. First, of course, is the exciting derivatives market. I hardly need to describe these further. But I will draw your attention to forward freight derivatives. These new instruments have been developed by the Baltic Exchange in London and are now being traded by many finance houses. Then secondly there is the fast-growing Islamic banking and insurance market. Many of the products now on sale throughout the Muslim world were invented, developed and marketed from London. Indeed, London has become the centre for Islamic finance, helped enormously by Muslims working in finance houses in London. In fact, they have been essential to its success. Thirdly, London largely invented and is home to the world's largest carbon emissions market and is the global centre for emissions trading. This innovation has happy implications not only for a world needing to wake up to its responsibilities for the planet.

The result of this open market access and the favourable regulatory environment means that foreign financial companies have flocked to London. Today, 20 years after 'Big Bang', roughly fifty per cent of City firms are foreign owned and there are 200,000 professionals from overseas in the UK financial services sector. Almost 50 per cent of office property in the City is owned by foreign financial institutions, with German pension funds owning almost a quarter.

And one of our true success stories is the London Stock Exchange. Because of an encouraging business environment, the LSE adapted to customers' needs; putting in faster electronic trading and bringing more companies to the market. Today the LSE has the most liquid equity market and the largest institutional investor base. It is the most international of all the world's stock exchanges, with over 600 foreign companies listed. And, in 2006, 367 new companies joined the LSE whereas the combined total for NYSE, NASDAQ and Hong Kong SE together was 332. In 2006 $104 billion was raised on the LSE, compared to $69 billion on NYSE and NASDAQ combined. In first half of 2007 this pattern has continued, US$26 billion raised on the LSE. NYSE and NASDAQ raised US$21billion combined. And, in keeping with its international position as the global exchange, the LSE invented a new market to sit alongside its Main Market.

Called the Alternative Investment Market or AIM, it is designed to bring young, growing companies to the attention of global investors. And it has proved very popular. In 2006, for example, there were 341 IPOs on AIM of which 109 were from outside the UK, from 27 countries. In fact, 72 per cent of world's total IPOs in the first half of 2007 went to AIM. And it is very simple and cheap to list on AIM. The regulation of AIM-listed companies is undertaken by the independent nominated advisers, called Nomads, under the supervision of the LSE. The Nomads are responsible for proper, good corporate governance in AIM companies and their proper regulation, not the UK regulator.

Then another key success factor is the physical environment, both security and the physical infrastructure. The City of London Police is an independent Police force which specialises in preventing and detecting financial crime. It has also built up a great reputation for physical security and the prevention of terrorist incidents. If people working in London feel safe and enjoy living and working in an attractive city, then it will attract the best financial executives from around the world. In addition the City of London Corporation has focused on trying to ensure that the office buildings are modern, up to date and fit for purpose.

But the key success factor is people and we are spending a lot of time encouraging business education and the development of professional skills. London has a pool of skills talent which is second to none – and many of our people come from outside the UK. So, please keep coming to London and working in London, as part of your successful career path.

THE PUBLIC RELATIONS FOCUS AND THE MEDIA COVERAGE

As mentioned earlier, I thought that the City of London Corporation's public relations team, headed by Tony Halmos was first class. I developed a particularly good relationship with Greg Williams, Head of Press, who handled, with imagination, all the approaches from the media for stories about the work of the Lord Mayor. He had excellent contacts with journalists and many stories, both amusing and serious, would regularly appear in the *FT* or *Times* or *Telegraph*, as well as periodicals and industry specific magazines. In addition, *CityAM* newspaper ran a weekly Lord Mayor's column. The whole press team at Guildhall was very professional – Lesley Mair, Loretta Lui, Rebecca Sandles and Emma Hutchings.

A number of themes were developed which supported the key messages:
- London is a centre of learning: Dick Whittington – a role model for someone coming to London, as a place of opportunity, to learn, work hard and become successful.
- The role of Lord Mayor is to support and promote the financial sector: Many articles appeared describing my role or reporting a view I expressed about an issue. Articles appeared describing my business background and dealings with Finland and experience in China, all aimed at establishing credentials. There was extensive reporting of my overseas visits, demonstrating the important aspect of this work.

Lord mayor sees UK-listed mainland firms tripling

Old China hand sells London allure

125 *Article in* South China Morning Post.

- The City is a caring place, with volunteering and charitable giving: I wrote, as Lord Mayor, an article for the *FT* just before Christmas entitled 'How we all profit from million dollar bonuses', with the punch line 'At Christmas or any other time it is great to receive – but even better to give'.
- London's success is based on Free Trade and its openness: I was pleased when an article appeared headed 'Mayors disagree over LSE ownership'. It had been reported that Ken Livingstone had argued that any bid for the LSE should be referred to the competition authorities. In contrast to this I said that the nationality of LSE's owners was not a matter for concern.
- London's regulatory environment is better than that in the US: Numerous articles reported my views on risk rather than rules-based regulation. When John Thain, the boss of the New York Stock Exchange, attacked the poor standard of corporate governance for companies listing on AIM, I was pleased to be given the opportunity to respond that 'AIM is a market for grown-ups'. When, later in the year, I was asked about the damage to London's reputation caused by the Northern Rock crisis, I described it as an incident with no depositor having lost any funds. I suggested

126 La Tribune *reports on the Lord Mayor.*

instead that the media should rather focus on the sub-prime crisis across the Atlantic which was of enormous proportions, adversely affecting the whole global economy. Many journalists in foreign newspapers also repeated the message that regulation should be risk-based not rules-based. My favourite headline was in the *Daily Telegraph* on 18 October, after I had given a Press conference in Hong Kong. I had defended our regulatory system and the headline read 'Lord Mayor stands up for City'.

- It is important to get London's transport infrastructure right: The complaints I received about Heathrow gave me the ammunition I needed to have a go at the shabbiness and inefficiency of our main international airport. My speech at Mansion House, when Gordon Brown was my guest, gave me an opportunity and my comments were reported in the Evening Standard as 'people will only do business here if it is easy to use our airports – at present it is not'. Ken Livingstone then picked up the problem of Heathrow and the media and political campaign began.
- The Lord Mayor is a straightforward businessman to whom we can relate: If you wish to be credible with a large audience, you have to come across as a straightforward person with apolitical ideas. Many amusing stories appeared as diary items and CityAM's many readers in the City often expressed their interest in our regular columns there.

As I look back on the Mayoralty, given the key role is to represent, support and promote the financial sector in the UK (the City), I am grateful for the part played by the City of London Corporation's Public Relations Office – to Tony Halmos and colleagues. Thank you. I am enormously grateful.

127 *Another successful ETQ seminar organised by the British Council and chaired by Sir Paul Judge – this time in Shenzhen.*

Part VII

CITY OF LONDON – CITY OF LEARNING

128 *Launch at Mansion House of 'City of London – City of Learning' campaign. Professor David Rhind, CBE, Professor Sir Roderick Floud, Sir Paul Judge and the Lord Mayor flank Ed Balls, the Economic Secretary.*

Come to London to
Learn and Make your Fortune

The concept of coming to London to learn, to work hard and then make one's fortune is not new. In an earlier chapter, I described how Dick Whittington followed this route and was apprenticed to the Mercers' Livery Company.

From early medieval times, Livery companies provided training in the various trades and occupations through an apprenticeship structure. Bakers, butchers, glaziers, goldsmiths, skinners and stationers all protected and enhanced their trades by teaching skills to youngsters who would become the Master craftsmen and Liverymen of the future. Indeed training, as well as charity, is still very much at the heart of the Livery movement.

THE GROWTH OF THE PROFESSIONS IN THE FINANCIAL SECTOR

With the advent of free trade and joint stock companies, the 18th and 19th centuries heralded the development of the newer occupations, such as accountants, actuaries, company secretaries, insurers and surveyors. These 'professions', as they became known, merited special national status. After all, a professional was someone who professed knowledge in a particular department of learning. A professional was also someone who had ethics, including integrity and confidentiality. So they sought 'charter' status and became 'professional institutes'. They were, like the Livery companies, for many years, self-governing. Not only did they establish regulations for training, through a system of articled clerkship, but set the exams and adjudicated the papers. They controlled entry into the profession and, in the case of proven poor quality of work, unethical behaviour or criminal activity, they had disciplinary powers that extended to fines and expulsion of a member from the chartered body.

In recent years, self-regulation has been judged to be too cozy, too protectionist and also anti-competitive. So, beginning in the 1980s, self-regulation began to be complemented by independent watchdogs and independent supervisory bodies, initiated by Central Government. However training, in the form of syllabuses and exam setting, for the professions, is still largely the preserve of the professional bodies, complemented, as well as provided, by the universities and by private sector training providers, some of which have now been awarded degree giving powers.

The UK professional institutes expanded abroad, typically in the 1930s and 1950s, to the former dominions, such as Australia, Canada, India and South Africa, as well as to Hong Kong, Malaysia and Singapore. These offshoots eventually became self-governing and separated from their founding bodies. Today, the qualifications, which are given to successful examinees, of the UK based professional institutes, are very highly regarded, throughout the world. To have the right to use, after your name, the initials ACCA or ACII or FCA or FRICS or ICAS carries with it recognition of a qualification belonging to a professional – and therefore denoting experience and status in a particular field.

TRAINING IN THE FINANCIAL SECTOR

For decades, the main training in the financial sector in the UK was via the professional institutes. Youngsters were 'articled' to a principal. Training was undertaken 'on the job' and exam training was undertaken via correspondence courses. These latter necessitated study papers and questions being sent, by post, to the articled clerk who would answer the questions and return them, again by post, to the tutor organisation for marking and notification back to the articled clerk. It was a very soulless method of learning and didn't provide the opportunity for interface between teacher and pupil. In the 1960s, these correspondence courses were largely replaced by direct tuition, with courses being held at hotels, universities and purpose built training establishments by the new training providers.

In the post-war period, business schools, which had not historically been as popular in the UK as a means of providing business education, began to be established. The London Business School, The Judge Business School at Cambridge and the Cass Business School in the City, among others, were founded to provide an alternative means of training management.

Other universities followed, introducing undergraduate and postgraduate courses in financial disciplines. These universities, as well as the independent training providers, complemented the professional institutes, by teaching the subjects identified by the institutes, who also continued to set the chartered exams.

In this way, the UK developed the most sophisticated and advanced framework for the education of professionals and of executives in the financial sector. Based on comparisons with the provision of education in other countries, the UK became truly a centre of excellence for business education and professional skills development. It was the best in class.

MY OWN INTEREST IN PROFESSIONAL EDUCATION

My own interest in professional education was kindled by the fact that my father had escaped a relatively poor family background by training and qualifying as a chartered accountant and being offered a partnership in his local firm at the tender age of twenty-one.

Clearly he was bright. He had been educated at Burnley Grammar School, which he left at the age of 16, and then worked in an accountancy firm, studying in the evenings and at weekends. On passing the national accountancy exams, he took some further exams to join the RAF, coming top in the country. But an accountancy career in Burnley beckoned and he was very successful at it.

I therefore had a role model, which initially I tried not to emulate. The accountancy profession was furthest from my mind when I left Cambridge with an economics degree. But discussions with prospective employers left me in no doubt that a first degree did not really equip me for a career, so I too studied to become a Chartered Accountant. Training via correspondence courses did not appeal and, after writing a letter published in *Accountancy* in 1968, advocating direct tuition, I followed my own advice and studied at one of the training providers in North Wales. It worked. I came top in the country in one of my exam papers, earning me the grand sum of £5 and being given a piece of paper evidencing my award 'The Deloitte Plender Prize in Bookkeeping and Accounting'. The successful exam result was to help me when it came to being chosen for interesting assignments.

Some of my early career at Coopers & Lybrand in London was spent in the Training Department, preparing training courses and giving lectures on accountancy, auditing and business investigations. I then assisted in the recruitment of graduates from Oxbridge by participating in the 'Milk Round', which in turn led me to be offered a non-executive post as a member of the Cambridge University Appointments Board for four years from 1977 to 1981. The CUAB was the advisory body for the Cambridge University Careers Service, which had realised that almost 10 per cent of Cambridge graduates were applying for jobs in the accountancy profession. They needed help and guidance. I was pleased to be involved and to assist.

Throughout my career as an accountant I continued to be involved in recruitment and training and could see the benefit to the financial function in a company of having someone with that training and experience.

When later, in 1994, I was appointed Chairman and Chief Executive of Coopers & Lybrand (subsequently PricewaterhouseCoopers) in China, it was clear that a key priority was recruitment and training. We started with 50 people in the whole country. By 1999 we had 1,500 – albeit also with the benefit of a merger between C&L and PW. Now some nine years later, the firm has almost 10,000 employees, showing what an ordered education programme can achieve when the raw material (the graduates) is of good quality.

THE WORLDWIDE SHORTAGE OF FINANCIAL PROFESSIONALS

My own experience in China had shown me the huge shortage of accountants that the PRC faced. My discussions with colleagues in other Asian and Eastern European countries confirmed the same shortage – in particular Russia, Hungary, Poland, the Ukraine, Vietnam, Thailand.

When I was Sheriff in 2005/06, I visited China, Mongolia and Saudi Arabia with my predecessor, Sir David Brewer, CMG. The business programme, devised in discussion with the FCO and UKTI, included business education and financial training as one topic and, in Riyadh, I chaired a seminar on this subject on behalf of the Lord Mayor.

The more I discussed this topic, the more I read, the more I began to appreciate the size of the deficiency of professional skills in emerging markets. Yet, these markets were being opened up by investors from the developed world who, by virtue of the scarce human resources, were taking large risks. I had seen it in China, at first hand. On the other hand, these countries could not develop properly without a large cadre of professionals who were properly trained and who had some experience.

I learnt that Vietnam, for example, a country of 90 million people, had only 1,200 qualified accountants.

PROFESSIONALS ARE KEY TO THE DEVELOPMENT OF ANY ECONOMY

The studies commissioned by the Corporation of the City of London had consistently shown that the large pool of professional talent in the London area was a key success factor.

During the post-war decades many bright graduates from British universities had flocked to the City and the professions. In Germany, engineering and manufacturing had been popular. In France, administration in Government was a favoured choice. Thus, London developed a competitive advantage which has served its Financial Sector well.

Education and the acquisition of professional skills are essential to the development of any economy as well as to the well being of its people. The emergence of a financial services industry in a country can only be effective if there is a large base of professionals. Many countries want to become a regional financial centre and cannot achieve this without talented professionals.

LONDON IS THE CENTRE OF EXCELLENCE
FOR A BUSINESS AND PROFESSIONAL EDUCATION

On the other hand, London has developed over the years as the centre of excellence for business education and professional skills development. And, London has benefited from an influx of bright, aspiring young people, who are enthusiastic and imaginative.

For many years, before and after the War, foreign students and foreign graduates flocked to London for training and work experience. De-colonisation and Harold Wilson's 'East of Suez' policy in the 1960s loosened the traditional ties – and the US and Australia became alternative locations for education. Then the removal, in the 1980s, under the Thatcher Government, of free university places for foreign nationals had a further adverse impact.

But a number of factors have combined to make London, and the UK generally, a favoured place for education for UK nationals from regional towns and for foreign nationals.

British qualifications have maintained their standards and enhanced their reputation, compared to some other countries. British qualifications are increasingly seen as flexible and adaptable to customers' needs. For example, it is possible for a foreign national to become a member of the Chartered Institute of Taxation without sitting a UK tax exam. Passing an international tax paper and a local tax paper is seen as sufficient evidence of competence. The Securities & Investment Institute (SII) have been developing an exam in Islamic Finance in collaboration with the Bank of Lebanon. UK student and work visas have been, in many cases, easier to obtain than US visas, particularly post 9/11. London is increasingly seen as the prime international financial centre – the place you have to go to and get experience if you want a successful career in the Financial Sector. Finally, the UK is a very welcoming place for foreigners – with very many foreign languages spoken and with restaurants serving delicious dishes from all around the world.

The City of London had, indeed, become the City of Learning. But as I approached my Mayoral year, I realised that not everyone overseas knew this. In addition, it seemed to me that there was a window of opportunity. The emerging countries wanted professional training now. And if we didn't provide it, then someone else would.

Preparation for the Campaign

International Financial Services, London (IFSL) exists to promote the UK-based Financial Services Industry. Funded significantly by UKTI and the City of London Corporation, it also has members from the Financial Sector who provide funds and participate in events and overseas delegations, led by the Lord Mayor.

For some time, IFSL had an Education, Training and Qualifications ('ETQ') Working Group, chaired by Sir David Howard Bt, a former Lord Mayor. This group recognised the importance of training and new hires to the Financial Sector and to London. The group had also recognised the importance of the Mayoral overseas visits programme as a vehicle for promoting the City as a place for education and employment opportunity.

Rather than re-invent the wheel, I drafted a position paper in January 2006, suggesting that a significant element of the Mayoral overseas visits programme in my year should comprise promoting 'The UK as an international centre of excellence to be educated, trained and obtain a professional qualification', I recommended working with the professional institutes, the key universities with business schools, the British Council, UKTI and the other NGOs such as the Financial Services Skills Council. This was blessed by Sir David Howard, with the encouragement of Edward Whitley, IFSL's Chief Executive.

Together with Brian Davidson, IFSL's Deputy Chief Executive, on secondment from the Foreign Office, I embarked on a series of meetings with the various organisations:

- The universities offering financial and management training: City University, including the Cass Business School, London Business School, London Metropolitan University, Leeds Business School, London School of Economics, Reading University International Management Studies Centre.
- The professional institutes: ACCA, Association of Corporate Treasurers, Chartered Institute of Actuaries, Chartered Institute of Management Accountants, Chartered Institute of Taxation, Chartered Insurance Institute, ICAEW, Institute of Financial Services, Law Society, Securities and Investment Institute, The Bar Council.
- The private training providers: BPP, Emile Woolf, Financial Training, 7-City Learning.
- The sponsors and NGOs: The British Council, EDO of the City of London Corporation, The Financial Services Skills Council, The Treasury, UKTI.

The results were very positive. Most had recognised the overseas opportunity. Some, for example ACCA, had actively pursued it over many years. But others were struggling. Almost all were keen to participate in some programme to promote their expertise and to exploit the opportunity.

As with the Lord Mayor's Appeal, I knew that once I became Lord Mayor I could not direct or manage this programme myself. While the British Council were enthusiastic, as were the educational establishments, it needed a driver. Fortunately Sir Paul Judge, who had already agreed to chair the Lord Mayor's Appeal, said that he would also lead the international education programme to promote the UK as a centre for education, training and qualifications. Paul came up with the slogan 'City of London – City of Learning' which we then took around the world.

We identified 13 areas that make up a successful financial services centre and where London could offer real educational expertise:
- Accountancy
- Actuarial
- Asset Management
- Banking
- Dispute Resolution
- English for Financial Services
- Financial Trading
- Insurance
- Law
- Management
- Marketing
- Property
- Shipping

We then brought together the professional institutes, the business schools, the private training providers and the appropriate modern Livery companies to provide a huge base of expertise.

The rest of the summer and autumn was spent preparing for the promotional programme during my Mayoral year. Regrettably, Brian Davidson returned to the Foreign Office and went to brush up his Mandarin before being posted to Guangzhou. IFSL's future had been in some doubt and attracting senior quality staff was not easy. We therefore found ourselves in a situation where there was a shortage of competent resource to prepare and undertake the programme which the overseas countries clearly desperately needed and the UK providers were keen to promote. The City Corporation's EDO helped to the extent that they could but they were short staffed as well. The Treasury had expressed enthusiasm and Gordon Brown and Ed Balls were supportive, but we lacked an ongoing executive team to carry this forward. With a certain amount of pushing, on the part of Paul and me, and with the consistent help of some stalwarts such as David Rhind from City University, Gordon Slaven from the British Council, Simon Culhane from the Securities & Investment Institute and Professor Sir Roderick Floud, as well as help from the Treasury, UKTI, EDO and IFSL, a programme was put together.

129 *The ETQ Steering Group – left to right: Gordon Slaven, Sir Paul Judge, John Stuttard, Professor David Rhind, CBE and Professor Sir Roderick Floud (not present in photo).*

The Launch of the ETQ Campaign

The programme comprised a number of elements:

- A fact sheet produced by the Corporation of the City of London
- A website, superbly produced by the British Council
- A 'City of Learning' DVD produced by UKTI
- An updated publication by IFSL on the professions in the UK
- A booklet prepared by the Financial Reporting Council on Corporate Governance
- A presentation describing the City's strengths as a centre of excellence for business education and professional skills development
- Assistance from the Livery companies that represented the modern professions
- Seminars on the Mayoral overseas visits programme to around 20 countries, organised jointly by IFSL and the British Council
- A formal launch on 14 November involving the Economic Secretary, Ed Balls, whom we knew to be keen on the development of skills.

130 *Ed Balls, Economic Secretary to the Treasury, with the Lord Mayor.*

Sir Paul Judge had taken over in the driving seat – and he drove. We agreed that the main ETQ opportunities for the City were outside the European Union and Paul therefore accompanied me to all of the 14 non-EU countries I visited (excluding Ghana which was more for VSO) and chaired 23 'City of London – City of Learning' seminars we held in those countries.

The official launch took place on 14 November 2006 at Mansion House with around 180 participants. The Minister was enthusiastic and spoke of the quality of British regulation and the development of Islamic financial instruments in London. In my speech I spoke about the importance of education and of attracting young people to London:

> If the availability of skilled personnel is our key success factor, then it is important that we keep the supply going by promoting the UK even more as the centre for a business education and a professional qualification. Although London's reputation in professional education and skills draws many, it could attract many more – to the huge benefit of the City as well as to the young people – and the training providers.
>
> So, training in business education and providing professional qualifications represent together an important export opportunity for the UK's business educational establishment and its professional institutes. This is the first time that the leading players in the industry have come together to make a global impact.
>
> The campaign involves City-related UK professional institutes, key university business schools and training providers that offer post-graduate and professional qualifications in financial, maritime and business services, both in the UK and overseas.
>
> It gives me great pleasure to launch formally my promotional campaign for the year: 'City of London – City of Learning'. We have an exciting programme for the year ahead. We are aiming to develop a programme of promotional activity, complementing the existing activities of each organisation involved, to help make the UK's business education and professional qualifications a global 'Gold Standard' that all will aspire to.

We were up and running, with plenty of enthusiasm from Mansion House, UKTI and the British Council, alongside those who would benefit – the universities and the professional institutes.

Promotion Abroad

The campaign began with a seminar in Kuwait in December involving the Cass Business School, ACCA and the British Council, who organised the event and who did a simply fantastic job throughout the year. Sir David Green, the former Director-General of the British Council, had expressed support for the initiative. He appreciated the strengths of the UK's post tertiary sector of education and he knew that while the British Council did not currently operate very strongly in this sector, it was an opportunity for the future. His successor, Martin Davidson, CBE, whom I had first met in Beijing, thought the same way. The British Council was founded to promote British culture and education and this was one area where the UK excelled and where we could legitimately promote a strength that would have great benefits to emerging countries.

This also fitted in with the Treasury aim of assisting emerging countries in an effort to reduce global poverty. The UKTI understood that British business and professional education was an export opportunity of the future, something which Gordon Brown emphasised to me on more than one occasion during my Mayoral year.

Seminars and roundtables then followed in almost every country and city that I visited during the year: Qatar, Karachi, Lahore, Dubai, Accra, Almaty, Astana, Moscow, St Petersburg (the best attended), Chongqing, Guangzhou, Shenzhen, Hanoi, Ho Chi Minh City, Kuala Lumpur, Helsinki, Delhi, Kolkata, Mumbai, Warsaw, Sao Paulo, Rio de Janeiro, Mexico City, Johannesburg, Cape Town, Nanjing, Shanghai, Hong Kong, Beijing and Tianjin. In total, there were thirty.

In addition, I spoke at many dinners, seminars and conferences in London for the key training providers and visited City University, Cass Business School, London Metropolitan and the professional institutes to promote the programme.

The British Council did a great job organising most of the overseas seminars, with input from IFSL in London. But the real star of the ETQ programme was the chairman, Sir Paul Judge. He literally drove it right from the beginning, and showing great public service. He paid personally for his own air fares and hotel accommodation in order to chair the events in each city we visited. In an era where senior people try to take full advantage of perks and privileges, it was refreshing to see someone with such a big public heart. It was therefore a great pleasure when Paul decided to stand for election as an Alderman, in the vacant ward of Tower, and was duly elected in July 2007. Thank you, Paul, for your contribution to the ETQ programme in 2006-07. Without you, it wouldn't have been the success that it was.

ACHIEVEMENTS

There is no doubt that the profile of the UK, as a place to study for a business education or professional qualification, was enhanced as a result of the campaign. The contacts with many Governments and overseas universities was increased and the media coverage significant. MOUs were signed for Cass Business School and SII in Abu Dhabi, Dubai, Mumbai and Shanghai. In a number of places (Qatar, Chongqing, Shenzhen, Astana, Tianjin) there were requests for assistance to develop a financial training centre and these are now being progressed. But, perhaps most important, Government and the British Council appreciated the benefits of promoting the 'City of London as a City of Learning'. If there is a single legacy from my Mayoralty, this might be it.

131 *The Lord Mayor has an audience with the Vietnamese Prime Minister, Nguyen Tan Dung.*

Part VIII

PROMOTING THE
CITY OF LONDON ABROAD

132   *Exchange of gifts with Shanghai Vice Mayor, Tang Dengjie.*

Promoting the City of London Abroad

As described above, the content of the Lord Mayor's role has changed, as the businesses of the City have become more global in nature and as international travel has been made easier.

WORKING OUT THE PROGRAMME OF OVERSEAS VISITS

In preparation for each Mayoral year, Kay Brock, as Private Secretary and Chief of Staff at Mansion House, writes to the leaders of the City's businesses. She asks them to name those countries which they consider a priority for a Mayoral overseas visit, from the point of view of their businesses, and to specify areas of business which might be promoted and also to describe issues which should be discussed. In parallel, the Foreign & Commonwealth Office (FCO) and the UK Trade & Investment (UKTI) gather information, both locally and in the UK, and make their own recommendations as to countries which the next Lord Mayor might visit. There then follows a period of iteration when views are exchanged, also involving the City of London Corporation's Economic Development Office (EDO), prior to a meeting of the Lord Mayor's Visits Advisory Committee (MVAC), chaired by a former Lord Mayor (in my year, Sir David Howard Bt), on which all the above parties are represented. MVAC makes the final determination of the countries to be visited. The views of the City's businesses are paramount since the Mayoral visits are ultimately for their benefit and they provide the business delegations and the speakers at seminars. But the views of the FCO and UKTI are also most important since they act as the hosts in each country and administer the programmes. Further they will ensure that visits are carefully timed so as not to clash with the travel plans of other Ministers. When travelling abroad, the Lord Mayor has Cabinet Minister status and this can be very helpful when accessing the right people at a senior level. Consideration is given to countries where the future Lord Mayor has experience or special relationships. In my case, I was pleased that Finland and Denmark were included and that it was agreed that I should make two visits to China – all countries in which I have worked and for which I had responsibilities while a partner in PwC.

At MVAC, it was decided that I should visit 23 countries and the budget for this was duly approved. In the event, one country was added later – Mexico, after the new President invited me to visit his country – during a dinner I hosted for him at Mansion House. Another was taken off the list – Lebanon, after it proved impossible to make this visit, despite two separate attempts, because of security considerations. In total I was to spend over 100 nights outside the UK – quite a time commitment.

Each visit required a huge amount of work. First the dates had to be agreed between Jonathan Nethersole, Mansion House Overseas Visits Officer, on secondment from the FCO, and the Foreign Office posts and the UKTI. National holidays, and dates when Ministers might be away, had to be avoided. This could always cause confusion if the individual dealing with this question at the other end was new to the country. Then one of Mansion House programme managers was assigned to plan the visit in detail, in discussion with the FCO and UKTI, and with the business community in the City. I had spent many years at PricewaterhouseCoopers (PwC) organising visits, conferences and seminars in foreign countries. Topics for focus change. For example, regulation of the Financial Sector, carbon emissions trading, climate change issues and Islamic finance were not on the agenda five years ago. On the other hand, Stock Exchange listings and Public Private Partnerships (PPP) are as current now as they were 10 years ago. The businesses in the City need to be consulted as to the important topics for a Mayoral visit. This year, I had added Education, Training and Qualifications (ETQ) as a topic in order to promote London as the centre for business education and professional skills development. The planning of the overseas visits has to be fitted in with the other events, namely the State Banquets, key church services, Livery lunches and dinners, school speech days and the other annual programmes of events and meetings. As a result, Neil Chrimes (the senior programme manager, ex FCO), Lt Colonel Richard Martin (the City's Swordbearer) and Colonel Billy King-Harman, CBE (the City Marshal) all had their work cut out. It is, like the Lord Mayor's role, a 24/7 job.

THE INWARD VISITORS

But my involvement with foreign countries was also as great in the UK as abroad. During my year, a large number (I counted over 100) senior visitors and foreign ambassadors came to see me at Mansion House.

One of my first guests was President Nazarbayev of Kazakhstan for whom a conference was organised, prior to a lunch in the Private Dining Room, in November 2006. This contact with His Excellency in London was an excellent way of developing relations with him and this important fast growing country, as well as ensuring a very warm welcome when I was later to visit him, in March 2007, at his new Palace in Astana.

Then in January 2007, at the suggestion of the Foreign Office, I entertained the newly elected President of Mexico, Felipe Calderon, for a Sunday evening dinner in the Private Dining Room. He wanted to pursue a policy of economic liberalisation and reform in the country, with greater involvement by the private sector. And he promoted the development of trade and investment with other countries, with the strap line 'More of the world in Mexico and more of Mexico in the world'. He was keen that I should visit Mexico with a business delegation and this was duly arranged for September 2007.

Another notable engagement was a lunch for the Mayor of Beijing, Wang Qishan, to whom we gave the Freedom of the City of London in a traditional ceremony in Mansion House. Presided over by the City Remembrancer, Paul Double, the ceremony required the new Freeman to promise to obey the Lord Mayor and to inform him of any wrongdoings or conspiracies, which caused the Mayor to laugh when this was translated into Mandarin. We were later to visit Mayor Wang in Beijing in October 2007 shortly after his promotion to the Politburo had been announced – cause for another smile.

Much later in the year, on 7 November, the President of the Czech Republic His Excellency Vaclav Klaus, came for lunch, as part of a visit to the UK prior to his country taking on the Presidency of the European Union. He expressed strong views on the subject of climate change, denying its harmful effects, and was opposed to the large bureaucratic structures that had been created in Brussels. Having said that, he is pro the EU and very pro British. I rather liked him for his bluntness although I wasn't convinced about his denial of climate change.

Berlin (23 & 24 November 2006)

It has become the custom in recent years for the Lord Mayor, together with the Chairman of Policy & Resources (P&R) Committee of the City Corporation, to visit those countries about to take on the Presidency of the European Union. This affords the opportunity of exchanging views on any measures emanating from Brussels or draft directives that might have an impact on the Financial Sector in the UK. As it turned out, my first foreign visit was to Berlin, with Michael Snyder, the then P&R Chairman, before Germany assumed the EU Presidency on 1 January 2007. Michael and I were joined by Andre Villeneuve, Chairman of LIFFE and of the City Corporation's EU Advisory Group. There we strenuously defended the principles, risk-based approach to regulation against the natural instinct of the German politician or bureaucrat to prefer hard and fast rules. We were much troubled, during our visit, to hear the comments made about hedge funds, following the

133 Andre Villeneuve, Chairman LIFFE, with the Lord Mayor.

remarks of a German politician who had compared them to 'locusts', although we were relieved that the Chancellor's adviser did not agree with pressures for more regulation at EU level. We spoke about the need to ensure a continuing spirit of openness and free competition, in the light of increasing nationalist pressures in certain European countries to protect domestic industries. As with each of my overseas visits I was impressed with the quality of the briefings from the FCO and the UKTI. In Berlin, the British Ambassador, Sir Peter Torry, spoke about the need for reforms in Germany and for greater labour flexibility. At a breakfast with Roland Koch, the Prime Minister of Hesse, where Frankfurt is situated, we were delighted to hear him praise London as 'Europe's Financial Centre'. However, he emphasised a belief, widely held in Germany, that German institutions such as Deutsche Börse should be owned by Germans. In response to this I emphasised that opening up the market in the City of London to foreigners, following Big Bang in 1986, was a key factor in the City's success. But, in Germany, this was not a message that everyone wanted to hear. The German Banking Association gave us greater hope and I was impressed with their views on the desirability of open access and competition in Europe. The Chief Executive Officer, Dr Manfred Weber, was the first person to raise with me the issue of greater transparency and rating of prime mortgage loans – something that would, in 2007, come to haunt a number of banks. At the time I was impressed, and even more so, with hindsight. Germans are naturally cautious.

KUWAIT (17 TO 19 DECEMBER 2006)

Since Fridays are holy days in Islamic countries, they tend to work on Sundays. This is of great benefit to busy Mayoral diaries in that it is therefore possible to travel on a Saturday and start working again the following day. Thus the Mayoralty really does become a 24/7 job and more engagements can be crammed in.

The UK has a special relationship with Kuwait, not least because of the role we played in the First Gulf War. We helped, together with the United States, to remove Saddam Hussein's Army from the country. But we also made unique arrangements for Kuwaiti émigrés to carry on business in London through special banking arrangements.

134 *The Lady Mayoress welcomes Eid Al-Rasheedi, President of the Kuwait Investment Office.*

The friendship that resulted from this, and the sense of gratitude, became evident to me every time I met His Excellency Mr Khaled Al-Duwaisan, GCVO, the Kuwaiti Ambassador to the United Kingdom and also the Doyen of the Diplomatic Corps. He became a good friend. This close relationship was reinforced by subsequent meetings with Eid Al-Rasheedi, President of the

Kuwait Investment Office (KIO), part of the Kuwait Investment Authority (KIA) which has had a presence in London since 1953, with the aim of investing surplus oil revenues to reduce the reliance of Kuwait on its finite oil resource. Both dignitaries were charming and keen to ensure good relations between our two countries. They came together to see me, prior to my visit to Kuwait, to emphasise this. The KIO is one of the most important Sovereign Wealth Funds operating in London and has brought much business and benefit to the City over the last 50 years.

Escaping a cold London December is compensation for working on a Sunday in the warmer climate of the Gulf and we received another excellent briefing on arrival from the British Ambassador, His Excellency Stuart Laing. My business delegation included the indomitable Lord (Charles) Denman, who has been treading the boards in the Gulf for over 50 years and is now in his 90s, and representatives of Standard Chartered (Sir Tom Harris), HSBC (Michael Hodges), Cass Business School (Hassan Hakimian) and United Insurance Brokers (Bassem Kabban). I had met Charles in interesting circumstances the previous year when, as Sheriff, I accompanied Sir David Brewer on his Mayoral visit to Saudi Arabia. After checking into a hotel in Jeddah, I went to my room to find Charles asleep on the bed. From then on, arriving anywhere, I would always confirm that the number of his hotel room was not the same as mine.

This became a running gag every time Charles and I met. I was reminded of it when explaining to business audiences at the beginning of an overseas visit that my name was not Ken Livingstone. I would add that 'he's the one with the bendy buses that block London's roads and he said recently that he would rather share a bed with President Chavez than President Bush. Frankly I wouldn't like to sleep with either of them'.

Regrettably my meetings with the Kuwaiti Prime Minister and the Finance Minister were cancelled due to a Government crisis, brought about by MPs demanding that loans from local banks to Kuwaitis should be waived. This had apparently happened after the Gulf War. So there was a precedent and it had become a political issue again. However, my meetings with the Kuwaiti Stock Exchange and the Governor of the Central Bank showed me how close London and Kuwait are in terms of our respective views on the regulatory environment and on open market access. This gave me the opportunity to raise the issue of licences for international banks and for international lawyers in Kuwait. I asked for greater freedom for them to establish operations.

A Roundtable with the Young Presidents Organisation, comprising up and coming businessmen, revealed a frustration at the political process in Kuwait which slowed things down and I heard the comment 'paying the price of democracy' – a statement expressed in many emerging countries that I visited during my year. We also used this roundtable to discuss climate change and emphasise London's role as a centre for trading in carbon credits. We discussed the possibility of British-Kuwaiti joint ventures in carbon capture and carbon trading.

All agreed that London was a welcoming place to work and live. All agreed that this had helped the City become the centre for Middle Eastern investment. This welcoming attitude was questioned later in 2007 after the Chancellor announced plans to tax non-doms.

A feature of overseas Mayoral visits is the police motor cycle escort that ensures one is driven fast across town and arrives on time. Another feature is the extent of security, particularly for senior foreign visitors. That night in my hotel I had two minders, one of whom slept in a chair outside my door. I felt very safe.

The first of our 'City of London – City of Learning' seminars, promoting London as a centre for business education, took place in Kuwait, well organised by Jo Maher of the British Council. We dubbed this initiative ETQ (Education, Training and Qualifications). Chaired by Sir Paul Judge the ETQ seminar involved Stephen Shields of ACCA, the accountancy body which has done such a great job in exporting its qualification all around the world.

During our visit to Kuwait we heard our first complaints about London as a place for foreigners to visit. In most respects, London is considered to have many advantages. It is very welcoming and has become the world's international financial centre. But there were a few serious gripes. Chief among these was the tight security at Heathrow, particularly the one hand bag policy that affected not just those leaving London but also those in transit. The point was made that Kuwaitis on their way to the US or other European destinations were now seeking to avoid Heathrow. On my return to London, I communicated this to Ed Balls, the Financial Secretary to the Treasury, and was pleased to see that this issue was addressed during 2007 at Heathrow, but not yet at all airports, and therefore not yet fully resolved.

The second complaint was our transport system – with a strong plea for Cross Rail to be built. Again, after further communication and discussions with the Treasury, we were pleased when the Prime Minister made an announcement in October 2007 that Cross Rail had been given the go-ahead.

Despite these observations, made during our visit in the spirit of friendship and cooperation, I learnt from the KIA that they regard London as their global office and that their investment in the UK is disproportionately larger than our share of global GDP. Still further they appreciate the skills that exist in London when investing in emerging markets such as China, India, Indonesia, Pakistan, Turkey, Egypt and Morocco.

On our overseas visits, rarely did we have time for sightseeing, but a meeting at the Arab Fund Building afforded the opportunity to look round this stunning testament to Muslim architecture, with each room dedicated to a particular Arab nation and its design style. We were also pleased to be entertained by the Kuwait British Friendship Society at the home of Mohammed Naki and his Finnish wife, Tulla. We were very surprised, on arrival at their home, to be greeted by a Kuwaiti attendant, dressed as Father Christmas, in the courtyard lit with fairy lights. But, given the time of the year and the Finnish influence, perhaps it shouldn't have been so surprising. It certainly demonstrated the multiracial tolerance that exists in Kuwait, as well as their friendship. The next time we were to see Mohammed and Tulla was at the British Ambassador's Residence in Helsinki during my visit to Finland in May.

Our visit to Kuwait finished with a Press conference and a reception at the British Ambassador's Residence. A very successful three days, with existing friendships enhanced and new friends gained.

GHANA (20 TO 24 JANUARY 2007)

In 1957, the Gold Coast was the first British colony in Africa to gain its independence, changing its name to the Republic of Ghana. Ever since the Ashanti Wars of the 19th century, the British have had enormous respect for the Ghanaian people. Monotheist, Ghanaians took to Christianity when it first arrived with the missionaries. Today, Ghana ranks as one of the most democratic and stable countries in Africa, After South Africa, it is considered to be the second least corrupt country on the sub continent. It has produced great leaders such as Kofi Annan, the former Secretary-General of the United Nations, and John Kufuor, the present President of Ghana and in 2007/08 Chairman of the African Union. Its economy is growing, and this growth is sustained, with significant exports of gold, bauxite, cocoa and tropical fruits. And it is becoming a regional financial centre.

On some overseas visits, where it is convenient and where there is sufficient accommodation, the core of the Mayoral Party stays at the British Residence. On this occasion, Lesley and I were fortunate enough to stay with the High Commissioner, Gordon Wetherell, and his wife Rosie. With previous postings to Chad and Ethiopia, they knew and loved Africa. Built in the 1950s, the functional residence in Accra was full of African statues, masks and other carvings, including Ethiopian crosses. The garden was lush and tropical.

The other house guests included Neil Chrimes, the newly recruited Mansion House programmer responsible for the Ghana visit; Charles & Nicky Sinclair (Charles was a VSO volunteer in Ghana in the 1960s and is Chairman of VSO's 50th Anniversary Appeal); and Gerry & June Pulman (Gerry was the City of London Corporation's Chief Commoner).

After travelling from London on a Saturday (to optimise the Mayoral diary), Sunday could be spent getting to know the country a little and also visiting a project run by VSO, the manager of my Lord Mayor's Charitable Appeal and the main beneficiary. VSO had chosen Ghana as the focus of my initial overseas engagement with the charity, not least because of its importance. VSO had 54 volunteers in the country on an ongoing basis. Mark Goldring (VSO's Chief Executive), and Anne-Marie Jubber (Manager of the Lord Mayor's Appeal) had flown to Ghana to accompany me on my visit but also to see for themselves the good work that VSO was doing in Ghana and to review progress. We were accompanied by two other VSO staff from London (Rebecca Lloyd and Ben Langdon, who took some excellent photos) and the dedicated Ghana country director, Ibrahim

135 Anne-Marie Jubber, Director of the Lord Mayor's Appeal, shows how to do it during a visit to a village in Ghana, hosted by VSO.

Tanko. First stop a school at Elmina on the coast, near where African slaves were exported in former times, to meet a group of senior VSO staff who had developed a National Volunteer Programme. In just four years, they had increased the number of volunteers in teaching posts in Ghana from just 53 to 8,500, at an annual cost (for the volunteer directors) of just £68,000 – an amazing return and a great role model for the rest of Africa, indeed for the rest of the world.

But Elmina is renowned for something far more sinister. St George's Castle, built by the Portuguese in 1482 and captured by the Dutch in the 16th century, became a holding venue for slaves being transported from the interior to America and the West Indies. The fort was capable of accommodating about 500 slaves at any one time, in awful conditions in two large rooms – one for men and one for women. There was then a corridor, which became narrower, leading to the exit from which they were taken, shackled, in single file across the beach to board the awaiting ships. In the year in which we commemorated the 200th anniversary of the abolition of slave trade in the British Empire, it was a humbling and moving experience to visit St George's Castle.

Each year, it is customary for the Chief Commoner (an elected Councilman) of the City of London to accompany the Lord Mayor on an overseas visit. Gerry and June Pulman had joined us on our trip to Ghana, not least because Gerry would be the Chairman of the Reception Committee to plan the State Banquet for President Kufuor's State visit to London in March. Monday 22 January was to be Gerry and June's day, where he was promoted from being a simple 'Chief Commoner' to 'Paramount Chief Commoner', as will become apparent.

In Africa, when travelling from one place to another, one always starts early, just after sunrise, to avoid the heat of the midday. Monday 22 January was no exception and we travelled in 4x4s (Land Rovers of course) from Accra to the region around Ho, up country, quite fast. Dusty red African earth with strip development, shops selling functional wooden furniture, iron gates and garden ornaments were interspersed with truck stops and Police checks. What struck us most were the schoolchildren, neatly dressed in their uniforms – yellow, fawn or pink shirts and brown shorts or skirts. But there was something else – the imaginative signs that heralded some service that could be provided en route:

- Daddy's Comfort Lounge
- Light in the Tunnel Children's Home
- Lighthouse Chapel
- Tinkabell Development School
- God's Finger Farmacy [*sic*]
- Rosary Radiator Specialist
- 'The Lord is able' Fitting Centre
- 'One for the Road' Pantomime Bar
- Blessed Assurance Insurance Brokers

We caught a glimpse of different cultures and religions living in harmony with each other – a chapel on one side of the street, a mosque on the other. We were enchanted by Ghana and its seemingly peaceful way of life.

After a coffee stop at the *Akosombo Hotel* on the Volta River, we arrived at our first destination – a village called Anyirawase – and were met by a volunteer, Elaine Marrey, and her boss from the Department of Social Works, Larry Bissabe. There we were to experience one of our most amazing events of my Mayoralty. For those of you old enough to remember the film *Sanders of the River*, starring Leslie Banks and Paul Robeson, this was it – but without the colonial overlay. Togbega Addai Kwasi Sekpe XII, the Togbe or Paramount Chief, sat on the edge of a circle of villagers in a golden throne, wearing gold rings around his arms, a gold chain around his neck and plenty of gold filigree. Around the circle was an amazing kaleidoscope of village life – the local choir singing in close harmony, swaying from side to side as, I imagine, the best Gospel choirs sway in Louisiana; the disabled folk, showing that they too could join in anything; the older women, the decision makers, anticipating respect from any visitor; and the children, loving it all and picking their noses as they watched the proceedings.

The Paramount Chief began with a formal speech of welcome. Thrust in the centre of the circle, I responded, beginning with the words 'Togbewo and Mamawo' (Chiefs and Queens). I continued, 'it is a great pleasure to come to the village to commemorate the 50th anniversary of Ghanaian independence'. I explained the purpose of our visit and thanked him for his welcome. And, then, when introducing Gerry Pulman, I referred to him as the 'Paramount Chief Commoner'. And it stuck. Thereafter, Gerry was the Paramount Chief Commoner.

It was a magical ceremony, involving wine being poured on the ground in front of us, as a libation. Gifts were exchanged and then, as suddenly as we had arrived, we were off to the next event, another village in the Ho Region.

VSO had been working in this area for some time. There were agricultural projects, involving disabled people, whom we met. We listened to their achievements. I turned to one amputee and told him what a great job he was doing – he burst into tears. Being Lord Mayor is not just about promoting the UK's Financial Sector.

136 *The Lord Mayor on a visit to a village in Ghana with VSO.*

When we arrived at Ho to see the Minister for the Volta Region, the Hon Kofi Dzamesi, we were met by a barrage of cameras, including TV Africa and National TV. Gifts were exchanged but not before I had advocated spending the five per cent mandated by Central Government for disabled people on community projects. The VSO project in Ho was supported by VSO volunteers Gerry and Moira McGeoch. He is a retired banker from Scotland, now working with VOLPHIG (Volta Physically Challenged Independent Group) which supports 1,500 disabled people. At the centre in Ho, Gerry and his wife attracted disabled folk, many of whom had been begging on the streets, and interested them in taking on a challenge looking after themselves – sewing, designing websites or making food for schoolchildren. It was heartrending to be presented with a walking stick by Godsway, a severely disabled seven year old girl, and then to speak to Emmanuel, a double amputee who was helping other disabled men and women at the VOLPHIG centre. We decided to make a donation out of Mansion House Charitable Fund to the project.

Back in Accra, further meetings took place with VSO volunteers involved in business enterprise initiatives and then, for me, a plane ride to Kumasi, organised by Andrew Holmes, Managing Director of Taysec, part of Taylor Woodrow, to meet the Asantehene, the King of the Ashanti. It was a small plane, a twin prop, accommodating just six people for the 40 minute journey to the capital of the Ashanti Region. The welcome on the runway was also something from the past – the son of a previous Asantehene met me, with the head of protocol carrying an enormous black and white umbrella. The convoy of official cars took us swiftly to the Palace where we were ushered into a large audience hall, filled with paramount chiefs in colourful national dress. The Asantahene entered the hall. Accompanied by bearers and umbrellas, he was festooned with gold filigree armlets, bracelets, necklets, a splendid crown and rings with a lizard on each. He sat down at one end of the room on a huge chair, that I assumed to be the Golden Stool, the fabled throne of the great king of the Ashanti nation. He was every inch a king. Heads were bowed as the audience began. I was told beforehand that I must not address any remarks directly to the king but converse with a linguist, placed opposite me. This I did. Question, from the linguist: 'Why had I come?' Answer:

137 *Audience with the Asantehene in Kumasi, Ghana.*

'To pay my respects to the King of the Ashanti, whose bravery is legendary, on the occasion of the 50th anniversary of the country's independence'. This dialogue continued for some minutes. But then an unexpected development. The present Asantehene is Otumfuo Nana Osei Tutu II. Educated at North London Poly and having worked for a while at Brent Council, he later received an honorary doctorate of philosophy at London Metropolitan University. He had no desire to remain silent, regardless of protocol. 'Now I want to say something' he began. The ice was broken and we had a most enjoyable discussion, followed by lunch at his palace. After lunch, the High Commissioner judged correctly that it was time to return to Accra and approached the seated king with the request 'Your Majesty, may I take your leave to return by plane to Accra with the Lord Mayor?' The answer was swift and clear 'No. I want the Lord Mayor to have tea with me in my drawing room'. Gifts were exchanged and the king and I took tea before being whisked back to Accra for the business programme to commence. I was interested to learn, in discussion, that both the Asantehene and the President of Ghana are keen masons and that masonry is extremely popular in Ghana – a mixture of religious symbolism, community spirit and charity that has waned in the UK in recent decades.

Education, training and qualifications were at the centre of my visit which was timed to coincide with the launch of the British Council's 'Management Express Programme', driving home again the importance of skilled personnel in the financial services sector. This message was also at the heart of the Ghana launch of my ETQ initiative and I hope this will enable the FCO and the British Council to build on the already substantial base the UK has in Ghana as the (sought after) source of qualifications in such areas as accountancy. I was also able to launch (with representatives of the two Universities) the England – Africa partnership initiative between the University of East London and the University of Ghana, which resulted from the visit of Minister Bill Rammell to Accra the previous July. This latter demonstrates the benefits of the FCO coordinating successive visits to a country by Ministers and Lord Mayors.

On the financial services front, I visited the Ghana Stock Exchange, which provided an opportunity to underline the importance of a risk based, principles based regulatory framework, good governance and, above all, skilled people. The visit to the Stock Exchange was followed by a financial services roundtable, involving a wider group of managing directors and also Ann Grant, a Vice Chairman of Standard Chartered and a former British High Commissioner to South Africa. We gained a very positive impression of the potential development of Accra as a regional financial centre.

But the highlight of the visit was meeting the President, John Kufuor, for an audience at his Palace and then at a Reception he held in the grounds of his Palace to welcome home Kofi Annan, the retiring General Secretary of the United Nations. I was able to compliment the President on the democratic institutions in Ghana, the strength of the Ghanaian economy and the spectacular success of the volunteering programme with VSO's assistance. We spoke about his upcoming State visit to the UK and his concern that the weather might be too cold for him to wear Ghanaian national dress, which leaves one shoulder exposed. However, in the event, I was pleased that he did wear it, with no adverse consequences. It was also a great honour to meet Kofi Annan at his homecoming party.

The Gulf and Pakistan (4 to 14 February 2007)

Both the Gulf and Pakistan are of tremendous importance to the United Kingdom, for different reasons. But one common feature is the need to cooperate to reduce terrorism and ensure global security. While this is not within the Lord Mayor's remit, visiting countries which have a common political agenda is always helpful to the effectiveness of the business relationship. I was accompanied by Richard Regan, one of the two Sheriffs during the major part of my Mayoral year, and Colonel Billy King-Harman, CBE, the City Marshal, whose 'day job' is acting as programme manager. Billy knows the Gulf well, having lived there for many years, and is helpful continuity when the Lord Mayor and Sheriffs change each year. The business delegation varied between 15 and 50 senior executives and included some old stalwarts such as Lord (Charles) Denman, Sir Tom Harris (Standard Chartered), Michael Hodges (HSBC), Andrew Yeandle (Strutt & Parker), Tracey Elner (Ashton Commodities), Anthony Belchambers (Futures & Options Association), Stephen Shields (ACCA), William Knight and Terry Stone.

Qatar

Qatar is the wealthiest country, on per capita basis, in the whole world. Rich in oil and particularly in gas, it has huge foreign reserves as well as reserves of energy. Over US$100 billion is being invested in infrastructure. Qatar is seeking to diversify and create a regional financial centre, the Qatar Finance Centre (QFC). Qatar is also trying to position itself as a centre of excellence for education in the Gulf. Its Sovereign Wealth Fund, the Qatar Investment Authority (QIA), has significant and growing funds to invest. There was therefore plenty to discuss.

Travelling again on a Sunday, for good diary reasons, we had another excellent briefing from the British Ambassador to Qatar, Simon Collis, before beginning our round of visits, starting the following day with a seminar on ETQ at Qatar Foundation Education City, and then meetings at the QFC. I was pleased to be invited, later, together with other City based businessmen and former ambassadors, to join a group advising the QFC on some of its developments.

A highlight in Qatar was the lunch with His Highness the Emir, Shaikh Hamad bin Khalifa Al Thani, and his wife, HH Shaikha Mozah, a most impressive lady who had visionary ideas about the development of education in the country. The palace was a blend of Italian and Turkish styles with some paintings of hunting scenes. The Emir is keen on hunting with falcons. But we discussed some serious issues such as the Emir's desire to ensure that Qatar's impending massive wealth from gas is securely invested for the benefit of future generations and on diversification of the economy. The Emir and Shaikha Mozah were also focused on Qatar's professional labour shortages (a recent unpublished study had highlighted these in stark terms) and on the importance they attached to education not just to meet HR needs but also as an essential element in Qatar's social development. We explored the possibility of greater cooperation between UK professional educational institutes and universities and the Qatar Foundation.

Qatar is one of the world's major sources of natural gas. My meeting with the Energy Minister, His Excellency Abdullah bin Hamad Al Attiyah, allowed us to hear about Qatar's major investment plans including $80 billion of project finance in the five years to 2012. The Minister spoke about diversification beyond LNG to new products and petrochemicals and he emphasised Qatar's focus on establishing long-term relationships with partners. One of these close relationships is with the UK and Qatar will be supplying a large percentage of the UK's future gas needs through Milford Haven.

We identified many opportunities for working together in areas such as marine insurance, certification through Lloyd's Register, project finance, Islamic finance and carbon trading, as well as education, showed the variety and prospects of the UK-Qatari relationship.

At a meeting with the Finance Minister, His Excellency Yousuf Kamal outlined his plans for the further development of the Qatar Financial Centre (QFC) including extending the QFC Regulatory Authority's jurisdiction to cover the entire financial sector in Qatar, including local banks. He urged early conclusion of a Double Taxation Agreement and stated that a 10 per cent tax rate would be applied at the QFC from May 2008. The Minister's focus was also on the longer term and he envisaged total diversification of Qatar's economy through a series of developments over a 20 year timescale.

A final dinner with the First Deputy Prime Minister and Foreign Minister, His Excellency Shaikh Hamad Bin Jassim Al Thani, gave a further opportunity to strengthen the relationship and for me to reciprocate the hospitality at Mansion House when he visited the UK on the eve of Qatar's Investment Conference in London in March.

ABU DHABI

Oil rich Abu Dhabi and its iconic neighbour, Dubai, form part of the United Arab Emirates, but are governed separately from a political and financial point of view. They also have very different characters. It was my first visit to both cities and I was impressed by the wealth, the vision and the buildings. In Dubai, I was less impressed with the traffic as the road system has not kept pace with the other developments.

Abu Dhabi has eight per cent of the world's oil reserves and is the world's fifth largest producer of gas. The scale of investment in infrastructure is enormous.

Its foreign exchange reserves are substantial such that the Abu Dhabi Investment Authority (ADIA), the Sovereign Wealth Fund, has the most to invest of any of the global funds. The country is seeking to diversify in every way – football, Formula 1 and tourism, with some expensive hotels (the *Emirates Palace*, the world's first seven-star hotel) – but also manufacture of steel and aluminum.

My visit to Abu Dhabi centred around finance and investment, with a significant focus on the ETQ. My meeting with the Governor of the Central Bank, His Excellency Sultan Al Suweidi, focused on the regulation of the financial sector and the Governor expressed an interest in the initiative to form an International Institute of Regulation in London. A meeting with the Department of Planning and Finance, led by the newly appointed Minister, Nasser Al Suweidi, enabled us to learn about the proposed diversification of the economy. During a visit to the project finance and development organisation Mubadala, hosted by the Chief Operating Officer Waleed Al Mokarrab Al Muhairi, we heard about the major investments being made by Abu Dhabi both inside the UAE and abroad, including stakes in Ferrari and the Carlyle Group.

Business meetings took place with ADIA and the Abu Dhabi Chamber of Commerce and Industry. Business opportunities, for example in carbon trading and Islamic finance, were identified and discussed over a buffet dinner hosted by the Ambassador and attended by some 70 leading members of the expatriate financial community.

My meeting with Sheikha Lubna Al Qasimi, the Minister of Economy, responsible for ESCA (the Emirates Securities and Commodities Authority), showed the vision of the UAE leadership as I witnessed a cooperation agreement signed between ESCA and Ruth Martin of the Securities & Investment Institute (SII) to provide joint training courses through an SII office in Abu Dhabi.

DUBAI

Dubai is not far from Abu Dhabi. As one leaves Abu Dhabi, the traffic flows quite fast but gets much worse as one approaches the centre of Dubai. We were immediately driven to the house of the Consul-General, John Hawkins, for a reception sponsored by Barclays Wealth, with an exhibition and auction of some bronze horses. I had a long conversation with His Excellency Easa Saleh Al Gurg, CBE, the Ambassador of the UAE to the Court of St James, about relationships between the UK and the Gulf States. He focused on the need to solve the Palestinian question as a priority.

In Dubai, my business team was strengthened with the presence of Mark Garvin (JP Morgan) and Michael Thomas (Middle East Association).

The Governor of the Dubai International Financial Centre (DIFC), Dr Omar Bin Sulaiman, had gathered around him an impressive team, led by Nasser Al Shaali, the CEO. They had modeled the Regulatory Authority on the FSA, initially led by the Chief Executive, David Knott, from Australia. Before my visit, I had heard from an old friend, Robert Owen, a non-exec of DIFC,

138 A dinner and speech engagement with the British Business Group in Dubai.

of the history of the development of the financial centre and its birth pangs. They seemed to have a clear strategy and were growing well. An essential feature of the success of any financial centre is a reliable legal system and during our visit to the recently established DIFC Courts, we were welcomed via video link by Sir Anthony Evans who is based in London, but could legally hear a case physically taking place in Dubai. Two final cogs were the Dubai International Financial Exchange (DIFX), trading in shares, sukuk bonds, conventional bonds and structured products; and the Dubai Mercantile Exchange (DME) which had been built and was ready to start business as a market for energy futures, focusing initially on Oman crude futures.

I was also pleased, during my visit to Dubai, to speak at an ETQ seminar organised by the British Council and to witness the signing of two cooperation agreements between the DIFC and the Securities & Investment Institute (SII) and the Cass Business School, part of City University London. Dubai is a most suitable city for a British business education centre. We spoke about this and the strategic partnership between Dubai and the City of London with the Governor, Dr Omar. Although many perceive Dubai as a potential competitor to London, there is much to do by way of cooperation. Working together will increase opportunities for growth and also reduce the risks by sharing best practice in regulation and by exchanging information.

PAKISTAN

Pakistan was on the list of countries for a Mayoral visit for a number of reasons. 2007 was the 60th anniversary of Independence following the partition of Imperial India. Given its geo-political position bordering on Afghanistan, Iran, and India, Pakistan has had to contend with security difficulties and it is an important ally in the fight against terrorism. But, Pakistan was becoming again an important country for investment and trade. GDP growth was around seven per cent per year and bilateral trade with the UK was now around US$1 billion each way. Standard Chartered Bank had recently acquired Union Bank for US$500 million and other international banks were looking for investment opportunities. Two Pakistani companies had recently raised US$1 billion on the London Stock Exchange. In addition, there were now over 800,000 people in the UK who were British passport holders of Pakistani origin. The need for dialogue and strengthening relationships had never been greater.

And there was a personal reason for a visit to Pakistan. I was keen to return to the country after an extremely interesting few days driving through it, from east to west, during the Peking to Paris Motor Challenge in which I participated in 1997. Then I drove the 10,000 miles in six weeks in my 1934 Rolls-Royce, painted FT pink at the request of the *Financial Times*, who covered the story. On that momentous journey, my fellow travellers included Simon Anderson, a former Coopers & Lybrand partner who had lived in Pakistan and spoke a little Urdu (and Farsi), Gordon Barrass, CMG, who had joined Coopers & Lybrand from the FCO and spoke fluent Mandarin, and Roy O'Sullivan, our cigarette smoking 40-a-day engineer. On that trip, we had been sponsored by Jardine Fleming, H&R Owen, Eagle Star Insurance and Standard Chartered who threw a wonderful party in Lahore. Then we voted Pakistan as having the worst roads of any country on our journey but the best tyre repairers. What we would find this time – 10 years later?

Comprising four very different provinces, Punjab, Sindh, North West Frontier and Baluchistan, Pakistan is a collection of people from different ethnic groups. It is not cohesive. The British had based their Army training centre at Quetta in the west, partly to try to keep the Baluchis under control. When I travelled through Baluchistan by road in 1997 I remember seeing armed guards holding very old and rusty rifles at the petrol station forecourts and, when petrol stations were hard to come by, there were always boys with buckets of 'Regular' to keep the old car going. One's image of the North West Frontier is coloured by historical reports of the British Army encountering difficulties with the local tribesmen in this hilly terrain. This image of the North West Frontier was amusingly portrayed to British audiences in the 1960s' film *Carry On Up The Khyber*, starring Sid James as the British Resident Sir Sidney Ruff-Diamond and Kenneth Williams as the scheming Khasi of Kalabar. On the other hand, Punjab, with its historic cities of Rawalpindi and Lahore, its gracious hill stations and the country's modern capital of Islamabad, is a different world. And Sindh, with its large migrant population of Muslims from India, is blessed with Karachi, a bustling sea port and a centre of enterprise, endeavour and intrigue.

KARACHI

It was Karachi where our visit to Pakistan began. We had been advised that the security situation was volatile. This was evident as we were driven in a convoy of armed rangers and armed police to the heavily fortified Deputy High Commission, Acton House, which was once the headquarters of the Karachi Ports Authority. Prior to leaving the UK I had telephoned Lord (Charles) Guthrie, GCB, LVO, OBE, former Chief of Defence Staff, who had given me the benefit of his understanding of the situation in Pakistan. I remember his punch line 'Pakistan is almost impossible to govern, but it has great potential'. We appreciated the pre-visit briefing from the FCO and UKTI in London. On arrival at Acton House, the Deputy High Commissioner, Hamish Daniel, OBE, gave my business

WHITTINGTON TO WORLD FINANCIAL CENTRE

delegation his thoughts on the political, economic and business environment. In short, politics were complex, the economy was doing well and there were plenty of opportunities for trade and investment.

Throughout my five-day visit to Pakistan, I was struck by the obsession on the part of the local media about stories of British Muslims being mistreated in the UK and being discriminated against by British police and the public. This mirrored the image in the British media of Pakistan as a breeding ground and a haven for terrorists. The poor impression of each other in the media was not at all representative of all the good things that were happening and of the goodwill that exists between the two countries. I decided that I would make a point of this during my speeches, urging a greater focus on the benefits of working together to increase trade and investment. The media were very attentive, with many TV and press interviews. There was a good deal of press coverage which, hopefully, resulted in greater goodwill as a result of the messages given.

My Pakistani hosts were most hospitable. On my first evening in Karachi, the Governor of Sindh Province, a London Trained physician, Dr Ishrat Ul Ebad Khan, entertained us for dinner at the Governor's Residence. This was a very special place, dating from Imperial times, but with Jinnah's quarters kept untouched since he died in 1948, shortly after Independence. The late President Jinnah is a national hero. It is arguable that Pakistan would not exist without his tireless fight. It was therefore a special moment for me on the following day to be taken to the Jinnah Monument to lay a wreath at his tomb. Accompanied by the Mayor of Karachi, Syed Mustafa Kamal, a naval contingent had been detailed to act as honour guard, with an accompanying band. Marching in step, with our hosts and the UK business delegation, I appreciated the spontaneous

139   The tomb of Jinnah, the founder of Pakistan, in Karachi.

140   The Lord Mayor gives a Press interview after laying a wreath at the tomb of Jinnah in Karachi.

briefing from our programme manager for the Gulf and Pakistan tour, Billy King-Harman. Billy was a star. He was always there when you needed him and, on this occasion, we needed someone to take us through the military niceties. Up the steps we marched and into the mausoleum where I was ushered to the iron railings to lay my wreath. An Imam said some prayers. Two buglers played the Last Post and then the Reveille. Other soldiers appeared, in their fine uniforms with red plumes on the caps, and I was taken to sign the distinguished visitors' book of remembrance, in which I wrote 'I, Alderman John Stuttard, The Rt Hon The Lord Mayor of the City of London, pay respect and homage to the Founder of Pakistan, whose memory is precious and whose life and actions are an inspiration as we strive for peace, partnership and prosperity'. On emerging from the mausoleum into the sunlight outside, I was faced with a barrage of television cameras, microphones and reporters asking what was going through my mind. I responded that it was 'a great honour and a very moving moment for me to come to the mausoleum to pay my respects to Jinnah, the Founder of Pakistan, a great man'. I then repeated, 'His life and his actions are a great inspiration to all of us as we strive for peace, partnership and prosperity'. It was indeed a very moving moment.

Our visit to Karachi was very full and productive. I spoke at an ETQ seminar organised by Marcus Gilbert of the British Council. Meetings at the Karachi Stock Exchange and the Institute of Chartered Accountants in Pakistan, together with two conferences on Financial Services and Legal Services, gave us the opportunity for dialogue on a number of issues, including the possibility of working closely together in a number of areas – regulation, stock exchange listings and, of course, training. The Governor of the State Bank of Pakistan is a lady, Her Excellency Dr Shamshad Akthar, who impressed us greatly.

It is often said that in the Muslim world women are sometimes treated unfairly and have difficulty in getting jobs. It was therefore a pleasure to accept an invitation from Standard Chartered Vice Chairman Sir Tom Harris to open a new bank branch in the Defence district of Karachi run entirely by women. Intended initially as a branch for women, it has, I have been told, attracted a lot of male customers because of the well spoken and well educated single lady bank clerks!

ISLAMABAD

Islamabad is a new city, built to house the national government. Here we were to meet a number of Ministers, not least His Excellency Zahid Hamid, the impressive Minister for Privatisation and Investment. A Thatcherite, he was bent on increasing the extent of the private sector and reducing the role of the public sector with the catchy strap line 'Government has no business interfering with business'. Many opportunities were identified for UK investment banks, brokers and professional services firms.

But, my meeting with Prime Minister Shaukat Aziz was the highlight of our business visit to Pakistan for many reasons. He was accompanied by no fewer than 12 of his Ministers. As a result, we covered a lot of ground. With a career in Citibank, followed by a long spell as Finance Minister, Shaukat Aziz was someone to whom I could relate. We spoke about global events, the world economy, the changing relationships, the need to fight corruption and the many opportunities for investment. He was also the second senior figure during my overseas visits to raise with me the difficulties of getting through Heathrow and, for some Pakistani businessmen, the difficulty of obtaining a UK visa. He was impressive and, with someone like Aziz as Prime Minister, the country was being well served.

Other Ministerial meetings in Karachi included a discussion with the able Dr Salman Shah, Financial Adviser to the Prime Minister. He pointed out some of the realities of the business environment. Many overseas companies had made good returns in Pakistan and he pointed to ICI and Siemens who had each had a presence in Pakistan for over 100 years without making a loss. At dinner that evening, at the Residence of HE Robert Brinkley, CMG, the High Commissioner, and his wife Mary, I sat next to the delightful Minister for Higher Education, Dr Atta-Ur-Rahman, an Honorary Life Fellow at King's College Cambridge.

LAHORE

Our next stop was Lahore and, since it was a Friday (a non-working day), a visit had been arranged to two VSO projects. The route from Islamabad was attractive, crossing a mountain range. We were accompanied by an armed escort of two jeeps.

The first project, the 'New Light Aids Control Society' was in Green Town, a suburb of Lahore, which had been established by the first person in Pakistan, Nazir Masih, to declare on television that he was HIV Positive. In many countries, it is assumed that AIDS is the result of sex, whereas bad blood can be the cause or, in the case of a child, it can be passed on by an infected parent. There is therefore much stigma attaching to anyone who is HIV Positive. Sufferers are often treated as outcasts and have difficulty getting hospital care. The volunteers at the project provide counselling, food and support. They help sufferers obtain medical treatment and publicise the manner in which AIDS is spread. They hope to reduce the stigma associated with the illness. At the centre, there were some 40 people, of all ages, listening to the presentations and receiving us as guests. Accompanied by Sheriff Richard Regan and Billy King-Harman, we shook hands with everyone at the centre.

The second project was even more unusual. The Pak Plus Welfare Society in the Shalimar Gardens district of Lahore had been established by Shukria Gul, who became HIV Positive from her husband, who later died of AIDS. This gutsy lady, with her daughter and son working as volunteers, counsels sex workers in the area and explains how these illnesses are transferred, in the hope that they can learn and reduce the incidence. She also helps them cope with the stigma.

It was quite a change some hours later to be received in the splendid Residence of the Governor of Punjab, Lieutenant General Khalid Maqbool. This grand building, dating from the era of the Raj, had large reception rooms, with classical columns, leading to a Moghul style dining room and next to a huge Edwardian style ballroom. With a string band playing in the adjacent drawing room, our discussions centred on links we could form in the field of education. Then our host announced that he had to leave early to catch a plane to Multan to meet the President, Pervez Musharraf.

Lahore is a delightful city which reached its peak of glory under the Moghul rulers, particularly Akbar the Great. It is a place of greenery and of gardens. It is also Pakistan's second largest city and a place of significant commerce. Sadly, it rained for the entire two days that we spent in Lahore, which prevented our visit to the border with India to see the spectacular Changing of the Guard at sunset. But then we were rather preoccupied with other events, including a meeting with the Lahore Chamber of Commerce & Industry and an ETQ seminar with the Institute of Chartered Accountants in Pakistan.

A truly memorable moment of our visit to Lahore was the visit to the Town Hall to see the Mayor, Mian Amer Mehmood. Greeted as we arrived by an honour guard of eight soldiers with red sashes wearing head gear with red plumes, they looked magnificent as they stood to attention, while the two buglers sounded our arrival. I'm always impressed when I see soldiers from the Pakistani Army, having retained the best of the British and then taken it one stage further. After a discussion with the Mayor and members of the Town Council, I was presented with the key to the City of Lahore – my first – which is now held in Mansion House in London.

That night, we met up with Asad Ali Khan, my former partner at Coopers & Lybrand in Lahore. When we passed through Lahore in 1997 in my 1934 Rolls-Royce, Asad gave us dinner at his home and arranged for me to give a lecture to all his staff on the car rally. A most interesting man, with a family that works partly in Dubai, partly in London and partly in Pakistan, he is a truly international representative of his new nation.

As we left Pakistan, I reflected on what I had seen and my views of the future:

- Politically, at that time, it was stable. Musharraf had been in power for six years
- Economically, it was growing at seven per cent
- The Alliance with the West to defeat extremism and terrorism was solid, producing results, but the victory was not yet there
- Economic reform was going well, with the private sector becoming a larger part of the economy
- International companies were beginning to invest more in Pakistan
- There was an image problem both ways – the Pakistani perception of the treatment of Muslims in the UK and the British perception of terrorists being nurtured in Pakistan. There was a need to correct this
- I felt cautiously bullish about the future

Then, in March 2007, the President suspended the Chief Justice and my optimism waned. When Benazir Bhutto was assassinated in December 2007, things seemed to get much worse. Now, some months later, at the time of writing, there have been democratic elections and Pakistan has been welcomed back into the Commonwealth.

As I look back, I recall two of the comments made:

- Lord Guthrie: 'Pakistan is almost impossible to govern, but it has great potential'
- Zahid Hamid, Minister for Privatisation and Investment: 'Government has no business interfering with business'
- In Pakistan, whatever the political climate, businessmen just get on with the job of growing their businesses, trading with others and, at the end of the day, making money.

GUERNSEY AND JERSEY (15 TO 18 MARCH 2007)

Technically overseas, Guernsey and Jersey are not foreign and they are very much part of the UK Financial Sector, working closely with finance houses in London, Edinburgh, Leeds and Manchester to provide services and products that the islands can offer.

Lord Mayors visit the Channel Islands every two or three years and I was delighted that a visit was suggested in my year. I recall many happy holidays as a teenager at *L'Horizon Hotel* in St Brelade's Bay. My father's uncle had retired to Jersey in the 1950s, followed by his son in the 1970s, and my aunt, Margaret Boothman, MBE, lives there as does her son, John Boothman, a commissioner in The Jersey Financial Services Commission. There were therefore personal reasons for a visit and the weekend afforded the opportunity for John to arrange a fund-raising dinner for the Lord Mayor's Appeal and for us to stay with Margaret at her home in St Lawrence. Lesley joined me for this visit and we were accompanied by FCO secondee, Jonathan Nethersole, who arranged the programme.

First to Guernsey, where we were met at the airport by the Chief Minister, Mike Torode, and the Chief Executive, Mike Brown, and then by the Governor, Sir Fabian Malbon, and his wife, Sue, with whom we stayed at Government House, an attractive 18th-century mansion with a wonderful garden. Guernsey has a population of just 60,000 but has a thriving financial sector, with particular strengths in investment funds, captive insurance, fiduciary work and private banking. In our meetings with the Director General of the Guernsey Financial Services Commission, Peter Neville, and at a round table hosted by Gavin Tradelius of Generali with the Deputy Chief Minister, Stuart Falla, we spoke about corporate governance, minimum standards of regulation, EU directives and how we could work together. Both Guernsey and Jersey use UK lawyers and accountants, in particular, to help their overseas clients maximise their returns and minimise tax. They are therefore an important source of work to the UK mainland-based Financial Sector.

Our civic duty was to visit the Bailiff of Guernsey, Geoffrey Rowland, at the Royal Court. There we learnt about the ancient charters which kept Guernsey part of the British Crown but independent of the UK. We also learnt that in Guernsey they too have a mace, like the one we have in London. The only difference is that they don't invert it when it is carried on an occasion where the Monarch is present. On a visit to Guernsey, HRH The Duke of Edinburgh had queried this and it was explained to him that this was a longstanding tradition in Guernsey. Mace etiquette is obviously complex and requires further research.

It is a short plane ride to Jersey in a six seater that flies low and provides a bird's eye view of the attractive northern coastline. We were met on the tarmac by Governor Lieutenant-General Andrew Ridgway, CB, CBE, Chief Minister Frank Walker, and Chief Executive Bill Ogley. As in Guernsey, we were accommodated at Government House and greeted by the Governor's wife, Valerie.

Jersey's population is 88,000. We learnt that Financial Services now accounts for two-thirds of Jersey's GDP and employs 22 per cent of the work force. Tourism is still very important; agriculture less so. The island's strength lies in its banking and, astonishingly, while 19 per cent of Jersey's bank deposits come from the UK, 48 per cent of Jersey's deposits are invested in the UK. Its contribution to the UK mainland-based Financial Sector is therefore substantial. Pierre Horsfall, CBE and Geoffrey Grime, Chairman and Director respectively of Jersey Finance, believe that Jersey is now perceived as having a strong reputation for probity and corporate governance and has strong links with the City of London Police to reduce money laundering and other financial crime.

I also took time to speak at a Securities & Investment Institute conference, as well as give a Press conference focussing on how Jersey and the City of London could jointly promote their services. I was later pleased to be joined on my subsequent visit to Shanghai and Nanjing by Geoff Cook, Chief Executive of Jersey Finance, and colleagues.

Our civic programme included a meeting and lunch with Sir Philip Bailhache, the Bailiff, at the Royal Court and we had a similar conversation about the Jersey mace, given by Charles II. As in Guernsey, it is also carried upright in the presence of the Monarch.

Saturday gave us the opportunity for some sightseeing, starting with an inspection of the stained glass windows and a reredos at St Saviour's Church near Government House. These were the work of 19th-century Jersey born craftsman Bosdet, whose stained glass designs compare to those of Byrne-Jones and William Morris. As a Liveryman of the Glaziers, I have enjoyed seeing many glazed and painted windows in recent years and we were introduced to Bosdet on a visit to Jersey organised by the then Master, Brian Harris, in 2003. Bosdet's most famous works of stained glass are in St Brelade's Church, which dates from the 6th century. If you go to Jersey, take time to see them and then walk on the long sandy beach afterwards. You will be uplifted.

It was also uplifting to see Aunt Margaret again at her home in St Lawrence, accompanied by the Governor and his wife. Margaret has been a long time supporter of St John and we saw her and her son, Clive, at a number of events during my Mayoralty. These included the post Mayoral Investiture at St John's Chapel when HRH The Duke of Gloucester dubbed me as a Knight of Justice of the Most Venerable Order of the Hospital of St John of Jerusalem. That night, in Jersey, her elder son, John, organised a fund-raising dinner for the Lord Mayor's Appeal at the Jersey Pottery. We finished the evening by opening and sipping some 1888 brandy that Margaret's father-in-law, Jack Boothman, had brought back from Cuba in the 1950s along with many years' supply of cigars. The Cuban brandy was very smooth and not at all sharp. I'm looking forward to returning to Jersey to finish the rest of the bottle.

Kazakhstan & Russia (27 March to 9 April 2007)

With rises in global prices of the world's energy, the economies of Russia and Kazakhstan have become increasingly important in recent years. For the City of London they are growing markets for investment, banking, insurance, maritime services, wealth management and education and training.

Kazakhstan

Since the break up of the USSR in 1991, an independent Kazakhstan has emerged as one of the world's major producers of oil and gas. The country possesses large reserves of uranium, chromium, lead and zinc, as well as manganese, copper, coal, iron and, even, gold. It is also a large wheat producer. With a population of just 15 million, landlocked and sandwiched between two large neighbours, Russia to the north and China to the east, Kazakhstan has sought good relations with countries outside the region. In recent years under the leadership of President Nursultan Nazarbayev this new nation has prospered, with GDP growing at in excess of nine per cent per year. Its economic policies have been liberal, embracing the private sector and welcoming foreign investment and participation. The President's master plan for 2030, 'Half Past Eight', envisages a country where there is prosperity, security, education and social welfare. The President is a visionary and gets things done, as I found out during my visit to Kazakhstan and saw, in particular, the stunning new capital of Astana – his brainchild.

A close business relationship has developed with many large UK companies, such as Shell, BG Group, HSBC, BAe Systems, Pilkington, Group 4, De La Rue, Denton Wilde Sapte and the big 4 accountancy firms, all of whom are active in the country. The UK is held in high regard for financial services, education and training, and corporate governance. Eight Kazakh companies are listed on the London Stock Exchange and a further 10 on the junior market, AIM. Of the 3,000 students chosen to participate in the country's *Bolashak* (meaning 'future') programme, 1,000 have come to the UK. In the country's new capital, Astana,

Foster and Partners have designed the eye catching *Pyramid of Peace*. VSO has had over 100 volunteers in the country. The relationship with the UK spans a number of fields and is very close.

Before the start of my visit to Kazakhstan, I had received an excellent introduction to the country. The President came to London in November 2006 for a conference which we helped organise at Mansion House and for lunch in the Private Dining Room. Prior to that, I had met the Kazakh Ambassador, His Excellency Erlan Idrissov, on a number of occasions. He had earlier arranged for Kazakh horseman to participate in my Lord Mayor's Show. Always charming and very enthusiastic about his country and my visit, he accompanied us during our stay in his country, a gracious and helpful gesture. Since my visit was timed to coincide with the beginning of the Spring Festival, it was suggested that I should wish everyone a *Happy Nauryz*, a Happy New Year. I learnt from Erlan that Kazakhs have a great sense of humour, giving nicknames to everything. For example, the new Samruk (Bird of Phoenix) Tower in Astana has been nicknamed *Tuper Tubes*, which means Lollipop.

I also had the benefit of meeting, on a number of occasions, Sir Richard (Dick) Evans, CBE, who had done business with Kazakhstan in his capacity as Chairman and MD of BAe Systems. He had also helped establish the State airline company, Air Astana, and is now Chairman of the Kazakh State holding company, Samruk. From these informed sources, plus the FCO briefing from the British Ambassador Paul Brummell, I felt ready for my visit to Almaty, the old capital, and then to Astana, the new capital of modern Kazakhstan.

Our Mansion House programme manager was Richard Martin (otherwise known as the City's Swordbearer). Joining Alderman & Sheriff David Lewis and me, there were 15 in the business delegation, including Sir Paul Judge, Sir Tom Harris (Standard Chartered), Sir Tom Troubridge (PwC), Chris Gibson-Smith (Chairman of the London Stock Exchange), Trevor Barton (PBN), Bassem Kabban (UIB), Charles Hanbury-Williams (HSBC) and Angelica Phillips (Norton Rose).

Almaty is a very pleasant city. Built in Czarist times, it has a Russian feel to it, but it is very definitely Kazakh and at the cross roads between China and the west. After a call on the Mayor (the *Akim*) at City Hall, where I was given a gold-plated apple, the symbol of Almaty, he entertained us at a restaurant in the hills above the city. The entertainment included traditional folk music, played by stringed instruments that looked very central Asian.

I learnt about the horrors of the Stalinist period when many Kazakhs were sent to the gulags in Siberia. There was then an influx of Russians and Germans so that ethnic Kazakhs were reduced to less than 40 per cent of the population. Now, with voluntary repatriation, the balance is being restored. Since independence, Kazakhstan has been denuclearised and has been a stable force in the region.

While Almaty might be the old capital, it is still the financial heart of Kazakhstan, headquarters to the Almaty Regional Financial Centre (ARFC), whose Chairman, Arken Arystanov, I met on my first day. At a conference organised by the *Financial*

Times, his message was simple. After independence, the country had developed well but much of the wealth was in the hands of a few companies and there was a need to redistribute this through privatisation and public listings. There was a need to improve financial awareness and education. Building a financial centre in Almaty was a necessary first step. The regulatory environment needed to be established. The accounting and auditing profession needed to be developed. The UK could help with these tasks.

Chris Gibson-Smith spoke as Chairman of the London Stock Exchange and referred to the welcoming reception which the many Kazakh companies had received when they listed in London. The London Stock Exchange is well placed to develop its activity with Kazakhstan companies. We discussed the issues of Kazakh businesses going global: corporate governance, the need for competent independent non-executive directors, a clear business strategy, management capabilities and good communications. It was also clear that Almaty lacked professionals, particularly accountants, and it was most appropriate that the British Council should organise another seminar on ETQ, chaired by Sir Paul Judge.

A meeting with the Chairman, Grigori Marchenko, of Halyk, one of the country's major banks focused on the development of the financial sector. He stressed that banking and pensions were the most strongly developed and that Kazakhstan was about five years ahead of Russia as regards banking and about 10 years as regards pensions (pension funds in Kazakhstan were worth around 11 per cent of GDP, compared to less than one per cent in Russia). The main growth potential, in his view, lay in the non-banking financial services. The insurance sector was growing at around 60-70 per cent per annum, albeit from a very low base (there were for example only around 100,000 life assurance policies in a population of 15 million). Mutual funds and leasing were other areas of high growth potential.

Before we left Almaty, we had time to visit a VSO project for disabled children before flying on to Astana, built from scratch in the desert, to the north of the country. On arrival, I was welcomed by the Akim of Astana and given a model of the Samruk Tower – the Lollipop.

Astana is a city built with great vision, the President's vision. Its wide avenues and imaginatively designed and well constructed buildings give an air of authority. The centrepiece is the President's Palace, the White House. Situated between the Parliament and Government buildings on one side and a park and the Foster Pyramid on the other, the palace is a blend of classical western and eastern architecture. Covered in marble of different colours and in a dominant position, it looks like an Asian version of the White House in Washington, perhaps even a little grander. Inside, the vaulted reception room for foreign visitors is decorated with murals. The conference room is tastefully designed and has state of the art technology. The audience halls are stunning, inlaid with marble and furnished with paintings and objects depicting Kazakhstan's nomadic and romantic past. Often, when a country's economy flourishes, national literature, architecture and art also flourish. There is money to support the writers, the architects and the artists. This is happening in Kazakhstan today.

My audience with the President was warm and friendly. We had met before. I was an admirer of what he had achieved. He spoke about his desire to develop the economy and to broaden share ownership in the country. The City of London could help, enormously, in the next steps, to develop a financial sector to support the country's future economic development. I complimented him on his achievements and on the quality of his Ministers and Akims. He graciously took me on a personal tour of the palace. Each room was a work of art. A gift I will treasure is a beautifully bound coffee table book with photos of the palace and an explanation of the décor in the various rooms.

President Nazarbayev insisted that we should visit the Pyramid designed by Lord (Norman) Foster, with ideas taken from the Seven Wonders of the World. In the lower ground floor there is an opera house which holds 2,000 people. Above it is a reception area which similarly accommodates 2,000 people. On the top floor, in the apex of the pyramid, there is a conference centre with a hole in the middle, like a doughnut, above the reception hall, reached by a grand circular staircase, surrounded by plants resembling, as intended, the Hanging Gardens of Babylon.

During my Mayoralty, I became accustomed to opening buildings. My visit to Astana was to be no exception. At the invitation of the British Ambassador, Paul Brummell, I was delighted to open the British Embassy in the new capital, a floor of a modern building. Functional and cost effective, it would not have made

141   New PwC office opened in Astana, Kazakhstan by the Lord Mayor. Country Managing Partner, Alper Akdeniz is on the left.

the grand statement perhaps necessary during the age of the Great Game, but then the game had changed. The new office was fit for purpose.

I was also pleased to open the new PricewaterhouseCoopers office in Astana, in a similar modern building. The ceremony was quite a spectacle, with Alper Akdeniz, PwC's Managing Partner, presenting me with a Kazakh costume, a splendid cloth hat, a fur hat and a very pretty Kazakh girl in traditional costume who, I was told, could not be taken home with me, not even in the diplomatic bag!

My meeting with the Prime Minister, Karim Massimov, gave me the opportunity to explore cooperation in areas such as business education and professional skills development, raising finance in London, corporate governance and the strengthening of

the commercial legal environment. He suggested that the UK could assist with the introduction of accounting standards, common law, privatisation and education of professionals.

Meetings at the Supreme Court, and with Dick Evans at a conference organised by Samruk and its sister organisation, Kasyna (the investment fund for sustainable development), confirmed this agenda.

Support for the new commercial court formed as part of the ARFC was an important theme of the visit. Two British judges had conducted a training seminar for the new judges of the court in advance of my visit and the Bar Council had signed an MOU with the Kazakh Union of Lawyers on the proposed establishment of an Anglo-Kazakh Lawyers Association. I made the case for the use of English common law to underpin the ARFC, drawing on the example of the Qatar Finance Centre. Prime Minister Massimov said that he was thinking along the same lines, commenting that in his view the presence of an Anglo-Saxon common law system did much to explain why Hong Kong had become a major financial centre while Macao had not.

I heard at each meeting about the shortage of skilled professionals across the financial services sector in Kazakhstan. I stressed that the UK was ideally placed to support business education and professional skills development. Finance Minister Natalya Korzhova announced that, following my discussions with Prime Minister Massimov on this subject, he had agreed to establish a centre for the development of international standards in accountancy, and on professional skills more widely, to be set up under the Ministry of Finance. She would visit the UK to meet potential British partner organisations. I also stressed to the Finance Minister that, in the short-term, part of the answer must lie in the easing of work permit restrictions, for example in bringing in expatriate accountants.

I attended the signing of an MOU between the London School of Economics and the Civil Service Agency on the delivery of training programmes for senior officials, both in London and Kazakhstan.

There was much to follow up. My visit provided a stimulus to co-operation across the entire financial services agenda, including opportunities for UK companies and organisations in professional skills development, judicial co-operation, promotion of share ownership and links between the London and Almaty financial centres.

Kazakhstan is going through a good phase in its history. It has new found wealth, which is sustainable. It has a new found vision. Its people are confident, enterprising, amusing and friendly towards the west, particularly the United Kingdom. We should respect that friendship and work together, as the country becomes a major player in the region.

RUSSIA

For centuries, Russia has been a great power. Post the collapse of the USSR, the country lost its direction. But now, with new found wealth and strong leadership,

Russia is re-establishing its place in the world as an important economy and trading partner.

In recent years, there have been political tensions between Russia and the UK, arising partly from Russia's natural desire to regain its global position and partly from the differences in political and social cultures and the legal environment. This results in periodic tension and unacceptable incidents, for example the Litvinenko affair or the closure of British Council offices or when the British Ambassador is harassed. Russia's global image and reputation has suffered from a number of seemingly autocratic and undemocratic decisions and there are serious concerns over the rule of law.

On the other hand, business relations between Russia and the UK have, on the whole, been good. Periodically, one hears complaints of unfair treatment or strange court judgements. Corporate governance in the country is weak. There are arbitrary tax changes that adversely affect business strategies. Corruption is a major issue. But there is so much business to be done and Russians like dealing with UK institutions. Many wealthy oligarchs have chosen to reside in London, where it is safe and where assets are secure. Despite the challenging political and legal environment in Russia, successful foreign businessmen understand and learn to live with the conditions under which they must operate. Russia is an important place in which to do business.

I had met our Ambassador, Sir Tony Brenton, KCMG, in London when my visit to Russia was discussed. In the political climate which then existed between Russia and the UK, he had found himself the target of abuse and, on one occasion in St Petersburg, a mugging. But he was resilient and believed in a forthright and constructive response to the situation. He sought a good long term relationship between the two countries. After all, Russia and the UK had been allies for a very long time. Special trading ties had been established back in the second half of the 16th century, during the reigns of Elizabeth I and Ivan the Terrible; we had been allies in the Napoleonic Wars and then in the Second World War. Even now, there were some very positive aspects to our existing governmental and business contact. We were working together on anti-money laundering and counter terrorist financing. The UK was the largest single foreign investor in Russia, with BP and Shell being very active. In recent years, there had been major new stock market equity issues by Russian companies of Global Depositary Receipts (GDRs) on the London Stock Exchange, for example: Rosneft, Sistema, OAO Severstal and Comstar. In 2006, Russian GDRs accounted for six per cent by number and a staggering 48 per cent by value of funds raised. And, as final demonstration of the closeness of the relationship, I was informed that the registration number of the British Ambassador's car is 001CD1, because the UK was the first country to recognise the Soviet Union after the Revolution.

Travelling (again) on a Saturday, we arrived in Moscow from Astana for lunch at our hotel, the *Metropole*, hosted by the Municipality of the city. The *Metropole* is a wonderful example of Russian art nouveau design, centrally situated within walking distance of the Kremlin. The First Deputy Mayor, Yury Roslyak, introduced us to traditional Russian food of smoked fish, thick soup and pork and, of course, vodka, with the comment 'there is no bad vodka in Russia, only too little of it'. But we spoke more seriously about the issues facing capital cities: traffic problems, increasing property prices, disparity of wealth and, in Moscow's case, an increase in gun crime and issues caused by immigration from CIS countries.

Russia has two of the world's great museums, the Hermitage in St Petersburg and the Kremlin in Moscow. Being a Sunday, we had the opportunity to indulge in some sightseeing and it was a delight for me to revisit the Kremlin and see some of the Czarist costumes and treasures including the fine collection of 16th-century English silver. Most domestic silver of that period in the UK was melted down in the 18th century at a time when new designs were being created by the Batemans and others. On the other hand, the Ambassadorial gifts from Elizabeth I and, particularly from James I and Charles I, have survived in a unique collection in Moscow.

For the business visit to Russia we were joined by representatives of various educational establishments, Alderman Alison Gowman of DLA and Igor Sougorov of VTB. Joining us locally in Moscow were Mike Kubena (Senior Partner of PwC in Central Europe and the CIS) and Roger Munnings of KPMG.

Meetings with Chairman Dr Sergey Ignatiev at the Central Bank, with President Alexander Potemkin at MICEX (the Exchange), with Chairman Oleg Vyugin at the Federal Financial Markets Service and with Chairman Neil Cooper at the Russia British Chamber of Commerce, all pointed to similar conclusions. The Russia/British relationship in financial services was close, with much to offer each other. London was regarded as the financial capital of the world and a natural place for Russian companies to do business. But in Russia, there were issues over the certainty of interpretation of law and over the adequacy of corporate governance and financial reporting which needed to be resolved. This was very much the focus of my meeting with the Finance Minister, Alexei Kudrin, who listened carefully when, as Lord Mayor of London rather than a former partner in PwC UK, I raised the issue of the renewal of the PwC operating licence in Russia in connection with the firm's role as auditor of Yukos. I pointed out that this issue was being carefully monitored in London as an indication of the interpretation of regulations in Russia. He graciously responded that, as the Minister responsible for licensing auditing firms, he believed that each of the Big 4 global firms had contributed greatly to the development of the accounting profession and the improvement in financial reporting and that he saw no reason for changing the status quo. I was pleased to learn that PwC's Russian licence was renewed some weeks later. This was an indication of the pragmatic approach which the Russian Government can adopt when dealing with international business matters.

My meeting with the Mayor of Moscow, Yuri Luzkhov, gave me the opportunity to thank him for his civic welcome and to hear some of the issues affecting the capital. He referred to the Moscow city council as being the 'State Duma' but then laughed and corrected himself by saying 'not yet the State Duma'. I thought to myself that there are other mayors I know who think the same way, namely that capital cities should, as in ancient Greece, become nation states again. Perhaps Mayor Luzkhov gave them the idea. He added that his budget of US$32 billion was larger than that of the Ukraine. He was concerned about rising crime, traffic and immigration. I was pleased to present him with a model of Mansion House and he gave me a glass plate depicting St George killing the dragon. It was a beautiful souvenir of my visit to Moscow. I learnt later that St George had been adopted by the capital city after being introduced to Russia via the Orthodox Church in Constantinople and then Kiev.

In Moscow, I attended and spoke at four events: a Capital Markets conference held jointly between the London Stock Exchange and MICEX; an ETQ seminar organised by Martin Hope of the British Council; a seminar for insurance companies considering raising capital in London; and a Carbon Trading seminar at the British Embassy. At the last of these, UK and Russian companies and government officials discussed the development of carbon markets and their potential for tackling the common challenge of climate security. I explained the leading role of the City in innovating carbon trading instruments. Other speakers discussed the significant projected growth in carbon markets, the effect this is already having on company valuations; and the key next steps for Russia to push forward implementation.

142   *The Lord Mayor receives an engraved glass plate from Yuri Luzkhov, the Mayor of Moscow.*

At each of the meetings, seminars and in Press conferences, I delivered key UK messages: the importance of predictability in the legal and fiscal (including tax) environment; and of high standards of transparency and corporate governance.

In addition to the business agenda, there were two dinners at spectacular venues. The Moscow City Government hosted a reception and dinner at the Smirnoff Mansion, an Art Nouveau gem built around 1900, but with each major room decorated in a different style – Egyptian, neo-classical and William Morris. Attractive models served the canapés and drinks. The other was a dinner at the Restaurant Turandot, hosted by HSBC and Denton Wilde Sapte. I was informed that a staggering US$68 million had been spent on this building to make it look like an 18th-century French chateau, with ornate wood carvings and plaster ceilings. The dining room housed a large collection of Chinese porcelain. At the second banquet, I sat next to Dr Sergey Storchak, the Deputy Minister of Finance, who told me of a very wild and unspoiled part of Russia that I must visit, Kamchatka, near Petropavlovsk, where the landscape is tundra, with geysers, volcanoes, deserted countryside and rivers teeming with fish. Kamchatka is one of the few places in the world that cannot be reached by road.

It was the Russian Ambassador in London, His Excellency Yuri Fedotov, who advised us that the only way to travel from Moscow to St Petersburg was by train. So we took his advice. Leaving Moscow at 23.30 from the St Petersburg Station, accommodated in single cabins with wash basin, and nearby restaurant car, one had the feeling of being part of an Agatha Christie murder thriller. This feeling was amplified when the restaurant car's menu seemed limited to caviar, blinis and vodka. James Bond, eat your heart out. As the train rumbled across the Russian countryside, ploughing through the snow, one could not help thinking of Dr Zhivago, with Omar Sharif in the title role and Julie Christie as Lara. All too soon, the train arrived in St Petersburg's Moscovsky Station and we were driven to the *Astoria Hotel* after a welcome by the head of the International Department, Alexander Prokhorenkho, and the British Consul-General, William Elliott.

I had forgotten what a beautiful city St Petersburg is. On a previous visit in 1990, with our son, Jamie, and some Finnish friends, Lars and Ritva Blomquist and Heikki and Lisa Hakonen, we had visited the Hermitage and the Yussupov Palace where Rasputin had enjoyed his final dinner, before being poisoned, shot and finally thrust under the ice. The city had seemed dilapidated and tired, with an air of faded grandeur. But this time, the city was more prosperous, cleaner and for the most part restored. We were to discover that President Putin was born in Leningrad and had supported the restoration and redevelopment of the city in recent years. It looked splendid.

A major concern amongst local inhabitants was the proposed construction in the south east of the city of the Gazprom Tower, which many regarded as an outrage which would spoil a World Heritage city of such beauty. Another was the proposed extension, described as a carbuncle (an expression borrowed from the Prince of Wales), to the Mariinsky Theatre, known in Soviet times as the Kirov, in order to provide extra facilities for this internationally recognised centre of opera and ballet. We were taken to a performance of Janacek's *Jenufa*. Although I had vowed never to see another rendition of this work – in my view musically uninteresting, with a depressing drawn out plot yet a euphoric ending – the production by Valerie Gergiev was outstanding. *Jenufa* is one of the most draining operas one can imagine, with the baby being killed at the end of the second act. But in the third act there is this incredible twist of emotions as Jenufa and Laca find renewed happiness in their marriage and the opera finishes with the pair celebrating their love for each other. After the performance, we went backstage. I teased Gergiev for playing with our emotions so cruelly, yet so successfully. We then all repaired to the nearby Backstage Restaurant which was decorated in the style of a ballet practice room.

But back to work. Our visit to St Petersburg began with a briefing at the *Astoria Hotel*, built in 1912 and now beautifully renovated and centrally placed next to St Isaak's Cathedral.

After this, in order to get a better understanding of the plans for the city, the Chief Architect and Chairman of the Committee on City Planning & Architecture, Alexander Viktorov, gave us a description of the major projects envisaged in the next few years – a dam in the harbour, relocating the berths for freight and cruise ships, a new ring road around the city linking the north of Russia with the Baltics, creation of a financial district, a new football stadium and an award winning project by Norman Foster to redevelop the old Army Barracks 'New Holland'. It was impressive.

This sense of vision and purpose was emphasised in a meeting with the Governor of St Petersburg, Valentina Matvienko, a very powerful lady who was keen to promote the city as a place to invest. She kindly invited me to return in June for the St Petersburg International Economic Forum and the White Nights Festival, an invitation I was later to accept.

Stephen Kinnock, the director of the British Council in St Petersburg, had organised an ETQ seminar in new offices just off Nevsky Prospect with over 200 people present. This was the largest number we had at any of the 30 ETQ events in the year. It showed the level of interest in British business education in the city. It was therefore doubly sad to learn later that the Russian Government had forced the office to close when relations between the two countries deteriorated towards the end of 2007.

The city government had arranged a short whistle stop tour of the Hermitage where we learnt that there are so many rooms full of treasures that, if you spend just one minute in each, it will take you seven hours to see every room. Catherine the Great had built up an enormous collection of 2,500 paintings, for example Sir Robert Walpole's Old Masters, 10,000 carved gems and 10,000 drawings. In pre-Soviet times, the Hermitage possessed 53 Rembrandts, although over 20 had been sold since 1917. In total the museum has over three million items. The Governor kindly gave me a double volume set of books with wonderful illustrations of some of the exhibits.

At an investment seminar I pushed forward the UKTI agenda on regeneration. I also spoke at a 'Going Global' conference, where I met Peter Gerendasi Senior Partner of PwC Russia, and then had time for a final Press conference.

Prior to catching the afternoon flight back to London, we made a scheduled stop at Victory Monument and then a quick visit to the spectacular Catherine Palace.

During the Second World War, Leningrad was besieged for 900 days in a battle which lasted an amazing 1,125 days. More than one million people were killed. Victory Monument was built on the spot where the German line was held and it

143 *The Lord Mayor pays his respects at the Memorial to those who died in the siege of Leningrad in the Second World War.*

now includes a museum with film footage from that era showing the deprivation and hardship suffered. On leaving I laid a wreath at the monument.

By contrast, the 18th-century Catherine Palace and adjacent park at Tsarskoye Selo is a statement to the splendour of the Tsars. Many rooms have been designed in different styles, from different countries. Most stunning of all is the ballroom. In the years before electricity, it was lit by thousands of candles which, together with over 300 mirrors, made the room simply blaze. It must have been an incredible sight for distinguished guests as they gathered to witness the opulence of Imperial Russia. The palace also contains the famous Amber Room, sometimes referred to as the 'Eighth Wonder of the World', which was stripped by the Nazis but has been painstakingly restored by the Russian Government.

LISBON (16 & 17 APRIL 2007)

In the run-up to Portugal assuming the EU Presidency on 1 July 2007, Michael Snyder and I spent two days in Lisbon meeting senior Government figures and repeating many of the messages given in Berlin five months earlier. The usual FCO briefing, this time by British Ambassador John Buck, preceded meetings with the Governor of the Bank of Portugal, the Secretary of State for the Presidency, the Financial Markets Regulator, other officials and businessmen. The Portuguese wanted hedge funds to be more transparent and they also agreed with a principles-based approach to regulation and greater cooperation between financial sector regulators rather than a single EU regulator. We were very much on the same page and there seemed to be a lot of common ground between the UK and its oldest ally.

China (22 to 27 April 2007)

Since I spent five years in China as Executive Chairman of PwC and six years as a non-executive director of the China Britain Business Council (CBBC), more than one visit to China was considered appropriate. With a schedule of seven cities, in the event I made three separate visits because the annual Communist Party Congress was called for the week beginning 15 October and therefore disrupted my autumn visit. As it turned out, this was a blessing in disguise since, on the third visit, I was able to see a number of high ranking officials who had just been promoted and were therefore in a very good mood. I am grateful to the C-BBC and in particular to its Chief Executive, Stephen Phillips, and also to Yan Foye, who had arranged many Mayoral visits to China.

Chongqing

I first visited Chongqing in 1996, when I was working in China and met a firm of accountants whom we were considering as merger candidates. The city was not ready, at that time, for a foreign accounting firm, with little foreign investment and an aura that resembled paintings of smoke ridden, labour intensive 19th-century European manufacturing towns. Two rivers meet at Chongqing, the Yangtse and the Jialing, and it has been a busy river port for centuries. During the Japanese invasion of China, the Nationalist Army moved to Chongqing which was almost out of range of Japanese bombers but, more important, protected from attack because of the thick fog that habitually engulfs the river valleys and the city. The planes simply couldn't see the targets.

During my first visit in 1996, there was a real pea souper of a fog and the working and living conditions looked positively Dickensian. We did, however, take a cruise ship down the Yangste to Wuhan and see the Three Gorges before the dam had been completed and the water levels rose. The Three Gorges have been painted many times by Chinese artists over the centuries and poems have been written about the extraordinary landscape and river scenes. Our few days floating down the river were quite magical, with delightful scenes, living up to its centuries old reputation.

My second visit was 10 years later, in 2006, with the previous Lord Mayor. New buildings had sprung up. Foreign investment had poured in and PwC had an office of more than 100 people. Now a year later, further changes had taken place and we learnt from Tim Summers, the British Consul General in Chongqing, that the UK was the top EU investor in the region.

Chongqing is one of the four municipalities in China, the others being Beijing, Shanghai and Tianjin, and has a population of 31 million. This special status means that Chongqing can be developed much faster than other cities, without the constant need for approvals from Beijing.

Our first visit to China during 2007 was organised by Billy King-Harman. Accompanied by Lesley, Alderman & Sheriff David Lewis and his wife, Theresa, we had a strong business delegation. Sir Tom Harris of Standard Chartered

Bank, Sir Paul Judge, Jack Wigglesworth of London Asia Capital, Peter Batey, OBE, of Vermillion Partners, among others, participated in a well attended 'Going Global' seminar prior to meetings with members of the financial community, the regulators and the Party Secretary, Wang Jang. A separate roundtable with Chongqing financial services officials enhanced understanding of London's regulatory system and strengths. This helped raise awareness of the benefits of listing in London.

The ETQ seminar, chaired by Paul, also went very well and Wang Jang wanted us to establish an education centre in his city. With such senior level support, discussions were progressed after our visit by Michael Brown of the Chartered Institute of Building. At the time of writing, it seems as though this is leading to a significant British educational presence in Chongqing.

During my Mayoralty, I promoted the UK's expertise in the field of carbon trading and climate change programmes. The European Climate Exchange (ECX) had been established in London, with early trading encouraged by the City Corporation and the Treasury. London had become the global centre of emissions

144 *The Mayoral party visit a clean development project (to reduce carbon emissions) at Chongqing Iron and Steel works, arranged by Consul-General Tim Summers (back row left).*

trading and was also a leader in assisting countries to establish clean development mechanism (CDM) projects. The world of climate change is full of initials but once you master a few it becomes understandable. Jed Jones of Carbon Options Limited and an adviser to BERR is an expert in this area and was invaluable in providing a basic understanding to me and others. So, it was most interesting and helpful, during our visit to Chongqing, to actually visit a CDM project at the Chongqing Iron & Steel Company and learn how it operated. An Oxford based company, EcoSecurities Group, had worked with the Chinese company to develop a project costing Rmb 411 million (approximately £35 million) which would capture and utilise the waste gases from the production process. With an annual reduction in carbon of 438,000 tonnes, the company could obtain Carbon Emission Reductions (CERs) which are credits issued by the CDM Executive Board under the rules of the Kyoto Protocol. These CERs could then be traded and used to fund the capital project to the tune of around seventy per cent of the investment. It was a good deal for Chongqing Iron & Steel and good business for EcoSecurities who had undertaken a staggering 374 projects in 36 countries using 18 different technologies. After seeing this particular project, I could now speak with authority on the subject of CDMs and CERs.

GUANGZHOU

Guangzhou is the capital of the Province of Guangdong, formerly known as Canton, where foreigners were first allowed to trade in China. On the Pearl River, Guangzhou is now part of a large conurbation which stretches all the way to Hong Kong. When the 'Opening Up' of the Chinese economy to foreigners began in 1979, Guangdong was the first area in the PRC to receive investment – typically from Hong Kong Chinese. With the common Cantonese language, it was easy for Hong Kong businessmen to establish factories making garments and other consumer products. Now, almost 30 years later, the economy of Guangdong is larger than any other South East Asian country, accounting for one-third of China's exports and 60 per cent of its trade surplus. Replacing low cost consumer products, Guangdong's industries now include pharmaceuticals, consumer durables and financial services. And it is said that 75 per cent of the world's microwave ovens are made in one factory in Guangdong.

Our Consul General in Guangzhou is Brian Davidson who, while on secondment to IFSL in the City, had helped me start the ETQ programme 'City of London – City of Learning'. A fluent Mandarin speaker, Brian had settled back well in China and was our host for the next few days in Guangdong Province. But, first we were to enjoy a concert given by the London Symphony Orchestra, conducted by Daniel Harding, at the Xing Hai Concert Hall. It was a delight also to hear the young Chinese pianist, Lang Lang, play Mozart's Piano Concerto in G Major (No 17), although the evening's performance was somewhat spoiled by mobile phones ringing every few moments. This is modern China.

In Guangzhou, there were two seminars 'Going Global' and 'Healthcare Insurance', the latter run by BUPA, and a roundtable with the Financial Service Office, before a meeting with the Vice-Governor and the Vice-Mayor. Education was a recurring theme. We also had the opportunity of visiting the new opera house designed by the imaginative architect, Zaha Hadid. It was also a particular pleasure to dine with Sonny Doo, a Hong Kong born PwC partner with whom I had worked from 1994 to 1999 when I managed our business in China, and his fellow partner, Alfred Leung. Sir Tom Harris joined us and announced that since this was the first day on which Standard Chartered could open Rmb accounts for its customers, they had decided to give me the very first Rmb account in Guangzhou, with the number: 401-888-888-1 as a thank you present for supporting the bank and mentioning Standard Chartered's name so many times at a recent Press Conference. It was a thoughtful idea and eight is a lucky number in Cantonese, meaning 'success'.

SHENZHEN

30 years ago, Shenzhen was a fishing village. Now, with high rise office blocks, golf courses and stunning municipal buildings, it is South East China's financial centre, with ambitions of competing with Hong Kong. The bar to full convertibility

of the Rmb gives Shenzhen an advantage when it comes to banking transactions in local currency. But in other areas, too, Shenzhen has developed its financial sector. Ping An Insurance, a life and property insurance company, was founded in China just 20 years ago by Chairman, Peter Ma, and is already the second largest life insurer in the domestic market. With 44,000 employees and 200,000 agents, it is growing fast under the leadership of its Group President, Louis Cheung. It has started to become global with HSBC taking a 19.9 per cent stake in Ping An, which itself has taken a four per cent holding in Fortis Bank. In Shenzhen, Ping An has created a state of the art school of financial services on a campus that would make any university jealous. Shenzhen also has a thriving Stock Exchange.

Our visit to Shenzhen included visits to Ping An and the Stock Exchange, but also participation in four separate seminars on 'Going Global', ETQ, Innovative Insurance and with the ACCA (the Association of Chartered Certified Accountants). I also witnessed the signing of an MOU between SII and Nankai University. Education and training were very much top of the agenda for our interlocutors in Shenzhen. Discussions between Paul Judge and the Shenzhen Finance Bureau about the establishment of a UK business education centre were productive.

Indeed, the agreement in both Chongqing and Shenzhen to establish a City of London Financial Training Centre – with strong local support – was the key tangible outcome of my visit to South China. The strong ETQ focus to the visit was in tune with a local acknowledged need to improve the capacity and skills base in financial services.

The visit also generated a number of useful leads from the 'Going Global' seminars – once again expertly organised by CBBC – which both Consulates-General will pursue.

MALAYSIA (28 APRIL TO 2 MAY 2007)

Arriving in a country immediately before 1 May is not ideal from a business point of view. Many politicians and businessmen take an extended weekend. However, after an exhausting visit to China, travelling to Malaysia on a Saturday gave us a Sunday free to recover as well as the bonus of the 1 May holiday in a country that I know well. As it turned out, Ministers were available on 2 May and were perhaps more relaxed than normal.

After leaving Cambridge University, I spent a year (1966/67) teaching English at a secondary school in Brunei, where Malay is the national language. I visited Malaysia at that time and have returned many times since then, both on holiday and on business. I always enjoyed the relaxed, yet determined approach to life, which has resulted in great prosperity since independence from the UK in August 1957. Now, 50 years on, the country is an example of racial harmony and moderate Islam.

We had stayed once before at the Carcosa, previously the Resident-General's Residence, on a hill top overlooking Kuala Lumpur. The famous colonial administrator, Sir Frank Swettenham, had arranged for it to be built at the end of the 19th century and he first took up residence in 1904. Constructed in a colonial style with large open verandas to attract the breeze, in lush tropical grounds of 16 acres, the Carcosa is evocative of a bygone era. Sir Frank also built another house in the gardens for the Governor of the Straits Settlement. Known now as Seri Negara (beautiful country), this equally attractive and grand house was originally given the name 'The King's House' and this is where we stayed. The British High Commissioner, Boyd McCleary, CVO, and his wife, Jenny, joined us for dinner that night, together with Sheriff David Lewis and Theresa, Sir Paul Judge and our programme manager Billy King-Harman, to begin our induction into present day Malaysia.

The country's GDP growth is around six per cent per annum and its industry is moving up the value chain. The financial services industry is still protected, although some opening up is taking place, with HSBC, Prudential and Standard Chartered seeking new branches and licences for new activities. Relationships between our two countries have improved significantly since the low reached under Mahathir's Premiership. Over 11,000 Malaysian students are now studying in the UK and a further 30,000 studying for UK exams in Malaysia. The country's legal system is closely aligned to the UK legal system. There are important trading links and the governments are close partners in countering terrorism and climate change. The Malaysian Government is encouraging the development of Islamic finance in the country, with ambitious growth targets.

During my visit, I had meetings with a number of senior figures:

- The Deputy Prime Minister, Dato' Seri Najib Tun Razak, who was concerned about climate change, pollution and professional education. We agreed to co-operate in all three areas
- The Governor of Bank Negara, the Central Bank, Tan Sri Dato' Sri Dr Zeti Akhtar Aziz, a seasoned operator and an example of how ladies can get to the top in a Muslim society. She was keen to explore links in the field of education and expressed great interest in Gordon Brown's initiative to create an international centre for financial services regulation. She gave comfort to some of my banking colleagues by encouraging strategic investments in Malaysia's domestic banks as a way of penetrating the banking market
- The Chairman of the Securities Commission, YBhg Dato' Zarinah Anwar, another lady in a senior position. Our visit to the Commission emphasised the importance being attached to Islamic finance and the market share that Malaysia has in this fast growing market
- The Second Finance Minister, YB Senator Tan Sri Dato' Seri Nor Mohamed Yakcop, who advised that liberalisation of the legal sector might take place in 2008 and encouraged collaboration between Malaysia's International Centre for Islamic Finance (INCEIF) and UK professional institutes such as the SII.

The High Commission had organised a number of events around Education and Training. One of these was a visit to INCEIF where I met the President & CEO, Dr Agil Natt (who holds a Masters Degree from City University), and Professor Rifaat Ahmed Abdel Karim, the Secretary-General of the Islamic Financial Services Board, whom many consider to be the founding father of Islamic finance. INCEIF had ambitions plans to expand the number of students to 250 full time and 5,000 through distance learning. They were keen to cooperate with UK institutions, echoing the Finance Minister's ambitions.

Another ETQ event was a seminar, chaired by Sir Paul Judge, which I opened and then a reception was held at the British High Commissioner's Residence for alumni of the Cass and Leeds Business Schools. Both of these were well attended, as was the British-Malaysian Chamber of Commerce Gala Dinner, chaired by Datuk Peter Wentworth of BP.

One can always dine well in Malaysia. The choice of Malay, Chinese and Indian food and, sometimes, a blend of all three, in an informal often outdoor setting, offers an exotic, tropical, eating experience. Our evening at the palace in Putrajaya of the Sultan of Selangor, Duli Yang Maha Mulia Sultan Sharafuddin Idris Shah Al-Haj ibni Almarhum Sultan Salahuddin Abdul Aziz Shah Al-Haj, was another highlight of my Mayoral year. I had met Idris, then Prince Idris Shah, in 1997 when we both participated in the Peking to Paris Motor Challenge, a journey of 10,000 miles which took six weeks. Idris, accompanied by his childhood friend, Penang born English businessman, Rikkee Curtis, was driving his 1932 Model A Ford called 'Humpty Dumpty' and I was driving my 1934 Rolls-Royce called 'Harrison', We had each decided that to reach Paris over such a long distance, with inhospitable roads, it was necessary to go at a slow speed. So we both poddled along at the back – and we both made it, in one piece. We had met many times after that, including in October 2001 when we toured Malaysia in our 1921 Silver Ghost with the Rolls-Royce Enthusiasts Club. It was then a great honour to be invited to the Coronation of His Royal Highness in March 2003 and to be given his Coronation medal. We had been able to reciprocate by arranging for the Sultan to be given the Freedom of the City of London and a splendid dinner at Guildhall in 2003. But now, on the occasion of my Mayoral visit to Malaysia, HRH invited us to his palace for a magnificent dinner with leading businessmen, senior members of both the Federal and Selangor administrations and friends. The palace, the Istana Darul Ehsan, is situated in a commanding position overlooking a lake opposite the mosque and federal government buildings in the new city of Putrajaya, just south of Kuala Lumpur. Decorated in neo-classical style, with many Islamic and Malaysian fixtures and motifs, it was designed by the Sultan's late father and completed after his death. Now it houses many model ships, another of Idris' hobbies, and a unique collection of first edition books on the Straits Settlement, North Borneo and Sarawak. The dinner menu matched the venue – marinated salmon, lobster, Wagyu beef and a plate of puddings (Malays have a sweet tooth). After dinner, we enjoyed a recital by the young violinist, Joanne Yeoh, who had studied music in the UK.

Our visit to Malaysia ended with a solemn ceremony – a wreath laying at the Cheras Road War Cemetery, early in the morning when the mosquitoes were at their hungriest. Apart from appreciating the sacrifice made by those who died in the Second World War and the Malayan Emergency of the 1950s, we gained an understanding of the unpleasant conditions under which our troops had to operate in the jungles of mainland Malaya. The Mayoralty has a close link with our Armed Forces and I was honoured to lay a wreath at Cheras Road.

145 *Wreath-laying at Cheras Road War Cemetery, Malaysia.*

The packed programme, with its clear focus on ETQ fitted well into the FCO's year-long public diplomacy campaign: 'Malaysia and UK: Forward Together', the themes of which are education, science and innovation. Education remains one of the UK's key priorities in Malaysia. The visit opened new opportunities. The prospects for collaboration in the fields of Islamic Finance and perhaps leadership looked, to the FCO and UKTI, particularly interesting. It was another helpful reminder to senior Malaysians that the UK is engaging seriously.

VIETNAM (2 TO 5 MAY 2007)

Vietnam is changing fast. In the last decade, since the Government decided to move away from traditional Communist central planning and state-ownership of assets to a free market economy that embraces foreigners, GDP has grown on average eight per cent a year. There has been a marked reduction in poverty and inward investment was up 60 per cent in 2006 to US$10 billion. With a population of 83 million, this is a country that no multi-national company can afford to ignore.

British Ambassador, Robert Gordon, CMG, OBE, who retired at the end of 2007, outlined some of the key drivers to economic success. Fifty per cent of the population is under 25 years of age. Vietnamese have a good work ethic and rates of literacy are high. Vietnam is close to large Asian markets. The relationship with the UK is also good, with a major push by financial services companies such as HSBC, Standard Chartered and Prudential – the Pru has 71 branches and a staggering 40 per cent share of the domestic life business. Vietnam is one of the stars in the Prudential's portfolio.

Initial impressions of Hanoi, our first port of call, are of a bustling Asian city, with some attractive French colonial buildings, with Chinese overtones. This latter is hardly surprising since Vietnam was part of China for a thousand years until 938 and a tributary for much of the time thereafter. Territorial disputes flared up in the 1970s, leading Vietnam to ally itself with the Soviet Union. Now Vietnam is following the Chinese model of a western economy with a single party (the Communist Party) government. And it seems to be working rather well.

Education and training was, again, a theme and discussions with the Minister of Education, Dr Nguyen Thien Nhan, focused on cooperation in post graduate training and professional skills development. The Minister plans to send between 1,000 and 1,500 graduates overseas for study to PhD level. This education theme was repeated at meetings with the Prime Minister, Mr Nguyen Tan Dung, with the Ministry of Finance and also with Mr Vu Bang, the Chairman of the State Securities Commission (SSC). I was also able to raise the issue of Vietnam being slow to grant licences to foreign banks and it appeared that the current hold up was due to lack of an MOU between the SSC and our own FSA, something that I was able to raise with the FSA on my return to London. I was pleased to learn subsequently from Peter Sands, Chief Executive Officer of Standard Chartered, that his bank had now obtained a licence to operate in Vietnam.

Ho Chi Minh City (HCMC), formerly Saigon, has a more international feel to it than Hanoi and is also the home of the country's stock market. Launched in 2000, the HCMC Stock Exchange now has 106 companies listed with a total market capitalisation of US$10 billion, and a growing proportion of trade handled by foreigners. Further meetings focused on education and training and I was pleased to visit the ACCA's training centre, managed by the Singapore firm, FTMS Training Systems, which produces most of the qualified accountants in the country.

Lesley accompanied me on this tour of South East Asia and had her own programme of visits to charitable and educational institutions. In Vietnam she opened a new VSO office in Hanoi and visited centres for autistic and disabled children in both Hanoi and Ho Chi Minh City.

Our visit to Vietnam was high-impact, with prominent and favourable coverage in the local media. The timing was good: as Vietnam sees new possibilities opening up as a result of WTO membership, it is becoming clearer that they need help in increasing the skills in their financial services sector. London's growing reputation – and the patient cultivation of this market by key financial services providers – puts the UK in an excellent position to play a key role structurally and educationally, as well as commercially. The FCO and UKTI will now follow up the many leads thrown up by this visit.

We left Vietnam with a very good impression of its prospects and of the opportunities for foreign companies.

India (19 to 26 May 2007)

As one of the BRIC countries, India merits a visit by a Lord Mayor each year. With GDP averaging eight per cent per annum and a huge population and economy, the developments in India are as important to monitor and take advantage of as those in China, with whom India is often compared. In preparation for my visit, I was extremely pleased to have a comprehensive briefing from Lord (Karan) Bilimoria, Chairman of the UK India Business Council. Karan is well known as the founder and Chief Executive of Cobra Beer.

India is a well established democracy and this sometimes impairs progress. Pressure groups, such as the one million domestic lawyers and the millions employed by the major Indian banks, prevent a more rapid opening up of the market to foreign participants. Corruption and poor administration slow down the necessary developments in infrastructure such as roads, ports and telecommunications. But the private sector is very active and powerful. As a result, the economy is changing fast – and Ministers are very well aware of the shortcomings and the need to remove obstacles to progress.

My visit to India included three cities, Delhi, Kolkata and Mumbai, accompanied by Sheriff Richard Regan, programme manager Neil Chrimes and a business delegation of around forty. Picking up on the recent high level report on developing Mumbai as an international financial centre, I focused on reducing protectionism and prohibitions to market entry, on regulation of financial services and on education.

Delhi

Travelling, again, on a Saturday gave an opportunity during the day flight from London to Delhi for preparation for the visit. It also gave an opportunity for a rest on the Sunday to counter the effect of jet lag and time change. We had been invited for lunch by the Finnish Ambassador, Asko Numminen and his wife Liisa, old friends from the time they spent in London. Their residence is the work of the well known Finnish designer, Antti Nurmesniemi, who is perhaps better known for his iconic horseshoe-shaped sauna stool. It was good to see the Numminens again as well as hear from another EU Ambassador his views on India and how it was changing.

146 Another successful ETQ seminar chaired by Sir Paul Judge – this time in Delhi.

Our own diplomatic representative, the British High Commissioner Sir Michael Arthur, KCMG, had been in India for four years and spoke of the diversity. He commented, 'in one day in India, you can observe four centuries'. At one end of the spectrum, India is a first world country with all the sophistication and life styles that go with that. At the other end, there are millions of people living on less than US$1 a day. Government is also very decentralised with 28 states controlling their own affairs. Our own relationship with India has matured greatly in recent years. There is a new paradigm, based very much on partnership, but also based on a long historical relationship of contact between our two nations.

I was pleased to learn, at meetings in Delhi with Corporate Affairs Minister Prem Chand Gupta and with Law Minister HR Bhardwaj, that the concept of a limited liability partnership would be steered through the Indian Parliament, thus enabling foreign lawyers to enter into partnership with qualified Indian lawyers.

Lauding the accomplishment, the *Daily Telegraph* reported this story in its issue of 29 May with the headline 'Lord Mayor's visit to India ended rather swimmingly – for Britain and Stuttard'. However, at the time of writing, some nine months later, this law had not been put into effect as a result of continuing lobbying by the Indian legal profession.

Similar considerations apply to the insurance industry, where there had been an expectation following Gordon Brown's visit to India, as Chancellor, in early 2007 that the limit of foreign ownership of Indian insurance operations would be increased from 26 per cent to 49 per cent. But both Commerce Minister Kamal Nath and Planning Commission boss Dr Montek Singh Ahluwalia unhelpfully linked raising the foreign ownership limit in insurance to concessions to India in GATS.

My meeting with the Institute of Chartered Accountants of India (ICAI) enabled me to stress the importance of mutual recognition which had been discussed with the Institute of Chartered Accountants of England & Wales, but I added that no Government to Government agreement could be contemplated while the ICAI had law suits outstanding against the ACCA for offering training packages in India.

My meeting with Finance Minister Palaniappan Chidambaram had the added bonus of seeing the interior of the North Secretariat building at the end of the splendid Raj Path, the broadest avenue in Sir Edwin Lutyen's imperial city. Perhaps not surprisingly, it had a feel of HM Treasury in Whitehall before its recent renovation, with open courtyards in a style similar to that found in Florence, large rooms with splendid views for Ministers and senior officials, small rooms for junior officials and some even smaller rooms for brewing tea. We spoke about the Government's desire to develop Mumbai as a financial centre and I emphasised the key success factors of open market access and education. He responded positively but it was clear that Parliamentary pressure groups would inevitably thwart best intentions.

During my visit to Delhi, various media interviews and seminars were arranged by the High Commission, including one on financial services and another on education and training.

Kolkata

I was the first Lord Mayor of London ever to pay an official visit to Kolkata (or Calcutta as it used to be known). Until the 1980s, Lord Mayors typically travelled to countries in Europe or cities in the US. By the time that Mayoral Visits Programme included emerging countries, Calcutta was suffering from significant economic decline. Multinational companies were leaving the city en masse and there was little a Lord Mayor of London could do to halt this and to stimulate trade and investment.

Founded by the East India Company in 1690, Calcutta was the capital of British Imperial India until 1911. It was Asia's greatest trading centre and in 1903 there were a staggering 30,000 Europeans living there. In today's Kolkata, there are just 100. The demise of this once great international city began when New Delhi became India's capital. This decline accelerated after the Second World War due to a combination of factors – severe famines, communal violence, mass immigration into the city, power shortages, strikes, and a violent Marxist-Maoist movement – causing businesses to relocate. For three decades the government was ruled by a left wing Communist-Marxist party and it was not until the late 1990s that economic regeneration began, stimulated by wider national economic reforms in India.

Today, although still ruled by the left wing CPI(M) Party, it has a reformist Chief Minister of West Bengal, Shri Buddhadeb Bhattacharjee, whom I had the pleasure of meeting during my visit. The British Deputy High Commissioner, Simon Wilson, told me that the Minister was keen to liberalise and that Kolkata was 'on the turn'. The Chief Minister confirmed this, saying that as head of both the State and the Communist Party he did not wish to 'stick to the old dogma'. He had visited Vietnam and had seen that economic reform, liberalisation and private ownership could go hand in hand with a Communist administration.

Kolkata is full of gracious buildings, dating from the 18th and 19th centuries, albeit some a trifle dilapidated. But many have been restored. One of these is the *Oberoi Grand Hotel*, which has spacious accommodation and a large courtyard, centrally located in Chowringhee. The huge and impressive Victoria Memorial was built between 1906 and 1921 to celebrate the life of The Queen Empress. It is a statement to the might of the British Empire at that time, with a dome the size of St Paul's Cathedral. There has been some destruction of Calcutta's colonial buildings but fortunately the city has been spared the ravages of 1960s urban regeneration.

147
Bikash Ranjan Bhattacharjee, Mayor of Kolkata, orders photographers to stop fighting at a Press conference in his parlour.

Being the first Lord Mayor to visit Kolkata resulted in a large amount of media interest. The Press conference was attended by over 30 journalists and

photographers, including five TV cameras. But the most memorable media experience was my visit to the Town Hall when I paid a call on Mayor Bikas Ranjan Bhattacharjee. After being greeted on the steps by his worship, looking informal in an open neck shirt, we fought our way to the Mayor's Parlour through rows of cameramen, swarming like locusts and fighting each other to get a shot of the two of us together. The Mayor chastised them like schoolchildren for being so unruly and warned that they might not be invited to the Town Hall again to capture a similar occasion.

148 *Fifteen cameramen fight to get a picture of the first Lord Mayor to visit Kolkata. A bemused Anthony Cooke, Chairman of the Baltic Exchange, looks on.*

Our mayoral discussions focused around improving Kolkata's infrastructure through PPP, cleaning up the environment, opening the domestic market for financial services focusing on banking, insurance and ship brokerage, business and financial education. He was also very keen to utilise our expertise at saving and renovating old buildings. This did not seem to me like old fashioned Marxist-Leninist Socialism, more like the pragmatic approach to government that I had witnessed in China.

MUMBAI

On the west coast of India, Bombay's outlook to the sea is dominated by the famous Gateway of India, built to commemorate the visit to India in 1911 by George V and Queen Mary. From its completion in 1924, the Gate heralded travellers arriving by ship, often a P&O Steamship, from Blighty and the Gate witnessed the departure of the last British soldiers from India in 1947. Today, the Gateway of India is an Indian tourist site as I discovered staying at the magnificent *Taj Hotel* in a splendid room that looked directly over the Gate. And, as the British Deputy High Commissioner, Vicky Treadell, informed us, Mumbai is the commercial and entertainment centre of India, accounting for over 30 per cent of India's industrial activity and over 40 per cent of its maritime trade, with ambitions to be a regional financial hub.

Earlier in 2007, the Government of India's 'High Powered Experts' had produced a report on the development of Mumbai as an international financial centre. This was well researched and well written, covering all the obvious issues such as openness and market entry, financial regime governance and regulation, the legal infrastructure and fiscal policy. In my view, it was a bit light on the importance of professional skills development. The report had provoked a great deal of interest and debate. It was a useful platform for discussions with our interlocutors, Dr Y.V. Reddy the Governor of the Reserve Bank, P.H. Ravikumar the CEO of the Commodities and Derivatives Exchange and K.V. Kamath the CEO of the financial services group ICICI.

My meetings were warm and friendly. Dr Reddy invited further contact on opening up the market to foreign finance houses, but my delegation was sceptical, given the significant protectionist lobby. I emphasised the need for India to permit free market access if Mumbai was to succeed as an international financial centre. This was understood but the reality is that change in India takes time. As with many large emerging countries, I heard two stories – the optimists speaking about continuing growth and pent up demand; and the pessimists speaking about the poor infrastructure, protectionism and corruption. Some large domestic companies were even talking of relocating professional activities abroad, a sort of reversing outsourcing. However, to be a global player, one has to have a strong presence in India and, recognising this, the City of London decided that it must have an office in Mumbai, to assist bilateral financial activity, with a strong advisory board led by Alan Rosling of Tata. I was pleased to open this tiny office in downtown Mumbai, although many suggested that it should have been sited in the new financial district of Bandra-Kurla.

Continuing the ETQ theme for the year, I attended a discussion over lunch organised by the UK Law Society, the launch of a new exam for the SII, a seminar for the Institute of Chartered Arbitrators, a lunch with the Baltic Exchange and, of course, an ETQ seminar organised by the British Council.

Each visit has a memorable moment and, in Mumbai, that was The Queen's Birthday Party which Vicky Treadwell had organised around a James Bond theme for 2007. After a sober toasting of the President of India (by me) and of The Queen (by the head of protocol of the Mumbai Government), and an excellent speech by Vicky, we had a Bollywood treat, with music and dancing, and some scantily clad models wearing mind boggling swimwear. It was certainly a night to remember.

But what of India and of the prospects for the City of London? Democracy and the political processes slow down development in many areas – infrastructure, professional services, financial services and development of an international presence in the financial sector. Yet, there is a progress and London is well placed to be a partner – on equal terms – as India develops.

DENMARK AND FINLAND (3 TO 10 JUNE)

It is customary for the Lord Mayor to ask the Chief Commoner to accompany him on one overseas visit each year. In March, Deputy Pauline Halliday was elected Chief Commoner and we asked Pauline and her husband, Peter, to join us on this week's visit to Denmark and Finland, under the care of programme manager, Richard Martin.

For eight years (1986 to 1994) I was chairman of Coopers & Lybrand UK's Scandinavian Market Group and worked a great deal in both Finland and

Denmark on share issues, listings and acquisitions. It had been some years since a Lord Mayor had visited Denmark and I couldn't possibly not go to Finland during my year, given the honour bestowed on me by the President, my role at the Finnish-British Chamber of Commerce and the welcoming noises I had received from Finnish friends and our British Ambassador, Valerie Caton.

DENMARK

First, to Denmark, travelling as ever on a Sunday, we were briefed over dinner by British Ambassador, David Frost, and stayed with him and his wife Jacqueline, at their Residence in the leafy suburbs of Copenhagen. Danes are very practical people and our meetings with Peter Schutze of Nordea and Per Skovhus of Den Danske Bank revealed a lot of common ground when it came to dealing with EU issues, except that Peter was keen to have a single regulator in Europe. I was anxious to disabuse him of this, since a highly rules-based model, which might result, would not be one that he would appreciate afterwards. Both banks expressed admiration for the UK's Financial Services Authority and were thankful that the Continental (particularly German) focus on hedge funds seemed to have waned. They expressed concern about noises being made to regulate Private Equity further.

After a useful seminar on PPP at the Embassy and an award of a Mansion House Scholarship, the Ambassador hosted an interesting dinner party. I had my ear well and truly bent about the horrors of Heathrow – the increased security and lack of security staff to deal with this, coupled with the one piece of hand luggage policy. On my return to London, I wrote immediately to Ed Balls, Economic Secretary at the Treasury and, later in the year, David Frost brought a group of Danes to London to inspect the new Terminal 5 at Heathrow (before it opened!) and, then, to have lunch with me at Mansion House.

It was a pleasure to be entertained for lunch in the Tivoli Gardens (a sort of upmarket amusement park, with excellent restaurants) by a group of Danish businessmen, chaired by my old friend Jens Roder, President of the Danish Institute of State Authorised Public Accountants, with whom I worked at Coopers & Lybrand in London in the 1960s. Like me, he is an old car enthusiast and, for many years, was President of the Danish Jaguar Owners Club. Jens had arranged the lunch so that I could meet two Permanent Secretaries (Michael Dithmer and Peter Loft) and we exchanged views on financial sector regulation, on which there was a lot of common ground.

FINLAND

Valerie Caton and her head of Commercial Section, John Slate, had arranged an excellent programme. The fact that I knew most of the interlocutors, many of whom are friends, helped enormously.

Also, of great help and a particular honour for me was the involvement in my visit to Finland of the Finnish Ambassador to London, His Excellency Jaakko Laajava. Jaakko is a career diplomat and very wise counsel. Since he arrived in

London he has been instrumental in helping to convey Finland's strengths and was of enormous assistance when I organised a seminar in 2006 on 'A Balanced Approach to Energy – The Nordic Experience', involving many experts from Finland as well as the UK Minister for Energy, Malcolm Wicks, and the UK Government Chief Scientific Officer, Sir David King. It was a delight to be accompanied to Finland by Jaakko and his wife, Pirjoriitta.

The British Ambassador's Residence in Helsinki is one of the most gracious Foreign Office residences, dating from the beginning of the 19th century, in a Russian Czarist Empire style. It is built on a very solid granite base while the exterior, at ground and upper floor levels, is rendered and painted pink. In a dominant position at one end of the very attractive Kaivopuisto Park, it has a good size garden and sufficient space for entertaining. Unfortunately, during the cold war, when our Embassy staff numbers in Helsinki were higher, a modern building was built immediately next door and is now too large as a result of the downsizing that has taken place in the last 10 years. Finland, now a member of the EU, in a stable geopolitical position, does not demand the intense diplomatic and intelligence attention that was warranted in the 1960s and 1970s.

However, as an economic and trading partner, Finland has a special relationship with the UK. This dates back to the 18th century when the British fleet relied on the northern Finnish cities for its supply of tar, to keep the ships watertight, and to the early 20th century when Finland became the UK's main supplier of paper, for newspapers and magazines. There is a wonderful story, which Valerie's predecessor as Ambassador, Matthew Kirk, tells of the British Navy bombarding the northern city of Oulu, in the Gulf of Bothnia, during the Napoleonic War, and destroying the tar depot, only to discover that the British had already paid for the tar and that it was their own British asset that they were destroying. The Finns laughed all the way to the bank and they love hearing a Brit tell the story.

Finnish humour is very similar to British humour, based on word play rather than slapstick. The Finns are cultured people, well read – perhaps because of the long northern winter nights – and very open and frank. They say what they mean and they mean what they say. Friendship is important, indeed essential, as a precondition to doing business. Long standing relationships are very special. I have, as a result, been very fortunate to have had the opportunity of working with Finnish companies for 25 years. I have gained many Finnish friends and they are life long in their friendship.

My first encounter with Finns was being invited to Helsinki in December 1983 by an old friend, Lars Blomquist, to advise the Finnish sports goods company, Amer, on how to raise equity finance in London and list its shares on the London Stock Exchange. On late arrival at the hotel, I was informed that the four partners in the Finnish firm with whom Coopers & Lybrand was associated had already started their sauna and my first 'business' meeting was with four naked men thrashing themselves with birch twigs and being washed by a very large lady wearing a plastic apron. You could say that on my first visit to Finland I was 'presented with the naked truth'.

My first Finnish business assignment was equally bizarre. At that time, Amer was known for its manufacture of cigarettes, as well as sporting goods, essentially the ice hockey stick brand Koho. The Chief Executive, Heikki Olavi Salonen, was a larger than life character who boasted that there were only two people in the world that had their own brand of cigarettes, James Bond and himself – 'HOS'. I explained to Heikki that, as part of our work, I needed some key information for the first page of the prospectus to explain the direction of the company. I needed to understand his strategy for Amer. At this point a Pavlovian reaction set in. 'Strategy', he said, 'if you want to understand strategy, then we go to the sauna.' The executive sauna was on the top floor of the office building. In Finland, saunas are usually sited in locations where there is a splendid view. From the top of the office building, the view was not that splendid, but it was unique, overlooking the factory, with a balcony and steps down to the roof. After a shower and then a hot sauna, Heikki turned to me and said 'John, have you ever rolled in the snow?' 'No, Heikki', I replied, 'I have never rolled in the snow.' 'Then we go', he commanded. And the Chief Executive of the mighty Amer Group Limited and I rolled in the snow on the roof of the tobacco factory while the good workers made cigarettes underneath. When I explained back in London what I had been doing during my visit to Finland, there was a bemused silence. It was difficult to be taken seriously.

Well, today, in Finland, there are still saunas, but the sauna culture among Finnish industry has largely disappeared, unless you are the factory manager of a paper mill in the deepest countryside, where the traditions live on. My best sauna experience was at the country home, near Kuopio, of Lasse Lehtinen – MP, writer, journalist, television personality and now an MEP. His sauna is a smoked sauna, a real cut above, where the room is heated by wood smoke being passed through it, until the fire dies out, leaving the stones hot. When you emerge from the sauna you feel, literally, as though you have been smoked. A guest some years ago of Lasse was the comedian, TV personality, writer and globetrotter Michael Palin, who expressed pleasure at being beaten by Lasse with birch twigs. He said that it reminded him of his schooldays at Shrewsbury School. My memory of Michael was slightly different. Even then he was an actor and we appeared together in Henry VI Part 2, in which I played the Lord Chief Justice. In our different ways, we both benefited from that early theatrical experience of being taught to play a part, annunciate beautiful verse and project one's voice to the back of an auditorium.

Valerie and John had identified three objectives for my visit:
- promote the UK as an attractive place for Finnish investment, especially from the hi-tech sector
- promote UK financial centres as a resource for Finnish companies
- boost the network of high-powered, well-placed Finns with strong links

to the UK, including through our scholarship and alumni schemes.

- The programme had been planned to meet these objectives and included a visit to Oulu, Finland's equivalent of Silicon Valley, as well as substantive discussions in the capital city.

My Mayoral visit to Helsinki included meetings with Leif Fagernas, Director General of the Confederation of Finnish Industries, Mauri Pekkarinen, Minister for Trade and Industry, Jyrki Katainen, Minister of Finance, Jouni Torasvirta, President of the Helsinki Stock Exchange and senior representatives of the Bank of Finland.

These meetings highlighted a number of interesting features about Finland and how Finns see themselves from the far Northern corner of Europe. The country has benefited enormously from being a member of the EU. There is a feeling of greater physical security for the country, which has historically been threatened as a result of its long border with Russia. Continuing GDP growth of around three per cent and declining unemployment combine to improve confidence. Terms of trade are, however, getting worse, with prices of forest products and electronics decreasing while prices of imports, particularly of oil and gas, are increasing. The population is aging yet, unlike other mature economies, there is little immigration to offset this. There is a need to increase expenditure on R&D and the role of the public sector is being questioned. There are concerns about the Finnish educational system, which many in the UK look to with envy. Not so the Finns, they believe that they have too many universities and that too many students are being educated for the wrong jobs, with too many people studying for degrees in 'soft' subjects.

Russia will always feature in the minds of Finns. For one hundred years, from 1809 to 1917, Finland was a Grand Duchy of the Czar. After independence in 1917, Finland's south eastern border was physically very close to Leningrad. Wanting greater lebensraum and attracted by the idea of seizing the city of Viipuri (or Vyborg) and the Saimaa Canal, the USSR began the Winter War. This, in turn, led to the Continuation War, where Finland was obliged to side with Russia's enemy, Nazi Germany. Despite fierce resistance from the brave and outnumbered Finns, the whole of the south eastern part of Finland, known as Karelia, was sequestrated by the Soviet Union, which also demanded reparations from the defeated country. In the post Second World War period, Finland's economy was boosted by a bilateral trade agreement with Russia, which still remains an important trading partner. Nokia has a very large presence in Russia and many Finnish SMEs have invested and are trading well. Finnish children are being encouraged to learn Russian at school. However, Finland is losing market share and forest industry companies have been wary of investing too much in a country that they know well. Recent rhetoric from the Kremlin reminds Finns of the days of the Iron Curtain, with Russian nationalism being fuelled. The Finnish reaction is to build relationships and seek to find common ground. Many will recall the policy of appeasement during the days of Kekkonen, who was President from 1956 to 1982, and they now seek a stronger position for Finland. They thus take great comfort from their membership of the European Union and some would like to see Finland become a fully fledged member of NATO.

Finland has always been sensitive to environmental issues. With such a small population living in a huge area of forest, with difficult agricultural growing conditions, and with thousands of lakes, nature and people are very close. This is borne out in art – paintings, literature, and glass design – and also in the lifestyle – there are rumoured to be millions of country cottages and saunas in the country. Energy is produced from biomass as well as fossil fuels. Finland is the only country in Europe currently to be building a nuclear power station, based on the latest technology which generates a fraction of the waste of previous generations. In fact 25 per cent of energy now comes from renewables. But there are concerns that if the percentage of energy from biomass is artificially increased then this could cause wood prices, and therefore pulp and paper prices to rise – a phenomenon which the US has experienced with its production of bio fuel from corn.

Other discussions centred on financial regulation, corporate governance, public private partnerships and professional skills development. On this latter subject, I was pleased to be present when scholarships were given to eight bright young Finns to study in the UK and also to have discussions with the rectors of Finland's leading universities, organised by Tuija Talvitie, the Director of the British Council.

In my efforts to promote the UK financial services industry, I gave several press interviews highlighting the opportunities for Finnish companies wanting to list in London, around the caption 'Is Finland missing its AIM?' This taps into a concern of the new Finnish Government that Finance Minister Katainen raised with me: how can Finland exploit its intellectual assets to secure future prosperity as its working population shrinks and global competition in traditional sectors gets ever tougher? Our answer was that Finland's younger hi-tech businesses needed to 'open the gate to success' by drawing on AIM finance to grow into world markets. The AIM Seminar organised by the FCO at the Embassy built on this message with detailed presentations to 62 interested Finnish companies. There was plenty of subsequent positive feedback from these companies and it seemed likely that two or three would seriously considering listing in the coming months, as a direct result of the seminar, with others in the longer term.

At a dinner at City Hall, hosted by the Lord Mayor of Helsinki, Jussi Pajunen, I was presented with the Silver Medal of Helsinki which, I was informed, is only given to foreigners who have performed meritorious service to the city. It was a complete surprise and I am greatly honoured to have received his accolade to accompany my other Finnish honour, Commander of the Order of the Lion of Finland.

Getting physical exercise during the Mayoral year was always a challenge. So I was delighted to accept a challenge of a sporting nature when I was invited to play tennis with Markku Vartiainen, a publisher and editor of the magazine *Finn-Niche*, against Minister Pertti Salolainen, former Deputy Prime Minister and Finnish Ambassador to the UK and now an MP again, and Olli-Pekka Kallasvuo, Chief Executive of Nokia, with whom I worked on many assignments during the 1990s. It was a close, hard-fought game, which our opponents won by a whisker.

Nokia is one of Finland's great success stories and I have been pleased to be associated with it particularly with its listing in London in 1987 and then during its restructuring in the 1990s under the able leadership of Jorma Ollila, CBE, who became a good friend.

Another delight was a dinner arranged by Johan Kronberg, Managing Partner of PwC Finland, at an attractive old house in Huvilakatu, where I was given a stunning ornamental glass plate by the distinguished Finnish designer, Heikki Orvola. All my old friends from the firm were present, with their wives, and a nice touch was the transport that had been arranged to bring us from the Embassy, a 1929 Peerless car owned by the Aminoff family. I had previously had contact with the Aminoff family, as an auditor and adviser, to their companies, including Electrosonic, the audio-visual display company with a UK presence in London and Dartford. The Electrosonic Board held their Annual Meeting in the Residence during my visit and we had a discussion about global business issues, before I was whisked away in the Peerless.

In Finland, Lesley also had her own programme and visited a children's care centre. Finland is well known for its educational city and care for the young and attracts many interested educationalists from around the world to see how a country can become top in class.

To understand Finland properly, one has to get out of Helsinki – to the forests and the lakes. The Embassy had arranged for us to visit Oulu, an old city in the north on the Gulf Bothnia, known historically for its wood tar, timber and salmon. I had been to Oulu before and was impressed by the technology cluster that has developed around the university with involvement from Nokia and other major Finnish companies, including many in the healthcare industry. Welcomed by the Mayor, Matti Pennanen, we learnt that Oulu is the home to the largest technology park in Europe and has over 30,000 students at the university, Twenty-five per cent of the city's population. With an aging population, apart from the students, a focus in recent years has been on health and well being, particularly for older people. A visit to the university had been arranged and we were met by the President, Professor Lauri Lajunen, and saw the new micro and nano technology centre and the new robotic research unit. Finns have great imagination and excel at the application of technology, as we have witnessed during the mobile phone revolution.

Historically Finland has been well known for its forest industry, which is still a very major contributor to GDP, exports and employment. So our visit to the Stora Enso mill, the largest integrated pulp and paper facility in Europe, gave an impression of the continuing importance of this sector. The mill is enormous, like a great cathedral, with huge machines producing 570,000 tonnes each year. With their focus on the environment, the Finns had begun to use eucalyptus wood from Brazil as a key raw material. Trees can grow and be harvested within seven years, so contributing greatly to the production of oxygen in the atmosphere and neutralising the effect of carbon emissions produced by the mill, which also uses wood for energy supply.

The Company had also arranged a dinner for us to meet local businessmen and it was a pleasure for us that this was hosted by Stora Enso's Chief Executive Jukka Härmälä and his wife Marjatta, Finnish friends who had also lived in London for some years and with whom we have stayed during previous visits to Finland.

Our visit to Finland concluded with a two night stay with Lasse Lehtinen and Eira Palin, old friends who had a country home at Varpasjärvi, near Kuopio. Overlooking a lake, without another house in sight, it is a perfect place to chill out. They had asked mutual friends Lars & Ritva Blomquist and Kalle & Ammi Isokallio to stay for the weekend. Lasse is a wonderful cook and a visit to his home is always a culinary delight. On this occasion, the salmon had been freshly caught and smoked and, for pudding, he had prepared a mustikka (blueberry) pie. Lasse and Eira are also very keen on music and we were entertained by an accordion player and a saxophonist, playing traditional Finnish as well as Russian folk ballads.

24 HOURS IN ST PETERSBURG

Each year the Governor of St Petersburg organises a Davos-like event known as the St Petersburg International Economic Forum. It is an excellent opportunity to inform oneself of developments in the city and in Russia generally. It is also an excellent opportunity to network and to meet many senior politicians and executives.

The Governor, Valentina Matvienko, had invited me to the Forum, and the accompanying Festival, when I visited the city in April. As no UK Minister would be attending the Forum in 2007, the British Ambassador encouraged me to represent the UK, which I was pleased to do. A short early morning flight on Sunday from Kuopio to St Petersburg enabled us to reach the conference venue in time for President Putin's keynote speech. He drew attention to the shift in economic wealth and GDP from the G8 developed nations to the developing and emerging countries. He pointed out the investment flows into and out of Russia – approximately US$150 billion. He stressed the growing importance of the countries in Central Asia. He criticised the international organisations for not being effective at eliminating protectionism.

Other speakers included President Nazarbayev of Kazakhstan, Sheikh Hamad Bin Jassim Al Thani 1st Deputy Prime Minister of Qatar, Jens Stoltenberg the Prime Minister of Norway and then Dmitry Medvedev who was, some months later, elected as the next President of Russia. It was a powerful line up of senior politicians who advocated free markets and a reform of existing world bodies.

I was received, for the second time in two months, by the Governor who encouraged greater contact with British companies in the programme to develop St Petersburg further. I also had the opportunity of meeting again Finance Minister Kudrin and other Ministers, including Alexander Zhukov, a Deputy Prime Minister.

I was asked about the possibility of investing Russia's stabilisation fund ($200 billion) through London and responded that I judged the mood of UK business to be equally positive. I commented that the City continued to welcome business from Russia with open arms, and had confidence in Russia's continued economic growth and reform. However, I counseled that in order to accelerate the excellent business relationship, Russia should continue to make progress on a predictable and rules-based system for dealing with foreign investors, as well as strengthening corporate governance for global Russian companies.

During these meetings, conversations on possible cooperation were positive and subjects included PPP, corporate governance and education and training, but there was an undercurrent of tension caused by disagreements between the two countries on interpretations of law, not least over the Litvinenko case. I was pleased to have been able to keep the business agenda and the business dialogue going.

The White Nights Festival which takes place in St Petersburg each June takes advantage of the city's northern location which provides almost 24 hours of daylight. The backdrop of this gracious 18th-century city provides a splendid setting for an extravagant evening of outdoor eating at the Peter and Paul Fortress by the River Neva, accompanied by music and opera. As we arrived, scantily dressed models handed out canapés and glasses of vodka or champagne. Then, at the appointed hour, the Governor arrived with a grand entrance, greeted by stirring music from no fewer than 12 identical white grand pianos. With actors and models on jet skis on the River Neva, the whole event reminded one of a James Bond film set. It was memorable. So was our large and comfortable Prokofiev Suite at the renovated *Astoria Hotel* in the heart of St Petersburg, by the St Isaak's Cathedral.

St Petersburg is one of the world's most beautiful cities and it is currently experiencing a renaissance.

POLAND (10 TO 12 JULY 2007)

A short visit to Poland demonstrated the importance to the UK of this Eastern European country, which the British Ambassador, Charles Crawford, was keen to promote. With a troubled past, pushed backwards and forwards over the centuries by Russians from the east and Germans from the west, Poles have had to be resilient and resourceful to survive.

One of the older members of 'New Europe' they understand and appreciate the benefits of being part of the EU, but they don't like the rules and regulations. Poland has only been independent for 30 out of the last 200 years, so the new found freedom is precious. But, it has to reach the ballot box, since out of 38 million people, only three million voted – for the ruling 'Law and Justice' Party. In the 17th century Poland was a huge and powerful country. In 1608, the Polish Army captured Moscow. Today, Poles feel that the rest of Europe owes it a living. Yet, many young Poles work abroad – in Germany and the UK – and they are skilled workers who work hard. Corruption is still an issue, as is poor Corporate Governance. In Poland, there are always crises. Governments come and go. For example, there seems to be a new Finance Minister each year. Yet everyday life and business carries on regardless. This is the Polish way of life. GDP growth is around six-and-a-half per cent per annum and the economy is diversifying. There is a belief that foreigners can help but a lack of understanding as to how this might be achieved. Germans and Italians are very active but UK companies have not really focused as much as they might on opportunities in Poland, having rather leapfrogged the country in favour of China, India, Russia and the CIS.

A topic of great interest at our meetings with Mayor Hanna Gronkiewicz-Waltz and Deputy Finance Minister Katarzyna Zajdel was the UK's experience in PPP for infrastructure projects, particularly in the light of Poland's preparations for Euro 2012. One of my business delegation, Stephen Chandler of EDS, was able to respond knowledgeably to this.

There had been rumours that the Government, run at the time of my visit by the two Kaczynski twins, would introduce a cap on fee rates that lawyers could charge. This would have resulted in foreign lawyers finding practice in Poland to be unviable. I raised this concern at my meeting at the Ministry of Justice.

We held another ETQ seminar, organised by the British Council, which attracted a sizeable audience interested in financial qualifications. Then, at a pleasant dinner at the Ambassador's Residence, sitting next to Presidential candidate Henryka Bochniarz, I referred to the diamonds in my Mayoral badge as being of Polish origin – a love gift from King Sigmund August (1530-1572), last king of the Yagielonian Dynasty who died childless, to the young Queen Elizabeth I (1560-1603). This running gag, begun in Russia, continued and the Press were keen to pick it up and write about this fantastical story.

Members of my business delegation, including Mark Garvin from JP Morgan and Gerry Albanese from underwriters Markel International, were impressed with the business opportunities in Poland and sought closer ongoing ties with the City of London.

BRAZIL (13 AUGUST TO 1 SEPTEMBER 2007)

The term 'BRIC' was first prominently used by Goldman Sachs in a thesis in 2003 to describe those economies which were developing rapidly and which, by 2050, would eclipse many of the current mature economies. So far as Brazil is concerned, this has not necessarily done the country any favours, as its GDP on a PPP basis is over US$10,000 per year, compared to India's US$4,000. Brazil is therefore bracketed with countries which are less well developed, yet the country is in many ways sophisticated and comparable to some EU countries. Brazil has enormous reserves of practically every natural resource – oil, gas, ethanol, minerals, forest and fertile agricultural land. It is the world's largest producer of beef, chicken, coffee and fruit. It has very well developed agricultural, mining, manufacturing and service sectors, as well as a large working population. It has the 9th largest economy in the world, although there is a large disparity of income and wealth in the country, with some very wealthy landowners and industrialists. With growing confidence, national pride and enthusiastic energy, Brazilians are discovering a new place for themselves in the world.

Since it was discovered by the Europeans in 1500, Brazil was a colony of Portugal until independence in 1822. During this time, the country supplied gold and got little in return except the Portuguese language and a European culture. Now, some 500 years later, the population of Brazil is a hotchpotch with people of African origin in the north and Europeans of Germanic and British origin in the south. But everyone is Brazilian; everyone speaks Portuguese; and everyone loves football, carnival and the family. As we were to discover, Brazilians are very warm, friendly, emotional, touchy-feely sort of people, who like music, laughter and enjoying life.

Neither Lesley nor I had visited Brazil before. We hadn't even met that many Brazilians before, yet we both had ancestors who had lived and worked there in the 19th century. Lesley's family, the McCalls, had run a meat factory in the south, in Bagé, canning cooked beef tongues encased in jelly, and selling them to the European market under the brand name 'McCall's Paysandu Ox Tongues,' advertised as 'ready for immediate use' in the 1892 edition of Mrs Beeton's *Book of Household Management*. At precisely the same time that Lesley's ancestors were cooking and canning in the south, my ancestor, the Reverend James Midgley, was chaplain in the northern city of Recife, where he was busy marrying, baptising and also burying Englishmen and women, in his role as consular chaplain. He arrived there in 1875, after an extraordinary posting as a missionary to East Africa with the explorer the Reverend David Livingstone, and he remained in Recife until 1892.

At the end of the 19th century and well up to the Second World War, the relationship between Great Britain and Brazil was very close. British companies built the railways and supplied the trains. Family businesses such as Vestey prospered as the natural resources of Brazil were harnessed and the market opportunities in the US and Europe exploited. This special relationship with the UK goes back to 1808 when the British Fleet escorted the King of Portugal from Lisbon to Salvador to flee Napoleon's invading army. Then, during WWII, with more than two-thirds of the British Maritime Fleet torpedoed in the Atlantic and with traditional trading ties cut, the US took advantage of the void and assumed the role of Brazil's main trading partner. I used this history and the history of our family involvement in Brazil during my speeches. I would say that our relationship was like that of a husband and wife, married for many years and taking each other for granted. As a result, it had cooled somewhat but there was still real affection and love. It was time therefore, on the occasion of the 200th anniversary of our first relationship, to renew our marriage vows.

Today, there is greater contact than in the last 50 years between Brazil and the UK. The countries are complimentary. Brazil has resources, food and a significant manufacturing capability. The UK has services and expertise, not least in financial services. President Lula made a successful State Visit to the UK in 2006, when I was introduced to him at the Banquet at Guildhall. He raised the profile of his great country. But Brazil is relatively unknown in the UK as attention has been directed eastwards to the Gulf, India, Russia and China. So, Lesley and I decided to brief ourselves about Brazil by taking a week's holiday in August to some of the attractive old Portuguese towns, beginning on the coast at Paraty. Sheltered in an attractive bay, Paraty was the port from which the gold, mined in Minas Gerais, was exported. Today, it is a sleepy fishing village with simple fishermen's houses, some elaborately decorated, and excellent cafes and restaurants, which come alive at night. In an unusual method of sanitation, the town's streets are flooded twice each day by the high tide. To prevent the houses themselves being flooded, there are one or more steps up to the front door, but there are a lot of damp walls. Despite this and because of its unique attraction and location, Paraty is being gentrified as a weekend place for businessmen and their families escaping São Paolo, with tourist shops and some extremely pleasant hotels such as the one where we stayed, the *Pousada Pardieiro*, recommended by our old friend, Tim Butchard, who was head of the British Council in Brazil until retirement in 2004. Unfortunately we hadn't be able to visit him while he was posted there, but the present head of the UKTI in Brazil, Martin Raven, kindly met us every time we landed in São Paolo to ensure that we were properly looked after. Violent crime is prevalent in both São Paolo and Rio de Janeiro, but in Paraty it was possible to stroll through the streets at any time of the day unmolested and feeling safe. Paraty is famous for its *Cachaça*, a local Brazilian firewater, and also for its beautiful coastal scenery, at the end of a huge natural bay with small islands and little coves. A boat trip is a must. Ours did not disappoint.

Brazil is a big country. To travel to the gold mining towns of Minas Gerais takes some time. Tim had suggested we fly to Belo Horizonte, the capital, which meant a drive along the coast from Paraty to Rio. It was a pretty journey. We also passed the site of one of Brazil's nuclear power stations at Ita Curuca (Indian for 'Bad Rock' which perhaps explains why the authorities had initial problems with the structure sinking).

Everyone we met in Brazil asked why we had bothered to visit Belo Horizonte and were surprised when we explained that it was to see the first few buildings that world famous architect Oscar Niemeyer had designed in the 1940s in the Pampulha District. A fan of Le Corbusier, he led the Brazilian modernist movement and his church (of St Francis of Assisi) in Pampulha was so unorthodox that for years the ecclesiastical authorities refused to consecrate it. They relented in 1959 by which time Niemeyer had been asked to design the new capital of Brasilia. Now, 100 years old, he is still consulted regarding any new buildings or changes to buildings in Brasilia and is a world respected architect.

The old colonial mining towns of Minas Gerais are magical as is the rugged and wild countryside. Gold was discovered in large quantities in the late 17th century in Ouro Preto, a town among hills with narrow, attractively cobbled streets, excellent restaurants and small shops selling jewellery and items made from gold and semi-precious stones. Brazilians like long meals. They are keen on pork and also enjoy wonderful puddings, made from exotic fruits. Surprisingly, for Latins, they mainly drink beer rather than wine with food. However, Brazilians of German origin have ensured that the lager is of an exceptional standard. But the gems of Ouro Preto are its churches, such as the Church of St Francis of Assisi, dating from the 18th century, which contains elaborately carved statues, with plenty of gilt, reflecting the availability of gold.

Our next few days were spent in Tiradentes, a smaller gold mining town founded in 1702 and named later after a revolutionary hero. Set, like Ouro Preto on a hillside, it is one of the prettiest towns one can imagine, with restaurants, cafes, art galleries and artists' workshops. Two of the more interesting shops sell cutlery, the brainchild of an Englishman, John Summers, who established a pewter manufacturing business in nearby São Joao del Rei. Our hotel was an old farm, with outhouses and duck pond, all owned and managed by Raquel, the wife of a local gynaecologist, Luiz Ney Fonseca. His hobby was cooking at the farm and his speciality was *Leitao a Pururucha*, a dish of special suckling pig cooked slowly for days and then finished off by heating the skin to make it crackle. They had invited friends to dine with us and these included Robert Ballantyne, an English resident of Tiradentes and a former member of the FCO. Our time in Tiradentes was relaxing, enabling visits to many churches, a steam train journey to nearby São Joao del Rei and many pleasant meals.

The last few days of our holiday were spent in the northern colonial town of Olinda, not far from Recife, with its modern international airport. The Portuguese first landed in Brazil in Recife in 1500. Olinda was founded in 1535 and many of the churches and monasteries date from the early 16th century. They were burned down by the Dutch who occupied the port from 1630 and were rebuilt after the Portuguese recaptured the city in 1654. Now, slightly run down, Olinda is a jewel, recognised as such by UNESCO, and waiting to be restored. Some work has already begun. The Monasteiro de São Bento was founded in 1582 and is Brazil's first law school. The Igreja NS do Carmo dates from 1580 and has splendid ceiling paintings. The cathedral, the Igreja da Se, was built in 1537 and has a terrace from which one can view the roof tops of Olinda and look out to sea. Then the Convento São Francisco, dating from 1577, destroyed in 1631 and rebuilt in 1700, situated on a promontory to catch the sea breezes, with magical cloisters.

Before our visit to Brazil we had met the Brazilian Ambassador, Jose Mauricio Bustani, and his wife, Janine, on a number of occasions. They had recommended places to visit and hotels which we would like, including the *Hotel 7 Colinas* in Olinda, set in gardens in an attractive part of the town. Janine had also helped me research my ancestor, James Midgley, who spent 17 years in Recife between 1875 and 1892. Until the 1930s, when it was demolished, there stood in the main street, Conde da Boa Vista, 'the little church of the English'. More exciting, there is still a *Rua Padre Inglês* where, we were informed, Protestant clerics, including perhaps also James, lived. Then, on the main road to Olinda is the British Cemetery, now padlocked and seemingly no longer used for new burials, that dates from 1814. My uncle James would certainly have presided over funerals here.

After a week, we had begun to understand a little of Brazil, particularly its colonial history and the role that the British, including our ancestors, played in the development of the country. It was now time for the official visit to begin and we returned to São Paolo, to be met again by Martin Raven, with his wife Pippa, and to be briefed by the British Ambassador, Dr Peter Collecott, and join our delegation, programme manager Billy King-Harman and head of Press Relations for the City of London Corporation, Greg Williams.

I had been impressed by what we had seen and heard of Brazil thus far. With its extensive natural resources, I was struck by the dynamism, imagination, innovation and colour. For many years in the recent past it has been struggling to liberalise and realise its potential. This is beginning to have a positive impact. GDP growth has been around five per cent per annum for the last three years. With a continuing balance of payments surplus, foreign exchange reserves have increased to US$160 billion. Foreign direct investment to Brazil in 2007 increased almost 100 per cent to US$37 billion, which is more than the total invested in the whole of Africa. Brazil is the heart of automobile manufacturing in South America as an aerial tour of São Paolo was later to confirm to us. Brazil is also leading in the field of ethanol fuel technology, using sugar cane as the base for this energy efficient fuel. Most cars have dual fuel systems and some even have three. And, as if to demonstrate real wealth, I was informed that Brazil is the second largest market in the world for Ferraris.

The business programme had been carefully planned by Peter Collecott and Martin Raven, with the following objectives:
- raise the profile of UK financial services and related sectors
- demonstrate to Brazilian companies the attractions of listing in London
- increase Brazilian interest in CDM projects and trading in carbon credits
- remind Brazilian decision makers of the attractions of PPP and our expertise
- promote the City of London as a centre for professional training
- encourage Brazilian companies who want to go global to invest in the UK.

SÃO PAOLO

São Paolo has become Brazil's main manufacturing and financial centre, although some key industries, notably insurance, are still based in Rio de Janeiro. As a result, the head of our UKTI, Martin Raven, is located in São Paolo, at the Centro Brasileiro Britânico which also houses the British Council. Funded from English language training courses, the Centre makes quite a statement, putting the UK firmly on the map and giving us higher profile. During my visit, we had many meetings there, including media briefings and a reception and dinner hosted by Britcham, whose chairman, Francisco Itzaina, works for Rolls-Royce.

The Brazilian Stock Exchange, Bovespa, is growing very fast and accounts for 75 per cent of all South and Latin American market capitalisation of listed companies. At a lunchtime meeting, I was pleased to witness the signing of an MOU with the London Stock Exchange, as well as meet the CEO, Gilberto Mifano.

I was similarly impressed with my visit to the Brazilian Mercantile & Futures Exchange (BM&F) which is now the fifth largest exchange in the world. Trading in derivatives and foreign exchange, using the open outcry method, and government bonds, BM&F was preparing for a launch of carbon emissions trading. The Exchange was also about to be demutualised and represents an opportunity for a foreign institution to become a strategic partner. Other areas being considered were trading in non-ferrous metals and a soya bean market. There was an air of dynamism about the BM&F.

At City Hall, with Mayor Gilberto Kassab, we discussed how we could co-operate in the areas of PPP, carbon trading and prevention of financial crime. I later spoke at a conference on PPP chaired by Ambassador Rubens Barbosa, a former Brazilian ambassador to Washington and London.

A well attended seminar on listing on the London Stock Exchange was organised by Ivan Clark, a senior partner at PwC. Graham Dallas of the LSE gave an excellent and well received talk on the advantages of raising equity finance in London. Traditionally, Brazilian companies looked to New York as a source of finance, but were increasingly turning their attention to London now that it has become the world's leading financial centre. When I left Brazil I learnt that discussions had taken place with a number of companies considering listing in London.

A roundtable with a group of bankers, including HSBC, Lloyds TSB, Caixa, Itau and the large Bradesco, confirmed that banking in Brazil was profitable, with rates of return around twenty per cent. Real interest rates are high and credit is growing at 20 per cent a year. The bankers present explained that it was important to keep returns high since the costs of operation were also high, particularly caused by inflexibility in the labour market. Perhaps in response to the years of high inflation in the 1990s, the Brazilian banking system is technologically very efficient, with faster clearing and settlement than we have in the UK.

During my visit to São Paolo, I was invited to celebrate the refinancing, via London, of the Brazilian branch of the Parmalat company and was pleased to meet some bright, able, young financial executives, including André Esteves who was about to relocate to London to work for UBS, with his wife Lilian and family. I also visited the nearby Alpine resort of Campos do Jordão to speak on the advantages of doing business in London at a conference on derivatives attended by around 600 delegates from many parts of the world.

Porto Alegre

There is a unique and amusing feature to every country I visited. In Brazil it was the 'Batadores', the motor cycle outriders that accompany VIPs around the cities and to the airport. Dressed in smart leather uniforms, with plenty of badges, the batadores in Brazil are kings of the road, stopping ordinary vehicles, and roaring ahead to forge a way through traffic jams. Normally we would have three bikes escorting us. In São Paolo, the batadores gesticulated with clear hands signals – and on one occasion with both hands in the air while the bike was still moving. But in Porto Alegre we had no fewer than six bikes guiding us through. After a hair raising journey, we screeched to a halt outside the *Sheraton Hotel* and I got out and shook the hands of all six, admiring the badges on the uniform of the captain. Without a moment's hesitation he tore off the badge, with its Velcro backing, and handed it to me. I responded with a set of City of London cufflinks. Brazilians are spontaneous and very friendly.

Porto Alegre is one of the largest cities in Brazil and, as capital of the country's southernmost state of Rio Grande do Sul, it is geographically well placed to take advantage of trade with Argentina and Uruguay. Largely populated by immigrants of European descent, it had the highest standard of living of all Brazilian cities for many years. It is also gaucho country with the export of beef being a key industry, on which Lesley's McCall family business was based. From 1888, the McCalls had two factories in Bagé, south of Porto Alegre, which closed in 1974.

At a meeting with Governor Yeda Crusius, I was given a warm welcome and I watched the Governor as she sipped maté tea out of her traditional gaucho cup. She later gave me a similar cup and also two books – one on gauchos and the other on her palace, the very grand Palacio Piratini. We spoke about working together on CDM projects (under the Kyoto Protocol), PPP and listings on the London market. We agreed to pursue this in discussion with the local business association (FIERGS) and via UKTI.

Rio de Janeiro

My parents were great fans of Fred Astaire. In one of his all time great films, in December 1933, he starred with Ginger Rogers in 'Flying Down to Rio'. My father would have been 20 years of age at the time. In one of our family albums, I have photos taken in Jersey in 1934 and in Blankenberge the following year with my parents acting out the parts. My father is wearing all whites for tennis (long trousers of course) and white tie in the evening. My mother looks like Ginger Rogers in some very pretty outfits.

So finally to arrive in Rio and stay at the *Copacabana Palace* somehow seemed familiar. To have the opportunity of a 48-hour stay, including a Sunday, was a real treat. It was at this famous hotel that many celebrities have stayed since it opened in 1923. It simply reeks of Hollywood and stardom and is a great place for watching life on the beach across the promenade. Rio residents typically live in apartments with no gardens, so the beach is their amenity, their park. And you see all mankind and womankind in all sorts of dress and undress. There is nothing quite like it. Back at the hotel, Anne Phillips, a longstanding English resident of Rio, is the helpful manager of the VIP lounge. The service at the hotel is excellent, even if some of the waitresses are dressed to look like Carmen Miranda, with fruit on their heads.

Rio de Janeiro has suffered in recent decades after the decision to move the country's capital to Brasilia as well as São Paolo becoming the financial centre of Brazil. The city has also suffered because of crime. Unlike other Brazilian cities where the wealthy areas are quite separate from the poor areas, in Rio the favelas (the shanty towns) are on the steeper, less accessible upper parts of the hills whereas the wealthier areas are immediately below. Rio has lots of hills, so they are jumbled up, side by side. When we met Mayor Cesar Maia during our visit, he spent the first 30 minutes speaking about the problems he faced dealing with drugs and violent crime.

Despite these negative factors, investment is returning to Rio and we were taken to an interesting development, the Castello, a former monastery on the outskirts of the city being financed by Cahill International through the London market. The Governor of the State, Sergio Cabral, is also very energetic and bullish. To help us get a better understanding and overall impression of the city, he lent us his helicopter for an aerial tour on the Sunday. You can't beat seeing Rio from the air. It is a magical place.

In Rio, Alderman David Wootton, a partner in law firm Allen & Overy, joined my business delegation which also included a strong insurance representation, from Benfield, Lloyd's of London and Willis. The prospect of liberalisation and opening up of the re-insurance market had attracted their interest.

Meetings with State Secretary for Economy, Energy and Industry Julio Bueno, the Brazilian Private Equity and Venture Capital Association, the Business Association of Rio (Firjan) and CVM, the Securities and Exchange Commission were all positive in terms of potential areas for cooperation – PPP, listings, financial services regulation, CDM projects, insurance and education and training. My meeting with Jose Gabrielli, CEO of Petrobas, demonstrated the importance of this global energy company and its potential for growth in the area of ethanol and bio diesel.

We were grateful to the head of HSBC in Brazil, Henrique Frayha, for arranging a reception for my delegation to meet local businessmen and to Tim Flear, Consul General in Rio, for his organisation and for finding two fascinating places to dine, when we weren't on official duty. Both were outstanding – the

Marius Restaurant, with seafood served in churrascaria (barbeque) style, and The Aprazivel Restaurant, which resembled a tree house, on a hill top overlooking the city.

The Rio branch of Britcham hosted a gala dinner at the Palacio da Cicade, the very grand former Residence of the British Ambassador, now owned by the municipality. The Governor, Sergio Cabral, was the chief guest and the chairman of Britcham, Marcelo Moura, had arranged that I would give the Governor the award of Personality of the Year. The meeting was warm and friendly and I invited him to visit London where we could discuss further his ambition of keeping the insurance industry firmly in Rio, rather than losing it to São Paolo. I was pleased when my after dinner speech was later described as simpatico and carioca, meaning friendly, good natured, agreeable and appertaining to Rio.

149 *The Lord Mayor with the Governor of the State of Rio, Sergio Cabral, and the British Ambassador, Dr Peter Collecott CMG.*

BRASILIA

In contrast, Brasilia is open, spacious and modern, with an artificial lake. In many ways, it resembles Canberra, built to house government and the civil service, with no commercial, industrial or financial heart. The architectural style is pure Niemeyer, some of it quite striking. But for me Brasilia is a trifle soulless, having been built in a relatively short time, rather than allowed to develop naturally.

Staying at the Ambassador's Residence enables one to discuss issues more easily and the briefings from Peter Collecott (and his Australian ex-diplomat wife, Judith Pead) were excellent. A dinner at the Residence involving Miguel Jorge, the affable Minister for Trade, reinforced the bilateral relationship. Meetings at the Ministries for Foreign Affairs and of Finance and Planning added to this and very positive noises were made about the prospects for PPP projects, the opening up of the re-insurance market and also of the international legal market. This last was progressed at a meeting with the Brazilian Lawyers Association when the idea of a working group to discuss and resolve the issue was mooted.

I was impressed by my visit to Brazil. The country has so much going for it. Brazilians are wonderful people, as we found out. They also have a saying 'Para Inglês Ver', translated literally as 'for the English to see' and meaning 'to dupe' or 'to make something appear better than it is'. This saying dates from the 19th century and has its origins in the abolition of slavery. Great Britain outlawed the slave trade in 1807 and increasingly enforced this principle on other nations by stopping ships on the high seas. It was a further 40 years before Brazil made such trafficking illegal and, in the intervening period, when slave ships were stopped by the British Navy the slaves were well hidden in secret compartments. Hence, things looked better than they really were. So 'Para Inglês Ver'. This saying is now used in Brazil, without much thought given to its origin and it always produces a smile. I was able to say in my speeches that I was impressed by what I had seen in Brazil and it was not just a question of 'Para Inglês Ver'.

MEXICO (1 TO 7 SEPTEMBER 2007)

After being invited to visit Mexico by the President, Felipe Calderon, this was arranged for the first week of September, immediately following the visit to Brazil.

Arriving on a Saturday evening, with Lesley, Sir Paul Judge and Billy King-Harman, we had Sunday to recover from the long flight before starting the formal visit on the Monday. Mexico is full of ancient monuments from earlier civilisations and Segolene Paxman, the wife of the British Ambassador, Giles, took us, with two of their daughters, to see the Teotihuacan pyramids just beyond the outskirts of the city. Guided by an archaeologist, Kim Goldsmith who is married to a Mexican and has been living on the site for years, we were interested to learn that those sacrificed were volunteers, believing that if their hearts were plucked out of their bodies while still alive the Gods would ensure a special place in the after life. A climb to the top of the Pyramid of the Sun, with Paul Judge, afforded a great view of Teotihuacan and the surrounding area. A very late Sunday lunch, Mexican style, with Giles and his family enabled us to get a leisurely briefing as well as enjoy our first taste of real Mexican food, including chilli en nogada and chapulines (grasshoppers).

The Deputy Head of Mission, Richard Morris, took us, with his wife Alison, to see a Mexican musical, drawn from the country's history and different musical traditions. The venue was the Palacio de Bellas Artes, the country's grand opera house, built in 1905 (and externally looking very fin de siecle empire style), but completed in the 1920s (and therefore internally looking very art deco and Tiffany style). The performance didn't start until 21.00, and then only after the audience had started to clap. With this air of timelessness and a dose of mariachi music we felt we had arrived in Mexico.

After independence from Spain in 1821, Mexico had a turbulent history of civil war, war with the United States and frequent assassinations. Despite these difficulties, the country has emerged as the 14th largest economy in the world and, with a population of 105 million, the largest Spanish speaking nation in the world. Mexico has a GDP per capita of around US$12,000 per year, marginally ahead of Brazil. The country's economy is very dependent on the US and as a member of NAFTA it has benefited when the US economy has performed well. By contrast it has suffered during a US recession and it is very much a feeder economy with 75 per cent of Mexico's manufactures being exported to the US.

This has prompted the new President, Felipe Calderon, to seek to increase the country's presence in world business markets, which are growing faster than the US, and he has called for 'more of the world in Mexico and more of Mexico in the world'.

Other issues facing the country include eradicating poverty experienced by a large percentage of the population, tackling public security and drugs, improving education and addressing fiscal reform. Tax revenues are too low and are very dependent on taxing oil revenues which are high, as a result of high world prices, but potentially declining as production declines. The state owned oil company, Pemex, accounts for 40 per cent of the Government's tax take. There is a need to encourage exploration and also to build refineries in Mexico rather than exporting the oil to the US to be refined. And, there is a need to liberalise the economy, which Calderon is determined to do.

The UK's relations with Mexico have always been strong. We were the first country to recognise an independent Mexico in 1821. The UK is today the 4th largest investor in Mexico, with all the large UK companies participating and HSBC one of the larger foreign banks. In reverse, the global cement company, Cemex, based in Monterrey, acquired the UK's RMC for US$5.8 billion in 2004. In 2007, the two Governments signed a Joint Declaration.

My first engagement was an audience with the President at his official residence, Los Pinos. He had made a special effort to see me, after our dinner in Mansion House, before flying to Australia for an APAC meeting. He welcomed me warmly and we spoke about the mutual need to raise the profile of each other's country. We spoke about the desirability of encouraging PPP projects in the country, about CDM projects, about the regulatory environment and about education and training – all areas for future cooperation. He apologised for not being able to host a dinner for me during my visit and suggested that I return with a business delegation. While I was meeting the President in his office, Lesley was being shown around the garden by his wife, Mrs Margarita Zavala. Later the President came out to greet Lesley with a big hug. They were both charming.

The usual round of Ministerial meetings followed, with Alejandro Werner of the Ministry of Finance, Dr Guillermo Ortiz Governor of the Bank of Mexico and Dr Guillermo Babatz Torres President of the National Banking Commission. The Finance Minister, Dr Agustin Carstens, also hosted a dinner for my delegation. Discussion focused on fiscal reform, regulation, corporate governance and the growing sub-prime crisis.

HSBC kindly arranged a dinner for us at their stunning new national headquarters and amazed us at the size of their operations, with 25,000 staff and 1,500 branches in Mexico. The education and training seminar, organised by the British Council, was well attended. And a major event was organised at the Club de Industriales, attended by over 300 businessmen and politicians, hosted by Don José Carral Escalante, OBE, aged 82, with the nickname 'Don Pepe'.

150 *Line up before lunchtime speech at the Club de Industriales in Mexico City. Flanked by the British Ambassador, Giles Paxman, and Club President Don Jose Carral Escalante, OBE (also known as Don Pepe).*

Other engagements included a seminar on carbon markets, where Jed Jones of DEFRA shone; a seminar at the Mexico Stock Exchange (the BMV) hosted by the President Guillermo Prieto Trevino and PwC CEO Javier Soni, where there was great excitement at the prospect of London as an alternative to New York; and a roundtable back at Los Pinos on PPP, where real progress was made by Stephen Harris of IFSL and Stephen Chandler of EDS.

I was delighted to read, later, that the first Mexican company, Fresnillo, had listed on the London Stock Exchange in May 2008, a decision stimulated by our seminar at BMV.

PwC Mexico organised a lunch for me at their headquarters office and I met some old friends from the past, including Rogerio Casas-Alastriste, the former Chairman who retired in 1986.

Giles Paxman had planned that we should visit Monterrey, the capital city of the northeastern state of Nuevo León. The city is in a valley surrounded by beautiful mountains including one that looks like a saddle, not surprisingly named Saddle Mountain. Monterrey has industrial strengths in a number of sectors – steel, cement, auto parts, glass and beer. It is the home to Cemex and I visited the company's head office for a roundtable with a number of Mexican businessmen.

But my first call, guided by our Consul Jonathan Clare, was to the Palacio de Gobierno to meet the Governor, José Natividad González Parás, and to see his magnificent palace dating from around 1900, a mixture of Prussian and Italian architecture. He later hosted a dinner for me in the hills above Monterrey.

An important theme of our visit to Monterrey was education and this merited a visit to EGADE, the graduate school of business. The Dean, Dr Alberto Bustani, a cousin of the Brazilian Ambassador to London, was enthusiastic about forming better ties with UK universities and business schools. EGADE has a very high reputation for creating entrepreneurs and, 20 years after leaving the business school, a staggering 68 per cent of all graduates are running their own businesses.

My visit to Mexico showed that there is enormous scope for developing the bilateral relationship further. I attempted to raise awareness of the City of London. In return, while Mexico is on the radar screen for many large British companies, we could do very much more together.

SOUTH AFRICA (3 TO 9 OCTOBER)

I first visited South Africa in 1964 while an undergraduate at Cambridge. It was the 400th anniversary of Shakespeare's birth. The English Academy of Southern Africa wanted to recognise this by bringing to South Africa a well known English Shakespearian theatre group or a well known actor. Sir Laurence Olivier and others who had been approached, perhaps Sir John Gielgud and Sir Michael Redgrave, were either too busy or too concerned about the unfortunate image developing in South Africa following the introduction of Apartheid and the Rivonia Trial which began in November 1963. So one of the organisers whose son was at Cambridge University approached him to see if he would bring a group of actors to play Shakespeare in South Africa. Stephen Gray had already produced *Love's Labours Lost* for the Experimental Theatre Group of Cambridge University which had toured France and Switzerland in December 1963. I had been a member of the cast, playing Holofernes, the schoolmaster. Stephen approached me to see if I was interested. I accepted. Others included Piers Pendred (a senior executive in the British Council), David Lascelles (a well known journalist with the *Financial Times*) and Richard Lee (a distinguished architect who was High Sheriff of Bristol in 2006-07). The Cambridge theatrical scene was torn apart. Should this group go to South Africa? Letters were written to *Varsity*, the University student magazine, by a group of luminaries, including Richard (now Sir Richard) Eyre, Tony Palmer, John Shrapnel and Graeme Garden, opposing the tour. Others, including the magazine's editors, supported it, referring to the protestors as 'Important Little Men'. The University Vice-Chancellor saw no reason to prevent the tour going ahead. So the group, known as the Cambridge University Shakespeare Group, departed for South Africa in June 1964 with the objective of performing two plays, *Love's Labours Lost* and *The Comedy of Errors*, over a period of two months.

The Government of South Africa was content that the group should play to mixed audiences, of black, white and coloured, in Johannesburg, Pietermaritzburg, Grahamstown, Port Elizabeth and Cape Town. But in Bloemfontein and Pretoria, they were to be whites only. The organisers argued that the group should also therefore play to black-only audiences and the townships of Heatherdale, Evaton, Luipaardsvlei, Daveyton, Springs (Kwa Themea), Mamelodi and Soweto were chosen for consideration. In the event, we played at five townships and these were memorable. Significantly, in Soweto, we played at the Orlando East Community Hall, which is now revered as one of the venues where black activism developed. Nelson Mandela had chaired ANC Youth League meetings there in the 1940s.

Robert Sobukwe founded the Pan African Congress at this hall in 1959. In the 1976 riots, it was the only municipal building and government office not to be torched. When the theatre group arrived in Johannesburg in early July 1964, Nelson Mandela had been sentenced to life imprisonment on Robben Island just two weeks earlier. The timing was historic and we were the first white group to play theatre in the townships to black-only audiences.

When British High Commissioner, The Rt Hon Paul Boateng, heard this story, he wanted to show me Fort Hare University in East London, where South Africa's black leaders had been educated. He wanted me to revisit the townships. My return to South Africa was to prove a very moving experience.

The country has experienced a peaceful transition since full democracy was introduced in 1994. With oversight from Nelson Mandela, the former President, and other leaders such as Archbishop Desmond Tutu, who chaired the Truth and Reconciliation Commission, the ending of Apartheid was smoother than had at one time been believed possible.

The focus in the last decade has been on effecting this transition. But there are some other deep rooted issues to be resolved. Despite falling unemployment, the country has one of the highest rates of income inequality in the world. Crime is on the increase and HIV/AIDS and corruption are major problems. Recently there has been an electricity crisis. To seek to resolve these problems, the Government of Thabo Mbeki has pushed a Black Economic Empowerment (BEE) programme which has three elements: increasing transparency, improving sustainability and capacity building and developing skills. Organisations are scored by a rating agency as to their success in complying with various measures. But this has not resulted in equality of opportunity and in a redistribution of income and wealth to the majority of black Africans. So, the Government has changed the measurement criteria and renamed the initiative the Broad Based Black Economic Empowerment (BBBee) programme. But the public have not been satisfied and Jacob Zuma was voted as the ANC Party President, lining himself up to be the country's next President.

Despite these developments, South Africa still attracts a large amount of foreign direct investment, particularly from the UK which in recent years has been the leading investor, accounting for over 25 per cent of all FDI. Barclays acquired 56 per cent of ABSA, Vodafone acquired 50 per cent of Vodacom, and BP, Shell, GSK, BAe Systems, British Airways, Cadburys, Virgin, Unilever, Rio Tinto, Standard Chartered, Independent Power and HSBC are all active.

The relationship between the UK and South Africa is good. The UK assisted in the peaceful transition from Apartheid; a statue of Mandela has been erected in Parliament Square in London; and, at the time of my visit, South Africa had just beaten England 36:0 in the Rugby World Cup. On top of that, we had a very popular High Commissioner, in the form of Paul Boateng who, together with Trade Commissioner Brian Gallagher, gave an excellent briefing on our arrival in Johannesburg. On this occasion, my business delegation included

Ann Grant (a former High Commissioner to South Africa, now a Vice-Chairman of Standard Chartered Bank), Ian Coleman (Emerging Markets Chairman at PwC), Sir Paul Judge (recently elected as an Alderman of the City of London), Anthony Nelson (Vice-Chairman Global Markets at Citigroup) and William Knight. Also accompanying us was Alderman and Sheriff Michael Bear and his wife Barbara, who know the country well. They were invaluable in helping us understand South Africa and they seemed to know almost everyone we met. Richard Martin was the programme manager from Mansion House.

JOHANNESBURG

Johannesburg is one of the world's great cities, founded in the late 19th century on the back of gold mining and the diamond trade. This led to its development as Africa's leading financial centre and a city of commerce. Johannesburg's wealth is evidenced by the Edwardian splendour of its public buildings, including the imposing Rand Club, and also by the well to do suburbs of Hyde Park and Lower Houghton where I stayed with a South African family during our theatre tour in the 1960s. They were involved with the Checkers grocery chain and were extremely supportive when five of our group decided to form a rock band, which we christened the 'Will Shake'. They hired drums and guitars for us. Playing Beatles and other 60s music, we performed on several occasions after our Shakespearean

151 *The Will Shake pop group – 44 years on.*

performances and, on one Saturday morning, at the Checkers store in Northcliff. For the sake of posterity, I have recorded the members of the Will Shake, namely David Collins (drums), David Lascelles (piano), Dick Lee (lead guitar), John Lornie (vocalist), Piers Pendred (rhythm guitar) and me (lead singer). Of course we played to packed houses but only on the African subcontinent!

In the intervening 40 years, Johannesburg has suffered from increased crime, particularly in the city centre, which has lost its financial and commercial heart to the neighbouring suburb of Sandton. There are attempts to regenerate the old inner city centre, but this has yet to be realised.

These issues should not detract from the importance of Johannesburg as a financial centre. It is not just the heart of South Africa's financial sector, which now accounts for a staggering 20 per cent of GDP, but Africa's financial centre. It was appropriate therefore that my visit should begin with a meeting, and lunch, with the Johannesburg Stock Exchange (JSE), hosted by the Chairman, Humphrey Borkum. I was pleased to hear about the excellent cooperation between the JSE and the LSE. I was also grateful to Geoff Rothschild who had arranged for Mandela to sign a copy of his autobiography for me, dated 3 October 2007, the date of my visit. This is a very special souvenir of my return to South Africa and one which I will always treasure.

My meeting with the Executive Mayor of Johannesburg, Mr Amos Masondo, emphasised some of the problems facing the city – migration of people from other areas, employment, urban renewal, improving the living standards of those in the poorer southern suburbs. He was excited at the prospect of the 2010 Football World Cup which South Africa will host and will use this as the catalyst for improving the environment of Johannesburg and surrounding areas. For example a new railway line is being built.

Other subjects of great interest were development of carbon emissions trading which was the subject of a conference at Eskom, the electricity public utility, and professional skills development, which we discussed with the Deputy Minister for Education, at the Gordon International Business School (GIBS) founded by Donny Gordon, and at the CIDA City Campus for students from underprivileged backgrounds.

But it was my visit to Constitutional Hill that proved to be the most moving of my engagements in Johannesburg. Originally the site of the Old Fort Prison complex, enlarged by Paul Kruger at the time of the Boer War, it was used to incarcerate political prisoners as well as common criminals. Mahatma Gandhi was imprisoned here in 1906. Nelson Mandela was kept in a cell in the Old Fort in 1962 prior to the Rivonia Trial. Today, the Old Fort and some of the older cells have been retained as a museum, but the main complex has been converted into the Constitutional Court building, using bricks from the demolished cell block. With great imagination, the architects have mirrored a penitentiary layout of walkways leading to offices and retained many of the features of the old prison, including a central staircase. Dr Ivan May, the Chief Executive Officer of the Constitution

Hill Trust, showed us around the museum complex and the new Court. I was privileged to meet Judge Albi Sachs, the former human rights lawyer. A ceremony took place to commemorate the agreement between the Constitution Hill Trust and Digital Links International, chaired by Sir Paul Judge, to provide refurbished computers to schools in South Africa. Then, I was honoured to accept a copy of the South African Bill of Rights, signed by the original signatories, as a gift to the City of London. I responded that I would ensure that this was placed in Guildhall next to the City's copy of the Magna Carta, 'our Bill of Rights'.

But there was more in store. One of Mandela's daughters, Zenani (known as Zeni) was a guest of one of the supporters of Digital Links, and had come to see her father's newly restored prison cell in the Old Fort. She was aged five at the time of his incarceration there, before being moved to Robben Island the following year. The papers in the cell included a copy he had transcribed of a letter he had written to her in August 1964. The original had long since disappeared but the sight of the copy was an emotional moment for her. Coincidentally, it had been written at the time of my first visit to South Africa.

That evening we witnessed a touch of old Johannesburg as we were entertained at the Rand Club by the Chairman, Peter Briggs, and his wife Judith. It had been founded by two of the great colonists, Paul Kruger and Cecil Rhodes, and contained some very historic memorabilia, including old photos of the club and of a grand dinner in 1898.

In marked contrast, the following day, after a radio interview with SABC and a roundtable on Islamic Finance, we visited a VSO project in Soweto. Determined to find the venue where we played two Shakespeare plays on 15 August 1964, we eventually located the Orlando East Community Hall and I went inside and stood on the stage that had witnessed more distinguished performers than the Cambridge University Shakespeare Group. Mandela had apparently used the hall for boxing

152   *The Lady Mayoress about to cut a tape to open a new water fountain in a township in South Africa.*

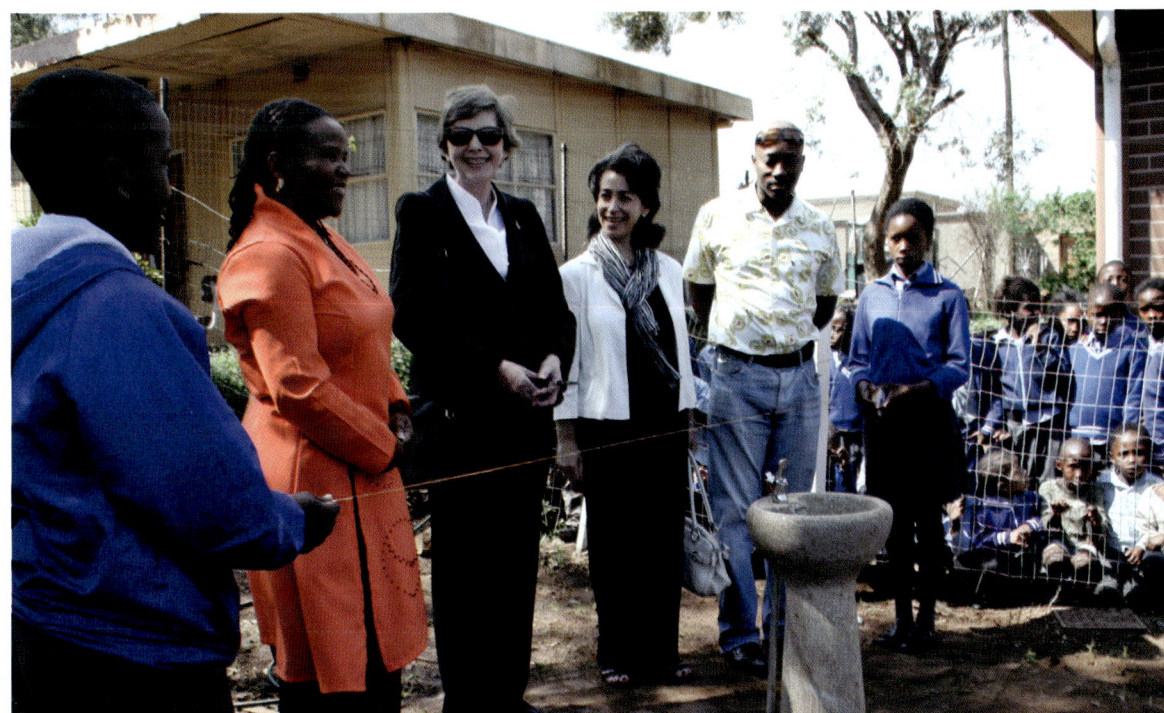

training as well for meetings of the ANC Youth League. Albert Luthuli, Oliver Tambo, Alfred Nzo and Robert Sobukwe had all spoken there in the 1950s.

Every time I visited a VSO project during my Mayoral year I was impressed. On this occasion, 12 volunteers had gathered together in Orlando West to describe their experiences helping to run hospitals and orphanages for HIV/AIDS orphans. We then visited the Aveiketsetse Le Bana community development project aimed at involving local communities in teaching children's rights and HIV/AIDS awareness. The children were taught that for every right, they had a personal responsibility. So 'I have a right to be educated' was followed by 'I have a duty to learn'. It was impressive stuff by any standards.

CAPE TOWN

The South African Government has two official locations, Pretoria and Cape Town. So the High Commissioner also has two Residences. It was a delight to stay with Paul Boateng at his Dutch style Arts & Crafts 1920s Residence in the Constantia district of Cape Town, one of the areas noted for excellent wine as well as gracious houses.

A Saturday afforded the opportunity of visiting a winery but not before we had attended a an event in a poor area of Cape Town, Hannover Park, where VSO had helped a local charity, Child Welfare, organise a soccer competition with teams from the townships of Khayelitscha and Hout Bay. We had paid for the kit, which was fought over as there seemed to be many more than 11 players vying for a place in each team. Before the competition began, the supporters from each side had dressed in local costume and performed a dance, like cheerleaders at an American football game. The Cape Coloureds from Hannover Park wore particularly bright costumes and were referred to as 'Klopsa Klopsa'.

Our stay in Cape Town included a meeting with the Governor of the Western Cape, Ibrahim Rasool, where we spoke about cooperation with the City of London in the maritime services industry. The High Commissioner raised the question of work permits for foreign professionals coming to South Africa, where apparently difficulties had been encountered. I raised the subject of restrictive practices in the accountancy profession in South Africa which hindered poor youngsters (who are mainly black Africans), from training as accountants. I later referred to this barrier with the media and I wrote as Lord Mayor an article that appeared in Business Day the following week. Other press interviews focused on the reasons behind London's success as a financial centre.

My meeting with the Mayor of Cape Town, Helen Zille, was also illuminating. As head of the Progressive Party, she carries the mantle of an illustrious predecessor, Helen Suzman who, for many years during the Apartheid era, was the only voice of opposition to the National Party. The Mayor was seized by the need to provide better education and encourage redistribution of wealth, particularly land. She was concerned about the dominance of the ANC. Clearly she was continuing a liberal tradition.

153 *The cheerleaders 'Klopsa Klopsa' before the soccer match at Hanover Park, Cape Town, organised by Child Welfare and VSO.*

EAST LONDON

Paul Boateng had planned an excursion on Sunday for us to meet the Premier of the Eastern Cape, Nosimo Balindlela, who received us at her farm near the village of Stutterheim not far from East London. Dressed in traditional Xhosa costume she gave us lunch outdoors before a formal discussion in her farmhouse, which

154 *Traditional greeting from the Governor of the Eastern Cape, Nosimo Balindlela, to the Lord Mayor and the British High Commisioner, The Rt Hon Paul Boateng.*

had a magnificent view of the wooded hills across a river. Politely she referred to me as 'Ta Ta' which means 'respected father' in Xhosa. We spoke about education and PPP, to improve infrastructure in the region.

A game drive at dusk in a nearby reserve preceded an early night before our visit to the renowned University of Fort Hare. Founded in 1916 it offered higher education to black Africans and was, for many years, the only university in Africa to educate indigenous people. As a result, it produced an elite. Such famous leaders as Oliver Tambo, Nelson Mandela, Govan Mbeki (father of Thabo), Robert Sobukwe, Mangosuthu Buthelezi and, even, Robert Mugabe, were educated there. We were welcomed by the Deputy Vice-Chancellor, Dr Tom, who had earlier in the week been appointed as the next Vice-Chancellor. It was a good time to be there. During a tour of the Art Gallery and Archives Centre we saw books and paintings dating from the period of struggle, including a memorable painting named *African Guernica* by Feni Mhlaba. Around 200 undergraduates and postgraduates attended the speeches by Dr Tom, Paul Boateng and me, with some interesting questions from a bright audience. I was grateful to Paul for suggesting a visit to Fort Hare as this helped, together with my visits to the townships, to put post Apartheid South Africa in a historical context and give us an understanding of the country's future.

155 *Visit to University of Fort Hare, South Africa, with Paul Boateng.*

Our week in South Africa was a highlight of my year. It was hugely enjoyable. But I had mixed feelings on leaving. One is always amazed by the energy, the resources, the capital invested, the climate, the scenery, the food and the wine. But the politics remain complicated and there are some serious issues to be resolved – elimination of poverty and the gap between rich and poor, improvement in education and professional skills, the enormous AIDS problem which is taking away so many trained people and leaving so many orphans. The period of transition to full democracy is over. Now is the time for these issues to be tackled head on. South Africa has the potential. It needs strong leaders, who listen, to make it happen.

CHINA (16 TO 20 OCTOBER AND 24 TO 27 OCTOBER 2007)

The timing of my second visit to China was thrown into disarray because the Communist Party Congress was announced for the week I was due to arrive in Beijing. It was even suggested that I should abort the visit, but I resisted this on the grounds that not everyone goes to the Party Congress and it would be possible to see the key people if one juggled the programme. So, after winning the battle, we divided the autumn visit into two parts, starting in Hong Kong. Alderman & Sheriff Ian Luder and his wife, Lin, joined us for the first week.

HONG KONG

Although I passed through Hong Kong four times in 2007, the official visit took place in the middle of October. As it happened, the Financial Secretary, John Tsang visited London the day I left for Hong Kong so I was able to meet him, together with Sarah Wu, the Director-General of the Hong Kong Economic Trade Office in London. He was bullish. The Hong Kong economy was in good shape, with annual GDP growth above six per cent, unemployment down at around four per cent and inflation below two per cent. Fiscal surpluses should enable taxes to be reduced. The property market, always a barometer of success in Hong Kong, had picked up in recent years. Banks had not been involved in the sub-prime market and Hong Kong was continuing to benefit from the growth in the Chinese economy. Interestingly, financial integration with the mainland was speeding up. The 'Through Train' concept should enable PRC nationals to invest in the Hong Kong stock market via Tianjin and the other concept of 'Qualified Domestic Institutional Investor' should enable PRC financial institutions to invest abroad.

These views were re-iterated when I arrived in Hong Kong and had meetings with Professor KC Chan, the Secretary for Financial Services, with Joseph Yam, Chief Executive of the Hong Kong Monetary Authority, with Michael Suen, the Minister for Education, and then finally with Donald Tsang, the Chief Executive. Donald Tsang said some nice things about London being the model for others to follow and how much he preferred the single financial regulator concept, notwithstanding Northern Rock. But he spoke mainly about the need to halt climate change and protect the environment, commenting that he was spending one-third of his time on climate change matters and that pollution in Hong Kong was getting worse.

Financial regulation, climate change and financial skills were the issues on everyone's mind and discussions in Hong Kong, as in other countries I visited, showed that there is much common agreement on these matters.

Hong Kong is noted for its food. The Cantonese like their ingredients fresh and the Cantonese cuisine is one of the finest in China. So a visit to the China Club, of which I am a life member, was a must – for dinner and also for lunch, hosted by the Consul General, Stephen Bradley. Decorated in revolutionary style with a priceless collection of 1960s Chinese Communist Party propaganda paintings, the China Club in Hong Kong is as much an art gallery as a dining club, thoughtfully planned by the socialite and charitable donor, Sir David Tang, KBE, whom I was later to meet again at Buckingham Palace on 19 February 2008 when we were both dubbed by The Queen on the same day.

It was also a pleasure to receive two separate invitations to dinner. The first was from my old friend and partner, Eddy Fong, who is now the Chairman of the Securities & Futures Commission, at the Hong Kong Country Club. He had gathered together a group of former partners, including the founder of Coopers & Lybrand in Hong Kong, Sanford Yung, as well as Nellie Fong, Marina Wong, Nick Allen and others I had worked with in the 1980s and again in the 1990s. The second dinner was at the home of Sir Michael Kadoorie, a leading Hong Kong businessman, from an illustrious trading family, whom I have met many times as a result of our mutual interest in vintage cars. His house on Hong Kong Island is situated on a promontory and has spectacular views.

During my visit to Hong Kong I gave media interviews and then a Press Conference after a speech to the Chamber of Commerce about the sub-prime crisis and the Northern Rock incident. Goaded by one reporter who commented that the Northern Rock 'crisis' must have hurt the City of London's reputation, I responded in a resolute manner. First, no depositor had lost any savings. There had been no crisis. It was an incident. Second, no bank had gone into insolvency. Third, the regulatory environment had proved to be robust. Fourth the media coverage at the time of the queues outside Northern Rock branches had inflamed the situation and made depositors more rather than less nervous. This scaremongering had been unnecessary because of the Bank of England's positive intervention to provide the necessary funding. I pointed out that the media had exaggerated the Northern Rock incident. Fifth, why didn't the Press ask about the much greater problem – not the Northern Rock 'incident' but the sub-prime 'crisis' in the US? The following day, the *Telegraph*'s headline in the internet version of the news story read 'Mayor pins Northern Rock crisis on the Press'. Well not quite right. Interestingly, in the hard copy version of the *Daily Telegraph* on 18 October, the headline had been changed to 'Lord Mayor Stands up for City'. Coming just three weeks before I stepped down, I could not have hoped for a better epitaph.

Nanjing

The literal translation of Nanjing is 'southern capital', in contrast to Beijing, which means 'northern capital'. This gives a clue to its historical importance, based on its location, near the mouth of the River Yangtse. At the end of the

14th century, it is rumoured to have been the largest city in the world, blessed with natural resources and an abundance of water. In winter it is mild, but in the summer it is one China's 'three furnaces' along with Chongqing and Wuhan, reaching temperatures of 40 degrees.

Today, Nanjing is a capital of the prosperous Jiangsu Province and specialises in electronics, cars, petrochemicals, iron and steel, and power, known as the 'Five Pillar Industries'. In 2005, Nanjing Auto featured in the UK newspapers when it acquired MG Rover from the administrators.

My visit was the first by a Lord Mayor of London to Nanjing. The focus was education and the promotion of the UK as a place for students to come to learn. Roughly 36,000 young Chinese are studying in the UK at any point in time and, as part of the promotion, the British Council had organised an event at Nanjing University. I also spoke on a 'Going Global' seminar planned by the CBBC.

Sun Yat Sen is highly revered in China and is considered by many to be the founding father of post Imperial China. He was the country's first Provisional President when the Republic of China was founded in 1912. Dying at the early age of 58, he was buried in a mausoleum built in 1929 on a hill side just outside Nanjing. I paid my respects to this great patriot by laying a wreath at his mausoleum.

SHANGHAI

I had met the British Consul General in Shanghai, Carma Elliott, MBE, before, in her previous posting to Jeddah in Saudi Arabia. Efficient and reassuring, she had suggested that we take the new train from Nanjing to Shanghai, a journey of just over three hours. It was a good opportunity to catch up with thank you letters (typically five a day on an overseas visit) which I typed on the pc brought by Neil Chrimes, Mansion House programme manager. I had a rule that I would always finish my letters before the end of each overseas visit, since there would never be time to do this once back in London. The daily Mansion House agenda rarely provided enough spare time to catch up.

I had lived in Shanghai for 2½ years in the mid 1990s. Then, the city was still suffering from years of neglect following the 1949 Revolution. But this had some positive features. Many of the splendid colonial style buildings had been left more or less intact. Shanghai had been spared the ravages of 50s' and 60s' town planning and architecture. It was therefore possible, when regeneration began, to leap decades in terms of building and systems design. Some of the older buildings had been preserved – along the Bund, perhaps the most famous waterfront in the world. The Hong Kong & Shanghai Bank's Headquarters, which opened in 1923, is a statement to the financial importance of the city at that time. The *Peace Hotel*, also on the Bund, formerly the *Cathay Hotel* where Noel Coward wrote *Private Lives* was under restoration. AIG is now back in offices on the Bund where its business first started in 1919. New daring modern buildings have also been constructed. The stunning Shanghai Museum is a must for anyone interested in the Chinese civilisation, with an amazing collection of early bronzes.

156 *Signing an MOU between the City of London and the Shanghai Municipal People's Government.*

The Pearl Orient Tower and the Shanghai International Convention Center in Pudong are just two of the many eye-catching new buildings that grace Shanghai's sister city, Pudong, created east of the Huangpu River on marshland. There are some wonderful restaurants to visit – 'M on the Bund', the 'Jade Restaurant' in the *Pudong Shangri-La Hotel* and the 'Villa du Lac'.

The Shanghainese are entrepreneurial people, with a keen sense of humour. They try to get things done, whatever the rules and the circumstances. As a result, with greater freedom to develop their own businesses and with greater encouragement from the municipal authorities, Shanghai is again becoming a city of global importance. There was a hiccup after the Tiananmen Incident of

June 1989, when those foreign companies who had newly established operations left because of the adverse foreign reaction. However, the Mayor, Zhu Rongji, who was later to become an effective Premier of China, established a Mayor of Shanghai's International Business Leaders' Advisory Committee, consisting of the chief executives of the world's leading companies. He was helped in this by Nellie Fong, the wife of my old friend, Eddy, whom I had seen in Hong Kong on this visit to the Far East. Nellie is now a partner in PwC. Today, almost every major global company has an office or a factory in Shanghai. The old buzz is back and Shanghai is, today, one of the most exciting cities in which to live and work.

Our hotel, the *Marriott*, was in Puxi (west of the Huangpu River), overlooking gardens and the Civic Centre, which was once the old racecourse. The oval outline of the track can still be clearly seen. The hotel was the venue for most of our meetings and seminars (one on ETQ and another organised by the ACCA). But the first event was a very cordial meeting with the Vice Mayor of Shanghai, Tang Dengjie, who, in the absence of the Mayor, who was away at the Party Congress, signed a new MOU with me, between our two cities.

It was a great pleasure for me to be welcomed at a Reception at the new offices of PwC in Shanghai. When I first arrived in 1994 we had just 12 people in our Shanghai office; today there are 2,400. Meeting old friends again – Betty Ko, Benjamin Ye, Yang Zhiqin, Dave McCann and Timo Lei – was a delight, as was meeting the new Managing Partner, Nora Wu, who hosted an enjoyable dinner for us.

Lesley and I later had lunch with my old friend and comprador, Ruby Chin, with whom I had worked in the 1990s. She was a miracle worker, charming officials and obtaining licences when others advised it was impossible. She had accompanied us to provincial cities, such as Chongqing, Hangzhou, Nanjing, Suzhou and Wuhan. She had journeyed with us down the Yangtse through the Three Gorges. She had taught us Chinese idioms and patterns of behaviour. She had helped us forge relationships with many local Chinese organisations. We were very fond of Ruby, now well into her 70s and not in the best of health. But it was lovely to see her again.

157 *Official signing, by Simon Culhane of the Securities & Investment Institute, for a new office in Shanghai.*

Education was very much on the agenda for my Shanghai visit and this included a formal opening of the new SII Shanghai office, a visit to CEIBS business school in Pudong, a speech at a seminar organised by the Law Society and an alumni reception for those who studied in the UK under the Chevening Scheme and the Lord Chancellor's Training Scheme.

Our visit to Pudong enabled me to view the new Lloyd's of London office and to open formally the Nelson Collection. Lloyd's has a spectacular collection of silver dating from the Napoleonic Wars when funds were raised to purchase gifts of silver, including dining services, for Nelson and his captains, known as the 'Band of Brothers'. The description had been applied originally by Nelson to those captains who served under his command in the Battle of the Nile in 1798. They were a closely knit group of friends and the term was taken from a quotation from the famous Agincourt speech in Nelson's favourite Shakespeare play, *Henry V*, 'we few, we happy few, we band of brothers'. A few choice pieces of silver had been sent to Pudong by Lloyd's as a display in the reception of their offices. As luck would have it, I was accompanied on my visit to Shanghai by a partner at PwC, Sir Tom Troubridge Bt, a direct descendant of one of the Band of Brothers, Sir Thomas Troubridge Bt. During my speech, I referred to this coincidence. The interpreter incorrectly translated what I had said as 'we are fortunate today to have with us Sir Thomas Troubridge who fought with Nelson at the Battle of the Nile'. For a moment, those Chinese present looked at Tom in some awe and amazement, as he had clearly aged very well.

Our visit to Shanghai finished with a ride on the world's fastest train, the Maglev, which links Pudong and the new international airport, covering 30 kms in exactly 7 minutes 20 seconds. With a top speed of 431 kph or 269 mph, it is breathtaking. It is also a tangible sign of what China has achieved in the very short period since the Opening Up.

BEIJING

These achievements were emphasised by British Ambassador, Sir William Ehrman, KCMG, when he briefed us on our arrival in the capital. William has enjoyed three FCO postings to China as well as an interesting secondment to Unilever China. He knows the country well. Coming at the end of the Party Congress, our visit provided an opportunity for reflection on the content of the speeches and on the new appointments and promotions. The President, Hu Jintao had confirmed continuing fast economic growth, but with more social safeguards. He had advised that China should expand and deepen the Opening Up that had taken place; that China should participate more in globalisation; that there should be a 'Great New Revolution' based on the work of previous generations; that trade and investment should be facilitated; and that the environment should be protected. Since the return of Hong Kong to China, the relationship between the UK and China has been good. The UK's FDI and exports to China have increased. Recently China has begun investing abroad, with no fewer than 340 projects in the UK. The UK has become a popular place for PRC students, variously calculated between 60,000 and 100,000 at any one time. There has been helpful dialogue on counter terrorism, money laundering and many other issues of global concern. The UK's financial services industry is developing fast in China, with major companies such as Aviva, HSBC, Prudential, RBS and Standard Chartered investing heavily.

Many of the senior Ministers and officials whom we visited had spent the previous 10 days at the Party Congress. They were still digesting the content of the speeches and the impact of promotions. As a result, they were absorbed in conferences and meetings. Despite this, we were warmly welcomed by the Mayor of Beijing, Wang Qishan, who interrupted his post Party Congress conference to meet me and my delegation. Earlier in 2007 we had given him the Freedom of the City of London at Mansion House. He was concerned with the need to do something about pollution and traffic congestion in Beijing. He was also in an extremely good mood, having been promoted to the 25 strong Politburo. And he was excited about the forthcoming Olympic Games with its stunning 'Birds' Nest' stadium, on which Arup have acted as consulting engineers.

Sovereign Wealth Funds have become the topic of much discussion in recent months. With rising prices of oil, gas and minerals, many countries have accumulated large surplus funds to invest. Current estimates are that these might total US$2.5 trillion. In some Western countries, this has become a matter of concern. The US, France and Germany, in particular, have protectionist tendencies and have expressed concerns about the real intentions of the sovereign wealth funds and have sought greater 'transparency'. Dubai World's takeover of P&O led to intervention by the US Congress which prevented the management of six major US ports falling into 'Arab hands'. Within the EU, there have been calls for greater transparency and a 'voluntary code of practice'. In my view many of these calls have been misplaced, some resulting from nationalist protectionist motives. Free trade and openness help economies. The PRC and the UK are living examples of the benefits of Opening Up. There is a good track record of sovereign wealth funds taking long term 'strategic investments' in companies as financial investments, not as vehicles for interference. Dubai World, the Kuwait Investment Authority and the Qatar Investment Authority are all examples of this. It has been suggested that without the investments being made by the sovereign wealth funds the global impact of the sub-prime crisis would have been much, much worse.

China's trade surplus, particularly with the US and Europe, has generated funds which are now being invested not only in US Treasury bonds and Eurobonds, as has historically been the case, but now in assets overseas. And China has its own sovereign wealth fund, the China Investment Company (CIC), with around US$200 billion, of which US$70 billion will be invested overseas. The Chinese Ambassador to the UK, Madame Fu Ying, recommended that I met the new Chairman of CIC, Lou Jiwei. I was pleased to do so, renewing an acquaintance in 1998 when he first became Vice-Minister Finance. It was an added pleasure to find that his deputy as Vice Chairman was another old friend, Jesse Wang, who had worked in London at the Bank of China. They were favourably disposed to London as a place for investment and I was pleased to learn that, after extending an invitation to Lou Jiwei to visit London, he had been welcomed by my successor as Lord Mayor, Alderman David Lewis, at the end of 2007.

My meeting with Li Ke Mu, the Vice Chairman of the China Insurance Regulatory Commission was equally friendly and very productive. I had been informed of applications being made by Royal Sun Alliance, Benfield, Locktons and BUPA to operate in certain business areas. I raised these at our meeting, together with the suggestions that the CII should operate in China to provide professional education and qualifications. I received a favourable response.

Meetings with the other regulators were also friendly. I had previously met both Liu Mingkang, Chairman of the China Banking Regulatory Commission (CBRC), and Shang Fulin, Chairman of the China Securities Regulatory Commission (CSRC). Liu Mingkang believed that, for China, there was a need to have both a principles/risk based approach as well as a rules-based approach. The culture demanded both and also a greater sharing of information between regulators and those involved in financial services. He wanted to ensure that foreign banks were treated equally with domestic banks and was keen to explore the lifting of the cap on foreign investments in the PRC economy. Shang Fulin spoke about the excellent relationship with the FSA. He referred to the vision for financial services in the 17th Party Congress, namely:

- Enhance financial security and manage risks
- Enhance competitiveness
- Encourage mutual growth of financial markets

I thought this sounded like Thatcherism. But then China has come a long way since the Opening Up. I raised with Shang Fulin the recent limitation (through 'Ordnance 10') on PRC companies wishing to list their shares and raise capital abroad. He explained that this was aimed at preventing domestic companies from transferring their assets abroad. Somewhat defensively, he argued that no PRC company had sought in recent months to list its shares overseas as the prices in Shanghai were so much higher than London. I have to say that I agreed, as this was indeed the case that price earnings ratios in Shanghai were ridiculously high. It was also clear that there is a perfectly understandable PRC Government policy to try to expand the Shanghai market to provide greater opportunities to PRC investors to invest in equities. Frankly, if I were the PRC Government, I would be doing exactly the same thing. However, in the longer term, this differential will not persist and it will be in the interest of the PRC generally to move towards a freer, more open market.

My meeting with Wang Jun, Vice-Minister Finance, was also friendly. Wang was responsible for the development of the accountancy profession in China and had significant discussions with both the ACCA and the ICAEW about cooperation. We spoke about this and I also offered him Freedom of the City of London – an offer which he pursued, gaining Party approval, and in February 2008 he was duly inducted, followed by a lunch at Mansion House.

It was 13 years since I first met Bo Xilai. The son of a General, Bo Yibo, who was on the Long March with Chairman Mao, Bo Xilai was destined for greatness.

158 *The Lord Mayor shares a joke with his old friend, Vice Minister Wang Jun, who was made a freeman of the City of London in 2008.*

His first major appointment was Mayor of Dalian. It was in this capacity that, in 1994, I went to see him to ask if Coopers & Lybrand could open an office in the city. In his role as Mayor of this important northern port, he was innovative in many ways. Dalian had always been international – at one time Russian, then Japanese. It was cosmopolitan and responded well to his ideas of becoming a major shipping and trading centre again, as well as having a top class soccer team, attractive parks, policewomen on horses and an annual fashion show and beauty contest. Promoted next to Governor of Liaoning Province, he was then appointed Minister of Commerce and was, in the Party Congress of October 2007, made Party Secretary of Chongqing, one of China's four municipalities. We spoke about possible restrictions to Chinese companies listing abroad through Ordnance 10 and he agreed to look into this. In response to a question from one of my delegation, Henry Manisty, he advised that there was no reason why Reuters should not establish operations in China. In conclusion, after speaking in Mandarin, he finished the meeting by saying in English that I was very 'handsome' and 'what good skin I had', at which my accompanying UK delegation, including the Ambassador, burst out laughing. He had meant to say that I was looking good. I replied to him that most people had not said this before about me but had instead commented on the attractiveness of my Mayoral badge replete with diamonds. The meeting ended on a high.

I have been a life member of the Beijing China Club since it opened in 1996. Formerly the palace of a junior Prince, the 400-year-old buildings in this complex now form a number of private and public dining rooms that serve some of the best Chinese food you can get, in a wonderfully romantic atmosphere. Ming-style furniture and lotus design lamps covered with red and green coloured lamp shades give this club a unique feel. There are three menus: Cantonese, Shanghainese and Sichuanese – the last associated with the club's immediate past, as the Sichuan Government's Rest House in Beijing for government officials visiting the capital. Deng Xiao Ping, the paramount leader of China who engineered the Opening Up of the PRC after Mao's death, came from Sichuan Province. Every year, he would celebrate his birthday with his family in a large room at the China Club. It was in this room where he allegedly made the oft repeated remark, 'It matters not whether the cat is black or white. It is a good cat if it catches the mice.' The interpretation is that 'it doesn't matter whether you are communist or capitalist, as long as the welfare of the people is looked after'. He was demoted twice for his capitalist leanings, but eventually rose to the top. Deng Xiao Ping is the reason why China is as it is today. The Chinese people, indeed the whole world, have a lot to thank him for. He is one of the world's great leaders in the 20th century, indeed of all time.

Lesley and I had lived in Beijing for 2½ years from 1997 to mid-1999, at the *Palace Hotel* in Wangfujing. The hotel, owned by the Peninsula Group, was part of Michael Kadoorie's empire. He ensured that we were well treated on our visit to Beijing and it was nostalgic to be staying there again, with its newly refurbished accommodation.

It was also a pleasure to visit PwC again in Beijing. Like Shanghai, the office had grown significantly and Frank Lyn (the head of PwC in China) organised a lunch involving some of my old friends, May Huang, Edward Shum, Allan Zhang, Charles Feng and Grace Tang. We exchanged gifts and I was presented with a silver model, a representation of the Olympic Stadium Birds' Nest.

There were a number of seminars organised in Beijing to coincide with the visit, including one of ETQ, the launch of a book on training material by the ICAEW and a breakfast with the British Chamber of Commerce at which I defended the UK Government's handling of the Northern Rock incident and pointed instead to the sub-prime crisis which had originated in the US.

TIANJIN

The last of our six Chinese cities was Tianjin, one of the four autonomous municipalities with special powers to develop without reference to Beijing. Our host was Mayor Dai Xianglong, whom I had met before in London in 2006 when I was Sheriff. After a very full and extended roundtable discussion, we signed an MOU between the City of London and the City of Tianjin with the aim of cooperating in the field of financial education. The mood music was good. It was clear that both cities had much to offer each other. After the usual, long but enjoyable banquet with many courses, we contemplated the return (three-hour) journey to Beijing, only to be informed that the motorway was closed due to dense fog. That did not present an insuperable hurdle to our host. He declared that the motorway would be specially opened for me and that we would be escorted back to Beijing by a police escort. Sure enough, in a thick pea souper, such as I have not witnessed since the 1950s in the UK, we eventually reached the outskirts of Beijing at which point the toll keeper, an employee of the city of Beijing, demanded payment of the toll not only by us but also by our escorting Tianjin police cars. The British Ambassador advised calm to allow the Chinese counterparties to sort out the problem, which they did after a halt of perhaps 20 minutes.

We reached Beijing in time for an early bed, prior to our plane home to London the following morning. It was this same flight number that some months later crash landed on arriving at Heathrow, with another friend on board, Matthew Kirk, formerly British Ambassador to Finland and now Director of External Relationships at Vodafone. Matthew was unhurt but shaken by the experience. Our flight home, by comparison, was uneventful, giving me the opportunity to type another few dozen thank you letters.

KOREA (21 TO 23 OCTOBER 2007)

Sandwiched between the last two visits to China, we were able to spend a few, productive days in Korea. My predecessor, Sir David Brewer, had had to abandon his visit to Korea because of an inward State Visit in the UK. I was pleased to make up for this and visit a country I had not been to before.

159 *The Lord Mayor and Lady Mayoress greet the Ambassador of Korea, Yoon-Je Cho, and his wife at the Mansion House Easter Banquet.*

The British Ambassador, Warwick Morris, was in the last of his three postings to Korea before retirement. He knew Korea well and pointed to the astonishing economic growth in the last 30 years since the Korean War left the country devastated. Proud of their 5,000 year history and with centuries of battering by their neighbours, plucky Korea was now the 12th largest economy in the world. Relations between our two countries were good, with the UK the largest recipient of Korean FDI in Europe. Standard Chartered Bank had acquired Korea First Bank in 2005 and, at my meetings with Korean Ministers, I was informed that the integration had gone well and that the Bank's contribution to Korea was appreciated.

Prior to our visit we had enjoyed meeting the Korean Ambassador to the UK, Dr Cho Yoon-je, on a number of occasions. The most recent was a dinner at his Residence at the end of September when he introduced us to Korean food. More important, he arranged for me to be received by the President, Roh Moo-hyun, who was stepping down in the New Year. The President told us that he had enjoyed his State Visit to the UK in December 2004 and the banquet at Guildhall. He was optimistic about contact with North Korea, although he did not envisage reunification in the short term. His country's ambition is to develop Seoul into a regional financial centre and he was keen to emulate London's success. We discussed financial regulation in the light of the sub-prime crisis and he declared in favour of a principles/risk based approach and a greater focus on corporate governance.

160 *The Lord Mayor is greeted by the Korean Prime Minister, Dr Han Duck-soo.*

These ambitions and sentiments were echoed at my other meetings with Kim Yong-duk, the Chairman of the Korean Financial Supervisory Commission (FSC), Lim Young-rok, Vice-Minister Finance, and Dr Han Duck-soo, the Prime Minister. All spoke in favour of an open market place and all wanted to see a financial centre develop in Seoul. But, as I pointed out at these meetings, this can only be achieved if constraints on market entry are removed. There was still a degree of nationalism and protectionism. For example, HSBC had agreed to acquire Lone Star's 51 per cent of Korea Exchange Bank, yet regulatory approval was not forthcoming and the offer lapsed. Foreign lawyers are also barred from practising in Korea. I pressed for changes, particularly in my meeting with the Prime Minister, and also gave the opportunity to Henry Manisty to plead for Reuters to be granted a licence in Korea to facilitate foreign exchange brokerage. A request was made by the FSC for assistance from London in the field of regulation and we were pleased to follow this up on our return.

At each meeting, I re-iterated the key success factors in London's rise to be the world's leading financial centre and repeated these again at a London Stock Exchange sponsored breakfast, at a lunch with the Korean British Chamber of Commerce and at a seminar organised by the Law Society of England and the Korean Bar Association. If Seoul really does want to become a regional financial centre, then Korea needs to adopt a more open approach to market entry by foreign companies and professions.

As always, it is a pleasure meeting the local PwC partners. In this case, the added pleasure was seeing again Taesik Suh, the President of the Korean Institute of CPAs, who had founded Samil, PwC's firm in Korea and the largest CPA firm in the country. We had worked together often when I was running the business in China.

Our final meeting was with the Korean National Pension Service which has funds of US$280 billion under management and a natural partner for the City of London. I was pleased to learn that there had been contact to see how we could assist. My business delegation included representatives from Deutsche Bank in London (Lord Aldington), Standard Chartered (Lance Browne), Schroder Investments (Sir Paul Judge), Aberdeen Asset Management (Robert Park), Standard Life (Alan Armitage) and HSBC (Simon Cooper). All had the door opened, albeit slightly, and agreed to follow this up with further meetings.

A MOMENT TO REFLECT

As the year progressed, there was hardly a moment to reflect. However, the FCO e-grams typically of two or three pages provided an excellent summary of each visit and of its achievements. Longer reports were produced later by each Mansion House programme manager which were then presented to the Court of Common Council, to whom I also gave a brief oral report.

The work involved in preparing for each visit was significant. First the date had to be agreed – not always easy. Then the content had to be determined and this required iterative discussions with the City business community and a huge amount of planning by the FCO locally in post, UKTI, IFSL, EDO and the programme managers who typically had a pre-visit recce. During my year, the British Council helped a great deal to organise the ETQ seminars.

The choice of executives who joined my business delegations was also key and the number on each delegation is important. Once the number exceeds 20, it is difficult to please everyone and ensure that they see the right people and get the benefits. Plus, it is a nightmare for the FCO to handle locally.

2007 was a fortunate year to be promoting the City of London. We had become the prime international financial centre in the world and everyone wanted to know the key success factors. And there was a great deal to promote – stock exchange listings, PPP infrastructure projects, project finance, forward freight derivatives, maritime services, carbon emissions trading, CDM projects, Islamic finance, professional services of all types and, of course, education and training.

Lord Mayors travel more than most Government Ministers. I spent over 100 nights outside the country. For me, that wasn't a problem. I have been travelling throughout my whole career with PwC and have lived abroad for more than six years. I found it stimulating to travel as Lord Mayor.

And what of the results? Well, in respect of each visit, I can point to specific achievements which are recorded above. I sincerely believe we helped promote the City and its services – and I think we added to the goodwill that already exists towards the UK in each of the countries we visited. Keeping up this programme and this level of contact is essential to maintaining London's position as the world's prime international financial centre.

161   *The Lord Mayor as head of a business delegation.*

Part IX

REFLECTIONS ON THE US SUB-PRIME CRISIS AND THE NORTHERN ROCK INCIDENT

20 June 2007
The Merchants & Bankers of the City of London
Mansion House

Grace before Dinner:

Heavenly Father,
Thy Son our Lord taught that the Kingdom of Heaven was
"like a merchant man seeking goodly pearls, who when he
had found one pearl of great price, went and sold all that he
had and bought it." Help us to value thy kingdom above all
things, that love of it may guide our actions; bless this City,
the Lord Mayor and Corporation in supporting all Merchants,
Bankers and Financial Institutions, bless Elizabeth our
Queen, and those who lead her government that commerce
may take place here and in this realm without let or hindrance
and for the well-being of all thy people. Grant that as we
thank thee for this feasting and fellowship, we may rejoice in
thy bountiful liberality and use the same to thy glory and the
relief of those in need, through Jesus Christ our Lord.
Amen.

Grace after Dinner:

> *Take my silver and my gold;*
> *Not a mite would I withhold;*
> *Take my intellect and use*
> *Every power as thou shalt choose.*
> *Take my will, and make it thine:*
> *It shall be no longer mine;*
> *Take my heart it is thine own*
> *It shall be thy royal throne.*

- Frances R. Havergal

For this and all his mercies may the Lord's Holy name be
praised.
Amen

Reflections on the US Sub-Prime Crisis and the Northern Rock Incident

THE ORIGINS OF THE SUB-PRIME CRISIS

'Sub-Prime' is a term that entered the popular vocabulary only relatively recently. Indeed it wasn't until there were indications of problems in the US sub-prime lending market that the public had an appreciation of what these things were. Writing in the *Financial Times* on 21 January 2007, John Plender commented that bad debts were creeping up in the US, particularly in the sub-prime lending market.

The sub-prime crisis, as we now call it, has its roots in the US where a mortgage lending market developed on a major scale, as a result of mortgage brokers persuading aspiring homeowners, whose credit was often suspect, to take out loans to buy or improve houses. In many cases, these individuals had no job or income and, apart from the houses they wished to acquire or improve, no assets. In the words of Marshal Carter, Deputy Chairman of the New York Stock Exchange, who paid a call on me in Mansion House on 10 September 2007, they were NINJA loans (loans to borrowers with No Income, No Job and No Assets). It has been suggested that, often, values were ascribed to the houses being mortgaged which were in excess of their true worth and that, often, borrowers' incomes were overstated. Because of the availability of credit and the desire for increased returns, banks in the US were persuaded to lend to these homeowners and these debts were then securitised (for example in the form of CDOs or collaterised debt obligations), rated as AAA and sold to other banks around the world. In a search for higher returns, global banks acquired securitised assets with higher coupons, without fully understanding the underlying nature of the assets and the likely risks.

In February 2007, HSBC announced large bad debt provisions in respect of its business in the US retail market and commentators suggested that this might be due to the bank's inexperience in this sector, a view that seemed to be confirmed when its US management was ousted later that month. The Chairman of the Federal Reserve, Ben Bernanke, was quoted as saying that he was following very closely signs of distress in the sub-prime mortgage market but that 'I do not think at this point it has implications for the aggregate economy'. In my view, albeit with hindsight, this shows that the Fed did not fully appreciate the implications of what the investment banks were actually doing. One of the main problems is that, in the US, there are many regulators. The Federal Reserve is responsible for monetary policy and the smooth functioning of the banking system. The SEC has responsibility for regulating the investment banks and focuses very much on investor protection. There is a different insurance regulator for each state. The Commodity Futures Trading Commission regulates the commodity futures, derivatives and options markets. There is then the Federal Deposit Insurance Corporation, the Federal Housing Finance Agency and the Office of Thrift Supervision. Having many different bodies responsible for regulating the financial sector is not helpful to effective regulation as the boundaries between financial businesses become blurred. As financial institutions change into conglomerates so, to be effective, the regulators need to be combined into one single regulator or, as a minimum, need to communicate more with each other and work together.

The word 'crisis' began to be used by journalists in February 2007, when referring to the sub-prime market, and US fund managers began to speak about the adverse implications for the economy, corporate profits and the stock market.

Despite this, in the following months, there were still a large number of optimistic statements being made. For example in June, JP Morgan advised that 'The problems being experienced by certain investors in sub-prime mortgages at present have not caused major market disruption but [do] outline a broader concern over asset valuation'. In July, Dave Shelock of the *FT* commented that 'problems in the credit market have not – yet – led to a liquidity' shortage'.

By mid July, the Chairman of the Fed reported that estimates of sub-prime loan losses were between US$50 and US$100 billion, if all were marked to market. Again, with hindsight, this estimate was to prove optimistic. By the end of July, the contagion appeared to have spread to Europe as one German bank (IKB Deutsche Industriebank) was bailed out by another. Companies such as Barclays, Bear Sterns, BNP Paribas, and Deutsche Bank, JP Morgan and UBS suffered and write downs were reported.

However, liquidity, per se, did not seem to be an issue until August, when the Federal Reserve, the European Central Bank and the Bank of Canada all decided to inject more funds into the market. It was evident that, not least in the holiday period, banks were becoming nervous about lending to each other when the true extent of losses on sub-prime activities (including asset backed securities) was not known. Yet, some commentators, notably Andy Xie wrote in the *FT* that 'Central banks share blame for credit bubble' and 'it's time for Central banks to stop bailing out markets'.

On 9 August 2007, Mervyn King, Governor of the Bank of England, announced that the Bank would not cut interest rates to bail out careless lenders hit by loan defaults. He commented that he was pleased to see that spreads were widening, reflecting a more realistic appraisal of risks, and that the sub-prime situation in the US did not represent an international financial crisis. He was concerned about injecting liquidity into the system on the grounds that banks had engaged in risky lending and any such support from the Bank of England would represent 'moral hazard' and lead to banks continuing to take on risky investments and not price risk correctly. He came in for severe criticism from the financial institutions in the UK for adopting this attitude and later (on 13 August) sought to reassure markets by re-iterating that banks could borrow, albeit at a penal rate, from the Bank of England if they needed to increase liquidity.

Then, towards the end of August, HBOS announced that it was bailing out its own Jersey-based debt financed fund. It seemed that the UK was not exempt from the impact of the US sub-prime losses. UK bank shares continued to fall, with Barclays, RBS, HBOS and Northern Rock all casualties.

It was clear that there was a major problem, which would have worldwide repercussions and, not surprisingly, the recriminations started.

During my visit to Brazil at the end of August 2007, I was interviewed by Sergio Leo of *Valor Economico*, the leading financial newspaper. After a discussion about my visit and the Brazilian economy, he asked for my views on the sub-prime crisis. I responded that the problems seemed to stem from a number of shortcomings, but two issues stood out:

- Poor corporate governance and poor risk management in the US banks, which resulted in high risk business being written in the first place
- Inadequate supervision and regulation by the US authorities, which focused too much on box ticking and compliance with rules, and not enough on the assessment and management of risks by a company

But within a week, the focus had turned to the role of the credit rating agencies who rated the securitised assets. The senior official at the Mexican Ministry of Finance, whom I met on 4 September, Under-Secretary of Finance Alejandro Werner, commented that 'this episode poses important questions for the Regulatory Environment, in particular the rating agencies who do not come out of this at all well'. He advised that banks had entered into more risky business in recent years. Then, on 5 September, EU Commissioner, Charlie McCreevy, attacked credit rating agencies, such as Moody's and Standard & Poors, for their conflicts of interest and poor methodologies. ECB President, Jean-Claude Trichet, also joined in.

I was less convinced by these attacks. First, the credit rating agencies seemed an easy scapegoat for a problem that, in my view, was down to poor risk management and poor regulation in the US. Second, I had been advised that credit rating agencies rated by reference to default and not by reference to asset values or liquidity in the system. The sub-prime crisis had, in my view, been caused by banks being too anxious to grow business and by not identifying and pricing risk correctly – and also by poor corporate governance and inadequate regulation in the US. I was, however, mindful of the charge levelled at credit rating agencies, namely potential conflicts of interest in their role rating instruments created by institutions who paid their fees.

The present liquidity crisis seemed to have been the result of the reaction of nervous banks, who had cut their own lending to match sub-prime losses and who simply did not know the extent of the impact of sub-prime losses on the balance sheets of their fellow institutions. It was these two factors that had led to a shrinking of liquidity in the wholesale markets.

On 9 September, the *Sunday Times* ran a story headed 'worst crisis in 20 years say banks', with money markets drying up.

On Tuesday 11 September, I chaired the monthly 'City No 1 Breakfast Group' meeting. Those present included Tom Huertas (Acting Head of Wholesale at the FSA), Sir Victor Blank (Chairman of Lloyds Bank), James Sassoon (Adviser to the Chancellor), Sir John Gieve (Deputy Governor, Bank of England), Mark Seligman (Credit Suisse) and others. The sub-prime crisis was discussed. Chatham House rules prevent me from disclosing who said what. However, Sir Victor Blank was unusually silent and it transpired later that, during the previous week, Lloyds Bank had been in unsuccessful discussions with the Bank of England about a rescue of Northern Rock. I recall leaving the meeting with two clear messages:

- There had been no sub-prime defaults in the UK. The UK system of regulation appeared to have worked
- Banks who acquired the securitised assets, such as CDOs, had not fully appreciated the underlying risks and had relied too much on the rating agencies whose role it is to rate securities on the basis of likely default and not on the basis of value.

THE NORTHERN ROCK INCIDENT

During 2007, analysts had commented (mainly favourably) on Northern Rock – its low cost base; its innovative products; and, occasionally, its funding model relying more on wholesale money markets rather than conventional depositors for its sources of finance. This had been encouraged by Northern Rock's own statements (eg in February) which were very bullish about prospects in 2007. Even in August, the bank had insisted that it had avoided debts connected with the sub-prime crisis. But rumours began to circulate and by mid August the name 'Northern Rock' appeared frequently in the media. Its shares plummeted on the grounds that its cost of borrowing would increase.

Extracts of media comments about Northern Rock in the last few years are interesting to read:

- *The Daily Telegraph* (9 December 2001) – 'Northern Rock has been one of the best performing banks in the past year. At 605p the shares should still have further to go. Keep buying'
- *The Daily Telegraph* (26 July 2002) – 'investors looking to bet on the ongoing strength of the mortgage market may still do better to take a look at Northern Rock, the most efficient lender'
- Merrill Lynch (31 May 2003) – 'Northern Rock has a simple but effective business model. Buy at 705p'
- Dresdner Kleinwort Wasserstein (3 September 2004) – 'The mortgage bank's low cost enables low pricing which drives volume growth and limits redemptions … at just 8.8 times forward earnings … the stock is very cheap. Buy at 706p'
- *The Daily Telegraph* Questor Column (27 July 2006) – 'Northern Rock

kicked off the bank reporting in style, with a 14.4% rise in underlying first-half profits and record lending of £14.8bn. The two key risks to the bank are whether it will hit a ceiling on market share – and a housing market slow down. Share price: £11.28 + 81.5p – Hold'

- *The Times* (2 October 2006) – Analysts at Keefe, Bruyette & Woods said Northern Rock's trading statement 'confirms all the positive trends we have come to expect from the company – excellent volume growth, stable margins, good control of costs and better than peers credit.'

- *The Daily Telegraph* Questor Column (3 October 2006) – 'Despite the price slide, a stout mortgage market makes this Rock as solid as ever. Stock: £11.58 – 10p – Hold for now'

- *The Daily Telegraph* Questor Column (3 April 2007) – 'Northern Rock has discovered the most virtuous of circles. Shares £11.36 – 9p. Buy'

- *The Times* (28 June 2007) – After Northern Rock's shares lost almost £500 million of its stock market value: 'Markets are right to be nervous about parts of the financial sector, but the jitters over Northern Rock look misdirected'

- *The Daily Telegraph* Questor Column (28 June 2007) – shares £8.34 – 113.5p. Questor says buy. Northern Rock's biggest threat is a sustained period of rising interest rates. But, it's a risk investors should take … yesterday's fall is an obvious buying opportunity

- Yet, interestingly, *Financial Times* (28 June 2007) – 'Northern Rock needs to reassess its strategy. It has funded its rapid growth by relying heavily on funding from the capital markets rather than using the deposits of retail customers'

- Then, at last, *The Times* (16 August 2007) – 'Northern Rock's business model has been called into question'

Interestingly Credit Suisse, who had been consistently pessimistic about Northern Rock's prospects, came out with the observation on 6 August 2007, 'Northern Rock's ability to access wholesale markets for its funding is a fundamental lynchpin in its business model' and commented that Northern Rock had a significant funding requirement in the short term.

But it was not until 13 September that the words 'liquidity crisis' were applied to Northern Rock after the Bank of England announced that it would provide 'such amounts of liquidity as may be necessary'. With the authorisation of the Chancellor (Alistair Darling), the Bank of England had stepped in to be 'lender of last resort'. Some journalists, for example Robert Peston of the BBC, commented that 'there was no reason for people with Northern Rock savings to panic'. However, the tabloids were less comforting and, with the share price of Northern Rock plunging and talk of emergency loans, depositors were not convinced that their savings were safe. 'Ministers could not be trusted' was a widely expressed view. As a result, queues of savers formed outside branches of Northern Rock on Friday 14 September and again on Saturday 15 September. Typically they were men and women in their 60s and 70s and, of course, the media had a field day. They reported that this was the first 'run on a bank' since 1866, although actually the City of Glasgow Bank collapse in 1879 was much more serious. However, it was some time since we had a situation where crowds queued in the streets to extract their deposits. Where would it end? There was talk of the 'crisis' spreading to other banks, for example the Alliance & Leicester and Bradford & Bingley, and of a loss of confidence and financial panic. *The Times* ran a story on Saturday 15 September headed 'I want to sleep at night knowing that my savings are safe. Who can I trust?' The newspaper pointed out that the UK's financial compensation scheme guaranteed only £31,700 out of the first £35,000 of a bank deposit and that the only really safe place was the National Savings Scheme. While factually accurate from a legal point of view, this sort of reporting did not help. It was, in my view, inconceivable that the UK Government would allow UK savings to be jeopardised in the way portrayed. The Governor of the Bank (Mervyn King), the Chairman of the FSA (Sir Callum McCarthy) and, finally, the Chancellor (Alistair Darling) all tried to allay fears and to calm the situation, to no avail. The FSA's advice was that Northern Rock was solvent, with a sound long term order book, but had short term liquidity difficulties. The British Bankers' Association advised that customers' deposits were safe. But, despite these assurances, the public was not convinced. Confidence was evaporating and the queues outside Northern Rock branches continued on Monday 17 September. Alliance & Leicester's share price plummeted on rumours of major liquidity problems and then rose again by roughly the same amount when they were found to be untrue. It was a time of rumour, a time of uncertainty, a time of fear. As a result, the Chancellor announced on Monday evening that the Government, after consultation with the Governor of the Bank of England and the Chairman of the FSA, would guarantee 100 per cent of all deposits with Northern Rock.

Not surprisingly, Sir Gus O'Donnell, Secretary to the Cabinet, whom I had invited to dinner in the Private Dining Room at Mansion House on Monday evening, sent his apologies at the last minute. The Northern Rock situation had become hugely political. It was important that a solution be found quickly to protect the UK's banking system and the reputation of the City of London. With the blessing of the Prime Minister, the Chancellor had been obliged to act.

Press comments on Tuesday 18 September included:

- Rational investors will not leave their money in a bank whose credit is evaporating before their eyes
- A catastrophe has been avoided
- US Treasury Secretary, Hank Paulson, admitted that bad lending practices were to blame for the present financial crisis
- Northern Rock had a business model which turned out to be flawed when credit dried up as it was almost wholly reliant on wholesale funding markets

- Downing Street insists that the Northern Rock crisis was the result of problems that originated in the US. Many journalists agreed, but it was still tempting to have a go at the new Prime Minister and the new Chancellor.

Immediately, of course, the recriminations intensified:

- The Northern Rock crisis reflects very badly on the Government's economic competence
- Regulatory officials were accused of helping Northern Rock to founder by not stepping in early enough
- It was suggested that the FSA should have identified the problems of Northern Rock's strategy earlier and should have prevented the bank from getting into trouble
- The Governor of the Bank of England should have reduced interest rates and injected more liquid funds into the market earlier to prevent the liquidity shortage which led to Northern Rock's collapse. He was then later accused of making a U-turn
- The Government should have acted sooner and (a) provided funds earlier (b) guaranteed deposits earlier – it was mentioned that the UK's financial compensation guarantee compared unfavourably with guarantees for the first 150,000 euros of deposits in some Continental countries. Alistair Darling was accused of having been caught 'off guard' at his first test.

My Reaction, as Lord Mayor, to the Northern Rock Incident

At the time, I was less convinced about the validity of the recriminations that accompanied the events relating to Northern Rock in the first fortnight of September.

- First and foremost, the funding strategy of Northern Rock was a matter for the board of directors. They had chosen an unusual strategy, relying more on wholesale markets than conventional savers providing deposits. Many analysts and media commentators had praised Northern Rock which had dramatically increased its market share of the mortgage loan business. Its non-executive directors were not inexperienced. Yet some other observers commented that this strategy relied on the continuing finance provided by the wholesale markets and that it was potentially risky. It was not until money market liquidity started to contract in the summer that this became a problem. But then, what a problem. It was suggested that the strategy and the risks had not been stress-tested enough. It's so easy with hindsight. However, the investors had suffered as the share price had fallen over the previous six months from £12.50 to £2.50
- The FSA had seemingly taken the view that Northern Rock's loan book was sound and that the bank's strategy was a matter for the board. If they got it right, the directors and the shareholders would benefit. If

they got it wrong, they would suffer. The FSA, like other regulators and commentators, did not envisage the extent of the contraction of credit and its impact on financial markets

- Until August, while there were predictions of losses on sub-prime loans, there was a perception that these were not as large as later transpired; that the US (and certainly the global) economy would not overly suffer; and that liquidity was not an issue. During August, these perceptions evaporated as did the wholesale liquidity market

- In August 2007, the Governor of the Bank of England took a hair shirt view that it was wrong to bail out banks that got into trouble because they took excessive risks. He was concerned about the 'moral hazard'. Some analysts and many banks criticised the Governor for not following the more supportive role adopted by the Federal Reserve and the European Central Bank. Then, in mid August he appeared to change tack and sought to reassure banks that funding was always available to meet their liquidity needs, albeit at penal rates. Finally, in early September, when it was apparent that the global credit crisis had impacted adversely on Northern Rock's liquidity, he agreed with the Chancellor and the Chairman of the FSA that emergency lending was necessary and should be made. During those five weeks, the wholesale liquidity market virtually dried up and, with hindsight, it is easy to see how his views must have changed. Some have not forgiven him for this, but he was re-appointed for another term as Governor, showing that he had Whitehall support which was seen, by the Treasury at least, to be justified

- The possible 'lifeboat' discussions, in early September, of Lloyds Bank acquiring Northern Rock, with the agreement of the Bank of England and the Treasury, turned out not to be feasible. First, this plan involved continuing Treasury support – and State Aid could be questioned under EU rules. Then, it could not be done secretly as in the 1973 banking crisis because it was a price sensitive disclosable event under Stock Exchange rules. Finally, the approval of Northern Rock's shareholders would be required, following a shareholders' circular, and the price alleged to have been offered for the rescue (later rumoured to be around £2.00) would probably not have been regarded by shareholders as enough

- No-one in the UK had seen a 'run on the bank' since 1866. The Treasury, quite rightly, advised the Chancellor not to rush in on Friday 14 September. To do so would set a precedent. How could the Chancellor save one bank and not the others? And would this extend to UK branches of foreign banks? If he guaranteed the depositors of one bank then effectively he would be guaranteeing the depositors of all UK based banks. Quite rightly, the Treasury would have advised the Chancellor to wait another day to see if the queues disappeared. When the weekend of 15/16 September failed to allay fears and the queues continued on Monday 17 September, the Chancellor had no option but to step in and make the guarantees in order to halt the bank run and, more important, prevent further runs on other banks.

Based on what I had heard and read, I took the view, at the time, that:

- The FSA's role did not extend to instructing the directors of Northern Rock to change the bank's funding strategy
- The Bank of England had correctly stepped in to offer Northern Rock funding as 'lender of last resort' but the Bank's communications had been less than convincing and reassuring to Northern Rock's depositors. Unlike in 1973, the Bank did not appear to have the power to 'arrange' a rescue of Northern Rock secretly
- The Treasury was right to delay offering guarantees to depositors until the Monday as it had not seen a bank run since 1866 and no-one could predict the events or the consequences
- The decisions made by the FSA, the Bank and the Chancellor had been logical and understandable at each stage
- The division of responsibilities between FSA, Bank and Treasury had not, per se, created the problem nor, perhaps, prevented its resolution. If all three functions had been the responsibility of a single bank regulator, the decision tree would not have been significantly different and the same considerations would have applied
- It is arguable that the present level of State guarantee of bank deposits was too low and should be increased closer to the European norm. However, this would probably not have prevented silver haired grandmothers (and grandfathers) from panicking and removing their deposits of >£100,000 which had been attracted to Northern Rock because of the higher rates of interest offered
- While some journalists had advised that deposits at Northern Rock were 'safe' after the Bank of England had stepped into offer funding as 'lender of last resort', the media had not helped the situation – not least by showing photographs of (albeit small) queues of pensioners withdrawing their savings (from a few branches) and by reporting websites jammed as a result of investors wishing to transfer funds to other banks. The reporting had not been balanced and had inflamed and exacerbated, rather than ameliorated, concerns amongst the public. The Press was not to blame for Northern Rock's mistakes but they had helped turn a manageable incident into a potential crisis.

I also took the view that, at this point in time, the Lord Mayor should seek to inject an air of calm into the proceedings; to urge considered reflection before precipitous reaction; to continue to support the FSA's risk based approach; and to urge directors to focus on risk management and corporate governance.

My City Banquet Speech (20 September 2007)

By happy coincidence, the 'City Banquet' was scheduled to take place at Mansion House on Wednesday 20 September, at which Sir Callum McCarthy was to be my guest of honour and Sir John Gieve would also be present. This would present an excellent opportunity to get across my views in public and before an audience of over 300 leading City figures, including the Press.

I had prepared a speech for this dinner some weeks earlier, with the help of the City of London Corporation's Economic Development Office and Public Relations Office, which focused on three matters:

- (a) growing concerns about the UK fiscal environment and a plea to reduce or eliminate stamp duty on share dealing;
- (b) the need to improve financial awareness and basic numeracy;
- (c) the ongoing encouragement of CSR by the City of London Corporation.

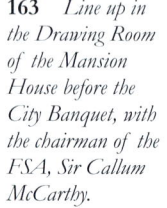

163 Line up in the Drawing Room of the Mansion House before the City Banquet, with the chairman of the FSA, Sir Callum McCarthy.

The Northern Rock incident and the views being expressed in the media changed all that. I decided to tackle the subject head on.

Having lived through the Secondary Banking crisis of 1973 (with Triumph Investment Trust and GT Whyte as my clients at Coopers & Lybrand) and having acted in a receivership role for an insolvent company in the late 70s (Dunbee-Combex-Marx), this was not unfamiliar territory. Having spent three years as Chairman of an Audit, Risk & Compliance Committee of a bank (Charities Aid

Foundation), I was aware of the issues. I had, during my Mayoral Year, met over 40 Governors of Central Banks and Chairmen of Regulatory Authorities and was therefore getting well versed in the issues of regulation. I had also supplemented this by reading all the media reports. But I needed help and I contacted, over the weekend, two friends who had an in-depth knowledge of the issues – David Lascelles, former banking correspondent of the *Financial Times* and currently a director of the Centre for the Study of Financial Innovation, and Peter Wyman, a senior partner of PricewaterhouseCoopers, who focused on corporate governance and the role of regulators. By Sunday night the speech had been re-written, covering the sub-prime crisis and the Northern Rock incident, and was supportive of the FSA (and its principles, risk-based approach to regulation). I counselled against a knee jerk reaction and I recommended time to reflect. I urged everyone to stick to their guns and to exercise calm.

David Lascelles was extremely helpful and supportive. His e-mail contained the following advice: Adopt the following theme:

> Ructions in the markets are rightly causing concern, and UK authorities are keeping cool heads. But looking at London's interests as a financial centre it is important that it maintains an awareness of the dangers of over-reaction. London's strengths lie in its sophisticated regulatory touch: the preservation of a system of regulation that is based on principles, that keeps things in proportion by evaluating risk. That way, we keep London competitive and innovative. The US (and even some Continental centres) are likely to respond with tougher rules. We should resist that temptation.

Peter Wyman's was equally helpful and supportive:

> A further thought: now may be the right time for some clear support for the benefits that have flowed from the financial innovation of recent years, coupled with a warning against knee jerk regulation which is likely to do much more harm than good. This is a bit pre-emptive, but who knows what will come out over the next few weeks – and the kind of guarantees Alistair Darling is offering seldom come without strings attached somewhere, if the City is going to need a champion it should be you! Regards (from New York).

Tony Halmos, Head of the City Corporation's PRO, was also helpful in terms of structure. He had assisted me in the preparation of certain key speeches during my Mayoralty. Unfortunately being at the Lib Dem conference at Brighton on City Corporation business prevented a greater involvement, but I am grateful to him for his contribution.

On Tuesday morning 18 September, I tested the basic messages in my speech with a small gathering of Aldermanic colleagues involved in the Financial Services industry, arranged by Alderman Roger Gifford (Head of SEB in London). The meeting emphasised the following points:

- Northern Rock had adopted a risky financing strategy. This incident emphasised the importance of risk assessment and the continuing need for risk-based regulation. It also emphasised the need to analyse and to price risk better
- The FSA's approach to risk based regulation is to be admired
- The liquidity squeeze is affecting most banks and will continue to do so for at least a year. Banks will have to bring back assets onto their books because refinancing of securitised assets will be difficult
- At this stage, it is too early to come to conclusions as to where blame should be attached. Don't blame anyone – at least not just yet
- There is a need for greater transparency in financial dealings

I gave my speech in Mansion House on Thursday evening. By this time, the panic was over and Northern Rock's share price had even started to rise again, to £3.15.

My guests that night (Thursday 20 September) comprised the great and the good of the financial world. Sir Callum McCarthy was my chief guest, on my right, and spoke well. Sir John Gieve, Deputy Governor of the Bank of England, was on my left. John arrived late, having attended a Treasury Select Committee meeting together with Mervyn King. King had spoken well but John received a mauling, not least from the chairman, ex-Treasury Minister, John McFall, who claimed he had been asleep on the job (by being on holiday) and referred to criticisms of his earlier service as Permanent Secretary at the Home Office. Not unnaturally, John arrived at the Banquet flustered and I tried to make him relax by saying that this was just one of those bad days and that tomorrow, hopefully, would be better. John recovered well as the evening progressed. In my view, Sir John Gieve had been appallingly treated by MPs who had not asked the right questions and who seemed intent on delivering a scalp. They couldn't get Mervyn's so they went for John's instead. In my speech, I was gracious in my remarks about the FSA, to which Callum responded that I had been too generous in my praise. My aim was to try to bring calm and reassurance – and that was achieved. My message was that 'your money is safe in the City of London' and that 'our system of regulation has been proved to work'.

DEALING WITH THE MEDIA AND THE PUBLIC REACTION

Some of the remaining seven weeks of my Mayoralty were spent, intermittently, dealing with the media, defending the regulatory environment in the UK and London's reputation as a financial centre. This was not a difficult task, but needed to be done, as there was a political and media hunt to find someone to blame, in addition to the board of Northern Rock.

This began almost immediately, with a briefing I gave, on Monday 24 September, to journalists from the PRC and Hong Kong. They asked if the Northern Rock crisis would hurt the reputation of the City of London. I responded that:

- This wasn't a crisis but an incident
- No depositor had lost money
- No bank had gone bust
- It showed that the regulatory environment worked
- The FSA, the Bank and the Chancellor had done well in preventing a crisis, but the Treasury now had a job on its hands trying to deal with the consequences of giving a guarantee to Northern Rock depositors
- The real question is 'how did the sub-prime crisis arise' since this is a real crisis, affecting global GDP growth and having a major impact on people's lives. What were the boards of the US banks doing? What was the US Fed doing when this business was written? What lessons can be learned?

The Director-General of the CBI, Richard Lambert, was so exercised by the whole affair that, on 26 September at the CBI North East Dinner, he criticised the UK tripartite system of supervision of the financial sector and commented that 'the standing of the UK as a world financial leader has also been tarnished'. Still worse, he said 'outside the movies, a run on the bank is something that happens in a banana republic'.

I did not agree with these statements. They were too sensational. The regulatory environment had, after all, worked. Yes, there had been queues outside Northern Rock branches, but these were small and short-lived. The media had exaggerated what had happened and had also inflamed the situation. The Chancellor had stepped in, as only he could, to stabilise the situation. And, after all, no depositor had lost any money. The losers had been the directors and the shareholders, as a result of the unlucky (and somewhat risky) choice of funding strategy adopted by Northern Rock.

In early October, Kitty Ussher, Financial Secretary to the Treasury ('the City Minister') wrote to me as a member of the Chancellor's High Level City Competitiveness Group to say that the Chancellor intended, after consultation, to prepare a discussion document on the Northern Rock affair. I responded on Friday 12 October praising his decision to reflect, to seek views and not to rush to introduce new regulations. I also commented that discussions with regulators in other countries during my overseas visits had confirmed that our regulatory environment in the UK was much respected.

On 17 October in Hong Kong, at a breakfast at the Hong Kong Club attended by about 120 people, I spoke about the need for London and Hong Kong to work more closely together in the field of corporate governance, professional skills development and financial regulation. I stressed that the Northern Rock incident proved that the system of regulation had worked in the UK. No depositor had lost money. No bank had gone bust etc. I commented that the media had inflamed a manageable incident. That evening Mark Kleinman of the *Daily Telegraph* ran a piece in the Internet version headed 'Mayor pins Northern Rock crisis on the press'. This was softened in the paper's hard copy version the following day

(18 October) when the headline ran 'Lord Mayor stands up for City'. I think that was one of the headlines I feel most proud to have been accredited with during my Mayoral year.

In Shanghai on 18 October, I gave a Press conference to about 25 journalists, responding to questions about London's regulatory environment.

In Seoul on 22 October, the Chairman of the Financial Supervisory Commission expressed his admiration for the UK system of financial regulation, with a single regulator adopting a risk-based approach. He asked for someone from the UK to be recommended to advise him further. Clearly he was not put off by the Northern Rock incident. When I met the President (Roh Moo-Hyun) later that day, he also expressed support for the UK regulatory system and interest in our new International Institute of Regulation. His supportive remarks were repeated by the Prime Minister (Dr Han Duck-Soo) at the end of a full day of meetings in Korea.

Back in Hong Kong on 24 October, two very separate views of regulation emerged. Joseph Yam, Chief Executive of the Hong Kong Monetary Authority, told me that Hong Kong had not really been affected by the sub-prime crisis and he warned against financial innovation without adequate regulation. He welcomed the change in global attitudes towards the assessment of risk and said that the Northern Rock situation could never have occurred in Hong Kong because the HKMA would have stopped it earlier. I wonder. He also advocated a separate independent regulator for the banking industry, rather than a single regulator for the industry as a whole with the tripartite arrangement in the UK for the banking industry. On the other hand, the Chief Executive of Hong Kong, Donald Tsang, later that day, told me that he favoured a single regulator of the financial sector and that he was frustrated by his colleagues in Hong Kong who were resisting attempts to adopt the London model.

At a Press conference in Hong Kong on that same day, I reiterated my views about the UK system of regulation. I said that the Press coverage in the UK of the Northern Rock incident had not helped, as it had created uncertainty and a loss of confidence, which had led to the Chancellor being obliged to announce a guarantee of savers' deposits at the bank. I suggested that instead of focussing on the Northern Rock 'incident', reporters should instead be asking why the sub-prime 'crisis' had arisen in the United States.

In Beijing, on 25 October, at a breakfast for about 100 members of the British Chamber of Commerce (Britcham) I gave a similar speech. In meetings with the PRC regulators (Liu Mingkang of the China Banking Regulatory Commission and Shang Fulin of the China Securities Regulatory Commission) as well as with Bo Xilai (Minister of Commerce), Wang Jun (Vice-Minister of Finance) and Lou Jiwei (chairman of the new China Investment Commission) strong messages of support, confidence and admiration were expressed about the City of London. The Northern Rock incident had not changed their views about the reputation of the City of London. Being a country I know well and respect, as well as one with growing global influence, this approbation from China's leaders was welcome.

SOME 'AFTER THOUGHTS' AND ANSWERS TO QUESTIONS THAT HAVE BEEN POSED

At the time of writing, not all the various reports commissioned into the Northern Rock incident have been published. However, I can offer some thoughts and some responses to questions that have been posed:

- History tells one that the unexpected will often happen – few economists or commentators predicted the oil price hike of 1973 and the subsequent Secondary Banking crisis. Similarly few people predicted the sub-prime crisis and the drying up of the wholesale money markets during 2007

- If something is too good to be true, then it isn't – Northern Rock's success, its growing share of the mortgage market and its higher than average interest rates payable to depositors were each somewhat unreal and were found to be unsustainable

- Risk assessment (and 'stress testing') is an essential and very necessary subject for a board of directors (as well as for a regulator). Most boards of companies have introduced this as a topic for board discussion. In some cases, a 'Risk Manager' has been appointed at senior level and in other cases (as at Charities Aid Foundation) the role of the 'Audit Committee' has been extended and renamed 'Audit, Risk & Compliance Committee'. The questioning of proposed new strategies and 'thinking the unthinkable' are essential qualities of non-executive directors. With hindsight, Northern Rock's funding strategy was risky, relying as it did on the availability of short term (three month) rolling finance in the wholesale money markets. In theory there was a risk that this market might contract, but money had been easy to obtain in recent years. The sub-prime crisis changed all that.

- Should the FSA have intervened and tried to deter Northern Rock from adopting a funding strategy which was unusual for a building society? The FSA has a role in relation to consumer protection and market confidence. While it examines companies in detail from time to time, responsibility for Northern Rock's business lay primarily with its board and its management. In November 2006, the FSA did issue warnings about the impact of the new Basel II rules (effective January 2007) permitting some banks, such as Northern Rock, to cut the amount of capital they hold by up to 30 per cent. In January 2007, the FSA alerted firms to the need to consider how they would operate in an environment where liquidity was restricted and reminded firms of the need to incorporate stress testing and scenario analysis into their business models. On 19 July, the FSA expressed concerns about possible deterioration in global credit markets. However, by their own admission, the FSA did not envisage a tightening of credit and the catastrophic impact of the contraction of global money markets on the position of Northern Rock. Earlier in this chapter, I noted the observations in the media about Northern Rock's future prospects – it was not until mid August that the alarm bells really started to ring, by which time the FSA was already holding daily meetings to review market conditions and their likely impact on vulnerable firms. From 16 August, a Northern Rock project team was established. But by then, it was too late. Short term market funding had disappeared. A lesson learnt by the FSA is the same as that for directors, namely that (a) anything can happen and (b) identification and stress testing of every risk should always take place. I was fascinated, and as shocked as many, when the FSA's own internal report was released in March 2008. This criticised the regulator for shortcomings caused by frequent changes in senior staff, inadequate review and discussion of findings and failure to engage properly with Northern Rock. This type of self-criticism is unusual and refreshing. Clearly there is much that the FSA can do to improve matters, by its own admission. But the impact of the sub-prime crisis took everyone by surprise, not least both the Federal Reserve and the other US regulators. In this context, the FSA's criticisms of its own performance are laudable but it would be wishful thinking to imagine that even if operating correctly it would have spotted the impending disaster. We should also not be deluded into imagining that additional rules-based regulation is required. Instead, both directors and regulators should be encouraged to focus more on the risks associated with any new or different strategy that is proposed. This requires much more than box-ticking.

- Should the Bank of England have intervened earlier to prevent the 'run on the bank'? The Bank was in much the same position as the FSA. The UK, indeed Europe, seemed to be almost immune from the sub-prime crisis and it was not until late July that the situation seemed to be getting worse. Even then, the Chairman of the Fed was estimating global losses to be a 'modest' US$50 to US$100 billion. Banks had been taking on risky business and the Governor did not wish to pump liquidity into the markets to bail out risky business. The banks did not approve of this decision. However, even if he had, the position of Northern Rock would not have been markedly different. He would have had to inject many tens of billions of pounds, for this to have worked its way through to Northern Rock. Instead, he looked to his role of 'lender of last resort'. These are unfortunate words. With talk of lifeboats, it makes it sound as though the ship is about to go under. Press and the Public interpret these words 'lender of last resort' as 'you're really on your last legs and no-one else will lend to you – therefore PANIC'. So the attempt to reassure depositors did not work. After all, these days, depositors can transfer tens if not hundreds of thousands of pounds easily from one bank to another via the Internet, in the same way that they had been attracted to Northern Rock because of its higher returns. The Bank of England has something to learn about its communications, since clearly they did not work on this occasion. Regrettably, it was not as easy in Autumn 2007, unlike in 1973, when the Governor (then Gordon Richardson) could have called in the directors of a major bank and the directors of a failing bank, for a fireside chat, to arrange a convenient bailout. At the time of the Northern Rock incident, with greater transparency, tighter Stock Exchange Listing Particulars, EU prohibition on State aid etc, these matters had to be dealt with in the public glare. It is, however, interesting to note that, some nine months after the Northern Rock episode, the Government decided to give the Bank formal legal responsibility for financial stability and to give it greater powers to intervene in the case of a failing bank. A Financial Stability Committee was appointed to scrutinise the Bank's work in meeting this responsibility and a 'special resolution regime' to enable the Bank to wind up a failing bank and to return depositors' funds up to a guaranteed threshold. It is also interesting to note that, subsequently, other bank bailouts have been facilitated in the UK.

- Should the Treasury have introduced larger guarantees earlier for depositors and should the bank run have been halted on the first day? It has been suggested that UK bank deposit guarantees should be at the same level as some countries on the Continent (circa £100,000). Yet, according to the British Bankers' Association, 96 per cent by number of depositors have balances in their accounts of less than £35,000. Yet, many had more than £100,000 on deposit with Northern Rock. After all, £100,000 only produces an annuity of £6,000, which is well below the poverty line, and not everyone has an index-linked pension, with many self-employed not having a pension at all. Saving during one's lifetime is, for many, the only method of providing for one's old age. The limit has subsequently been increased to £50,000 but, in practice, the government cannot politically afford to allow all depositors to lose their life savings. Then, in terms of speed of involvement, the Treasury had not seen a bank run for more than a century. Officials did not know how events would play themselves out. Caution about intervening on Day 1 (Friday 14 September 2007) was entirely justified. With hindsight, it is too easy to conclude that the Chancellor should have stepped in first thing on Monday morning, but he shouldn't be criticised for the fact that he didn't.

- Did the Treasury and the Bank have sufficiently experienced people to know how to handle these matters? After the Bank of England's role had been changed to focus on managing the monetary supply and fixing rates of interest, the expertise required was more in than nature of assessment of the economy and the way it is behaving. In former times, accountants, lawyers, merchant bankers and even insolvency practitioners were seconded to the Bank or spent the last few years of their careers monitoring the performance of companies and advising on insolvent situations. Lord Benson was recruited as an adviser to the Bank after retiring as Senior Partner of Coopers & Lybrand in 1975. Similarly the Treasury in recent years has followed a general trend in the Civil Service of becoming more detached from business and professional life. I recall in the 1980s a much closer relationship with the Civil Service, including frequent lunches, exchanges of view and personnel secondments. In the Northern Rock incident, once it was clear that funding was an issue, then knowledge and experience in areas such as insolvency, corporate restructuring, Stock Exchange procedures, mergers and acquisitions became more important. Were these available? Were they brought to bear at an early stage in this case? The formation of the Financial Stability Committee is a start in beginning to address that problem

- Does the Northern Rock incident suggest that the concept of a Single Regulator, focusing on risk, with a tripartite arrangement with the Bank and the Treasury, is wrong? My view is that even if there had been a single entity the same issues would have had to be faced and resolved. Perhaps internal communication would have been more effective if the Bank had also been regulator, but this would not have changed much. As for the risk-based method of regulation, the Northern Rock incident proves irrefutably that this is the right approach. A rules-based approach, relying on box ticking would not have helped at all. As I was keen to point out to overseas audiences, and they agreed, the Northern Rock incident proved that the UK system of financial regulation basically works. But lessons have been learnt and changes, as London has demonstrated over the years, will be made. Some further thoughts follow.

POSTSCRIPT

As this book goes to press (13 October 2008), one can reflect on the turbulent events of the last year. The global financial and economic environment has deteriorated greatly since the position which existed at the time I left Office in November 2007. Financial markets have seen their worst performance since the 1930s, as confidence has been replaced by fear. Financial credit has dried up and there have been worries over the future of the financial system.

Financial institutions have been hit hard, with some failing and others rescued. These have included such well known names as AIG, Alliance & Leicester, Bear Stearns, Bradford & Bingley, Dexia, Fortis, HBOS, Lehmans, and Merrill Lynch. Iceland is on the brink of economic collapse. Stock markets have plunged, with equity prices at their lowest levels for years. The world economy has not seen such trauma in the financial sector since the 1930s. Recession is forecast for most developed nations in 2009 as credit has tightened, consumer confidence has waned, fewer manufactured goods are being purchased and demand for raw materials has reduced, with a resulting fall in commodity prices. The IMF has urged for greater cooperation to prevent a full-scale slump.

In a bold and imaginative move, the UK Government has part nationalised UK banks such as RBS, Lloyds and HBOS, in addition to the earlier nationalisation of Northern Rock and Bradford & Bingley. Overall it has committed £500 billion to stabilise the financial sector and to restore confidence, by strengthening balance sheets and by providing credit guarantees and liquidity. Other European Governments have committed around £1 trillion as part of a coordinated rescue package to help ailing banks. And the US Government has followed the British example by injecting equity into US financial institutions as part of a US$700 billion support package which was eventually approved by US Congress.

Of course, the recriminations have started. Highly paid bankers are the first and most obvious target. At a time of elections in the US and, in the near future, in the UK, excessive remuneration and the guaranteed bonus culture have again come in for criticism, not least where banks have failed or needed bailing out.

The investigations and reviews are about to begin. Inevitably there will be legal actions, more regulation and a tightening up of procedures governing the sector. I hope, however, that the proposed solutions will focus on the real problem areas and not merely result in additional rules and more box-ticking.

It has been suggested, not least by the IMF, that there has been regulatory failure on a massive scale, with a failure to assess risk, and that regulators have been too remote from the business activities that they have been responsible for regulating.

It has been suggested that many problems in the UK have been caused by permitting building societies to operate like banks and to engage in activities beyond their competence.

It has even been suggested that the collapse of the financial sector heralds an end to the liberal economic capitalism ushered in by Thatcher and Reagan 25 years ago. I hope not. The world has seen real benefits from the opening up of markets. The former Communist countries, especially China under Deng Xiao Ping's leadership, are prime examples of the benefits of free market economics.

However, the relationship between Government, regulators and the financial sector must inevitably change. The financial sector provides necessary services to society. The ability to make money transactions and to provide a safe place for individuals to deposit or to invest hard earned savings is as important to society as the provision of water, electricity or garbage collection.

When taken literally, 'free market principles' described and espoused by Adam Smith and further embraced by Ronald Reagan and Margaret Thatcher have shown to be inadequate in ensuring a stable financial system, as evidenced by the massive Government intervention that has proved necessary. While not advocating a switch to Marxist or even Fabian principles, I do believe that governments cannot afford to leave the effective management of financial markets to market participants alone.

In his book *The Age of Turbulence*, completed in June 2007 when the crisis was brewing but not yet fully upon us, or recognised, Alan Greenspan, KBE wrote, 'Public sector surveillance is no longer up to the task' and 'We have no sensible choice other than to let markets work'. I was concerned to read this. While the capabilities of financial regulators to provide oversight have indeed diminished in recent years because of the complexity of financial markets, regulators are appointed by governments to protect people and to protect economies from systemic failure, as well as fraud.

However, in pursuing this line of argument, I would caution against a return to prescriptive regulation and moves which harm the freedom to innovate and to compete. The success of China and other former Communist states in the last 20 years is, as mentioned above, testimony to the effectiveness of Adam Smith's principles. Today, after a period of liberalisation, there is a need to reflect. But, we should not reverse the pattern of recent years. We don't want more regulation, but we do need better and more effective regulation. And how often has that cry been heard in recent years but not acted upon.

It also seems clear that a review of credit rating agencies is required – and will in any event be demanded – to ensure quality and professionalism, including independence.

However, I am less convinced about the calls to review 'mark to market' valuation principles. These were devised, I should hasten to add, not by accountants but by users of financial reports, investors and academics, to avoid the uncertainty attaching to the traditional method of permitting directors to value assets. If a security has been acquired with a view to holding it to maturity, then that is reason for not marking it to market. However, if the security has been acquired with a view to short-term trading, then 'fair value' is what someone will pay for it in the open market at a given point in time. If an asset can only be sold for, say, 50 per cent of its cost, then that is its value. Changing accounting rules to suit the owner's financial position is an extreme example of self-delusion. It also impairs transparency and does not represent a true and fair view of the state of the balance sheet. And, on this issue, 'mark to market' has an important political ally, Gordon Brown. In a speech he gave on 13 October 2008, when announcing the bailout and part-nationalisation of certain UK banks, he is quoted as saying, 'Some people are looking for a get-out-of-jail-free card and an easier way of registering their financial position than is the truth'.

There are many lessons to be learnt from the recent past and these will be discussed and documented in the months and years ahead. I venture to suggest that there are four areas, as a minimum, for serious consideration:

- Companies – Businesses and their boards must improve their approach to risk assessment, risk management and the pricing of risk. Problems typically occur when companies enter businesses or markets with which they are not familiar. My advice? 'Stick to your knitting' or 'If you want to venture out into new areas, then try to understand and manage the risks you face'. In many countries, banks have stopped being banks and have become supermarkets retailing complex financial products. The bank manager has become a salesman – paid to sell. What has happened to that cautious, perhaps rather boring, but upright and avuncular individual, who would eschew imprudent lending? Should we petition for his return? Should we encourage banks to go back to basics and, as before, constitute a safe haven for depositors, a place of prudent lending, as well as a secure means of money transfer? Then, compensation systems have come under criticism. These need to be reviewed to prevent excessive risk taking and to ensure that risks are properly managed. The public, and shareholders, will increasingly resist the practice of paying large bonuses when they are not earned. Finally, there needs to be more transparency in business undertakings
- Corporate governance – Non-executives must understand and question executives more about their strategies. They must demand options and alternatives. They must ask the 'what if' questions. They must be especially wary of dominant or over confident chief executives. In the US (and elsewhere), the roles of Chairman and Chief Executive must be split. But how can we also help non-executives, whose fees are modest compared with the risks they take? How can we ensure that they have the expertise necessarily required to fulfil an increasingly important role? The time commitment of non-executives needs to be increased and they need better support
- Regulation – Regulators must get closer to the businesses they are regulating so that they can better understand individual and systemic risk. They must also be more questioning of a chosen strategy and of the ability of executives to implement it. Box ticking is not enough. The role of the credit agencies needs to be reviewed. In the US, there also needs to be better coordination between regulators and, preferably, some amalgamation of regulatory bodies, so the regulator understands better those who are regulated
- Government – In the UK, we have seen some nationalisation and part-nationalisation of banks to prevent a wider crisis and economic depression. Over £2 trillion of public money is being injected globally into the banking system. It seems clear that the Free Market, so far as the financial sector is concerned, does not work so perfectly. There is a need for a greater balance between public oversight and private freedom. This requires a fundamental shift in political and economic thinking. Governments around the world must, in future, get even closer – and stay closer – to the financial sector, since financial services are necessary to the welfare of societies. And, in times of difficulty, there is a clear responsibility to act, as we have witnessed – in the public interest.

Index